THE

ISLAND WORLD OF THE PACIFIC.

KAMEHAMEHA III., KING OF THE HAWAIIAN ISLANDS

HARPER & BROTHERS, PUBLISHERS.

1856.

THE

ISLAND WORLD OF THE PACIFIC.

KAMEHAMEHA III., KING OF THE HAWAIIAN ISLANDS

HARPER & BROTHERS, PUBLISHERS.

1856.

THE

ISLAND WORLD

OF

THE PACIFIC:

BEING

THE PERSONAL NARRATIVE AND RESULTS OF TRAVEL
THROUGH THE SANDWICH OR HAWAIIAN
ISLANDS, AND OTHER PARTS
OF POLYNESIA.

BY REV. HENRY T. CHEEVER,

AUTHOR OF "THE WHALE AND HIS CAPTORS."

With Engravings.

The Sandwich Isles! the Sandwich Isles!
How fair on Ocean's brow they seem,
Reflecting the benignant Smiles
That from the Source of Beauty beam.

NEW YORK:
HARPER & BROTHERS, PUBLISHERS,
FRANKLIN SQUARE.
1856.

PREFACE.

Polynesia, or the realm of many Islands, within the last few years has been a rich field for the commerce, the literature, and the piety of the world. The name of one of the groups in it has become endeared to all Christendom, like Jerusalem or Antioch, where the disciples were first called Christians. The bare mention of it is enough to allure the interest of the Protestant world, for its associations connect it with the noblest triumphs of Christianity in modern times.

Numbers, too, of both Englishmen and Americans are now actual residents at those Islands, and many more are anticipating a residence there, for purposes of honorable trade and emolument; and it is a transplanted off-shoot from the old Puritan vine, in the form of New England missionaries, which has wrought sc marvelous a change in Polynesian society, that merchants can now abide there safely with their families, under the vine and fig-tree of a genial civilization.

These facts originate a natural desire, not only among sea-faring and commercial men who find a hospitable harbor there, but throughout the whole

English and American public, to be definitely informed respecting a people and a country where the outlay of Protestant benevolence has been so signally rewarded.

In these considerations, together with all the interwoven associations of boundless mineral wealth, indomitable American energy, and greatness yet to be, that come trooping into the mind with the words CALIFORNIA and PACIFIC, the present volume has its origin. And it is for the same reasons, also, that the author hopes to gain a hearing for this series of reverberations from a quarter of the world that bids fair to become the moral heart of the Pacific. After a few introductory chapters, therefore, historic, descriptive, and statistical, the book is made up of echoes and glances caught by the author after leaving the good ship Wales at Oahu.

The design of the whole is to present a true and life-like picture of the best part of Polynesia as it is seen now in 1850. Other writers, as Ellis in the Polynesian Researches, Stewart in his Journal of a Residence at the Sandwich Islands, Tyerman and Bennet, in the volumes compiled from their manuscripts of travel through the South Seas, between 1821 and 1829, by James Montgomery; Jarves, Dibble, and Bingham, in their several histories of the Sandwich Islands, have given to the world very accurate and entertaining delineations of Polynesian and Hawaiian society, usages, and annals, both civil and religious, up to the times when they wrote. But such has been the rapidity of changes in that part of Polynesia with which this volume has most to do, that the lapse of seven years suffices to effect a total revolution. This book is intended, therefore, to answer a want of the times, by affording, both to the wanderer abroad and to the stayer at home, a correct view of the Island World of the Pacific as it now is, just midway in the arch of the nineteenth century.

The scraps of vernacular Hawaiian occasionally introduced and translated, will be read with ease by remembering that *a* is always pronounced like the English vowel *a* in father; *e* like the English *a* in cane; *i* like *ee* in seen; *u* like *oo* in moon. The illustrative engravings are mostly reduced from original designs or sketches never before published, some of which were presented to the author on leaving the Island World for America by Rev. Lorrin Andrews.

Some writer has said, for substance, that it is a blessed mission to write books, which abate prejudices, unlock the hearts of men, strengthen the cords of human brotherhood, and make the kindly sympathies to flow. The author is not without hope that this mission may be fulfilled, in some good degree, by the present volume. Though not a missionary, it will be at once seen that he was a missionary's friend, which every self-respecting and sensible man will be who goes ashore at the Sandwich Islands, and uses his own eyes and ears instead of others'.

The writer publishes now what he saw, and what he thought and felt while seeing, as a book both for ship and shore. But should it gain only the ear and heart of seamen, whom as a class he loves and would labor for, his end will be answered. To them especially, and to the missionaries who have opened for them Bethels and Hospitals, and Homes in the Pacific, this volume is now dedicated by

THE AUTHOR.

New York, June 11th, 1850.

CONTENTS.

CHAPTER I.

INTRODUCTORY AND GENERAL VIEW OF POLYNESIA.

CHAPTER II.

PENGUIN ROOSTS AND ALBATROSSES OF CAPE HORN AND THE PACIFIC.

A

CHAPTER V.

NATURAL PRODUCTIONS AND PHYSICAL PHENOMENA.

CHAPTER VI.

HAWAIIAN RIGHTS AND WRONGS, POLITICS AND RELIGION.

CHAPTER XVI.

EARTHQUAKES, NATURE, ART, AND RELIGION AT HILO.

APPENDIX.

STATISTICAL VIEW OF THE RESOURCES, TRADE, COMMERCE, POPULATION, PIETY, POSITION, AND PROSPECTS OF THE HAWAIIAN ISLANDS.

ENGRAVINGS.

THE

ISLAND WORLD

OF

THE PACIFIC.

THE ISLAND WORLD

OF THE

PACIFIC.

CHAPTER I.

INTRODUCTORY AND GENERAL VIEW OF POLYNESIA.

The soil untill'd
Pour'd forth spontaneous and abundant harvests
The forests cast their fruits, in husks or rind,
Yielding sweet kernels or delicious pulp,
Smooth oil, cool milk, and unfermented wine,
In rich and exquisite variety:
On these the indolent inhabitants
Fed without care or forethought.—*Anon.*

He sat and talk'd
With winged messengers, who daily brought
To his small island in the ethereal deep,
Tidings of joy and love.—Wordsworth.

Ever since the revival of commerce that preceded the discovery of America, when Columbus was sent, according to his dream, "to unchain the ocean," the oceanic world of islands east and west has been acting like a magnet upon men's curiosity. To the mind of eager youth and sober manhood almost alike, there is an imaginative charm in the very word island; and when you add South Sea or Pacific, the fascination is complete and irresistible. Implying, as it does, remoteness, isolation, solitude, separateness, and linked as it is with romance and fable, adventure and song, it takes a powerful hold on the human imagination.

Island, in the Hebrew Scriptures, is any distant country approached by water. In what is called the Bishops' Bible, we find it always written *iland* or *yland*, from the Danish *Eiland* and Saxon *Iegland*, composed of *ie*, water, and *land*. Our present word island, according to Webster, is an absurd compound of the French *isle* and *land*, which signifies land-in-water land, or rather ieland-land; and it would be more accordant with etymology if it were always written ieland, that is, land made up out of and surrounded by water. This is, properly speaking, true of all land; both according to the cosmogony of Genesis and to the aqueous theory of geology, it is always land-in-water land, or earth standing in the water and out of the water. The great globe itself is but one of the islands in the vast ethereal deep of space comprehended within the limits of our solar system; and the far-reaching instruments of modern astronomy bring to light island-universes in the depths of immensity, whose outskirts the lightning could not reach in a million years.

God's glorious universe, therefore, may be contemplated as an infinitude of island-worlds—say rather an unexplored bay of islands in the vast ocean of His own infinity and eternity. Pervading all alike, both the vast and the minute, in an island-universe, and in the smallest islet of an earthly isle, is the radiant glory of the Creator, always visible, yet never fully revealed. Even as the Russian poet, Derzhavin, has sublimely written,

> Being above all being! Mighty One!
> Whom none can comprehend and none explore;
> Who fill'st existence with Thyself alone:
> Embracing all—supporting—ruling o'er—
> Being whom we call God, and know no more!
> In its sublime research, philosophy
> May measure out the ocean-deep—may count
> The sands or the sun's rays; but God! for Thee
> There is no weight nor measure: none can mount
> Up to thy mysteries. Reason's brightest spark,
> Though kindled by thy light, in vain would try
> To trace thy counsels, infinite and dark;
> And thought is lost ere thought can soar so high,
> Even like past moments in eternity.
> What are ten thousand worlds compared to thee?
> And what am I, then? Heaven's unnumber'd host,
> Though multiplied by myriads, and array'd
> In all the glory of sublimest thought,
> Is but an atom in the balance—weigh'd
> Against thy greatness, is a cipher brought
> Against infinity! O, what am I, then? Naught

The ISLAND-WORLD of the Pacific is presented to our contemplation in a great variety of interesting aspects and relations. The vast ocean in which it is imbosomed, sweeping in latitude from pole to pole, and rolling in longitude over a whole hemisphere, exceeds the area of all the continents and islands of the globe by ten millions of miles. Dotting it here and there, like stars in the air-ocean above, there are about six hundred and eighty islands of Oceanica, exclusive of New Holland, New Zealand, New Caledonia, New Ireland, and the Salomons. Yet such is the relative disproportion to the continental world of these small islands of the deep, to which the winged messengers of Commerce and Christianity are now eagerly flying on every breeze, that they are estimated to contain but forty thousand square miles, or less than the single State of New York; and their population, by latest estimates, is but little over five hundred thousand.

Within ten millions of square miles the whole surface exposed above the water, exclusive of New Zealand, does not exceed eighty thousand square miles. Latest French geographers, and the authors of the learned quartos on the Ethnography and Geology of Oceanica, attached to the United States Exploring Squadron, divide this vast realm of ocean and island into five portions.

First. Australia, including the Continent of New Holland and Van Diemen's Land.

Second. Melanesia, comprising all that part ot Oceanica inhabited by a dark-skinned race, with woolly or frizzled hair. It includes New Guinea and adjacent islands; New Britain, New Ireland, New Caledonia, New Hebrides, the Feejees and Salomon Islands.

Third. Malaisia; the name applied to the islands of the East Indian Seas, occupied by the yellow Malay race, including Sumatra, Borneo, Java, Celebes, Philippine Isles, and Sooloo Group.

Fourth. Micronesia; the name given to the long range of little groups and strips of coral rock and sand, scattered over the Pacific to the north of the equator and east of the Philippines, including the Pelew and Kingmill Groups.

Fifth. Polynesia; this designates the islands of Oceanica nearest to America, inhabited by light-colored tribes allied to the Malaisan, and all speaking in dialects of one general language. It is with this division of Oceanica only that we have to do in the present volume.

Polynesia proper includes,

1. The Navigator's Islands, otherwise called Samoa, having a population of fifty-six thousand.

2. Friendly Islands, or Tonga Group, with a population of eighteen thousand.

3. New Zealand, with a population of one hundred and eighty thousand.

4. Society Islands, or Tahitian Group, having a population of eighteen or twenty thousand.

5. Hervey Islands. The population estimated by Mr. Williams at fourteen thousand.

6. Austral Islands, named Rimatara, Rurutu, Tubuai, Raivavai, and Rapa, once populous, now supposed to contain but one thousand. The first of these islands I visited and explored in a whale-ship, and have estimated its population at four hundred.

7. Gambier Group. Population two thousand.

8. Paumotu Group, having eight thousand.

9. Marquesas, or Washington Group, estimated to contain twenty thousand, being the least Christianized or weaned from cannibalism and barbarity of all Polynesia.

10. Sandwich or Hawaiian Group. Estimated population before the late decimation by measles, one hundred thousand; now reduced, as by census of 1849, to eighty thousand six hundred and forty-one.

The total present population of Polynesia is therefore less than half a million, of which about eighty thousand have been gathered into the Christian Church by English and American missionaries.

These islands are classified, according to their origin, as coral, basaltic or volcanic, and continental The coral islands are two hundred and ninety in number. Basaltic, three hundred and fifty. Forty are of a mixed continental, volcanic, and coral origin, not clearly defined.

The entire area covered by the coral islands is estimated at nineteen thousand square miles. Area of the basaltic, sixteen thousand square miles. The coral islands are in all stages of formation, from the reef just breasting the breakers and peering out of the water, and the barren islet of coral sand and sea-birds, and springing palm-trees, to the verdant oasis of a thousand years, beauteous with its garland of bread-fruit, pandanus, and the all-answering cocoa-nut of the tropics, and surrounded with its barrier and fringing reefs.

The basaltic islands are of all shapes and periods of construction, from the simple volcanic dome or cone, scarcely at all abraded or disintegrated, to irregular mountain heights, having vast craters, with deep gorges between; lofty peaks, abrupt precipices, and sharp saddle ridges of basalt, lava, clinker, scoria, volcanic sand, and debris, some more and others less recent. These volcanic traces extend throughout Polynesia, and clearly show that in ages back all that vast ocean must have been the bed of an indefinite number of volcanoes, sub-marine or sub-aerial. Besides innumerable subordinate and side vents, it is computed in the Geology of the United States Exploring Squadron, from old craters now visible, that there could not have been less than one thousand volcanoes in violent, perhaps simultaneous action, from the Hawaiian Islands to New Zealand.

In the range of six thousand miles between New Holland and Mexico, there are some of the most extensive mountain chains in the world, lately surveyed and traced with precision by the scientific corps of the American squadron. The two principal are the Samoan, running through thirty-eight hundred miles, and the Hawaiian, through two thousand, besides others no less remarkable, all preserving a systematic regularity, which seems to exceed even that of continental chains. The height of summits in these chains, if measured from the bottom of the ocean, would surpass, it is calculated, the most majestic peaks of the Himalaya range. If only three miles be allowed for the depth of the Pacific near Hawaii, the summit of Mauna Loa, by measurement, will be thirty thousand feet above its base, or nearly six miles high.

The volcanoes now in action through Polynesia are confined to the four islands of Hawaii in the Hawaiian Group, Faloa and Armagura in the Tongan Group, and the north island of New Zealand. In Micronesia three are still smoking; in Melanesia, six or seven. These are all that are not now extinct of the great volcanic fires that once burned over this vast region. There are many things which concur to indicate that the islands remaining unsubmerged are but the tombstones of a buried continent, as wide and as long as that of South America, extending from the Sandwich Islands to New Zealand.

This being the origin, and these the physical features of Polynesia, it will readily be seen that in no part of the world are the sublime and beautiful found united in bolder contrast and variety. Lava-belching volcanoes throwing up vast mountains, and then shattering them again with earthquake throes and convulsions; torrents leaping precipices of a thousand feet; the blue, unbroken billows of five thousand miles of ocean thundering incessantly upon their coral coasts; placid lagoons and shore reefs beautiful with the coral shrubbery of a genial ocean; a tropical velvet verdure covering with its grateful mantle the steepest mountain crags; groves of the palm and bread-fruit like cedars of Lebanon; dells and valleys, and palm-covered plains, like the Garden of Eden, with every tree that is pleasant to the sight and good for food—these are some of the natural features and contrasts of beauty and sublimity in the fairy gardens of Polynesia. Their combined loveliness and grandeur of scenery can be appreciated only by those who have actually visited some of the South Sea paradises,

> "Round whose green shores the long Pacific roll,
> By trade winds borne across the world-wide waste,
> Surges unceasingly."

Well might it be said by the fair authoress of THE PARTING SHIP, bound for that beauteous island-world,

> Oft shall the shadow of the palm-tree lie
> O'er glassy bays wherein thy sails are furl'd;
> And its leaves whisper, as the wind sweeps by,
> Tales of the elder world.
> Oft shall the burning stars of southern skies
> On the mid-ocean see thee chain'd in sleep,
> A lonely home for human thoughts and ties,
> Between the heavens and deep.
> Blue seas that roll on gorgeous coasts renown'd,
> By night shall sparkle where thy prow makes way;

Strange creatures of the abyss that none may sound,
  In thy broad wake shall play.
From hills unknown, in mingled joy and fear,
  Free dusky tribes shall pour, thy flag to mark:
Blessings go with thee on thy lone career!
  Hail, and farewell, thou bark!

I have climbed the fantastic mountains of some of the basaltic Polynesian islands for two or three thousand feet, whose ridgy backs were so steep that I could sit astride them as on a horse, and pry myself along, looking down a thousand feet on either side. And again, I have gazed upon and roamed over densely wooded coral islets, as Rimatara, one of the highest, without rivers, or ravines, or proper hills; overlaid with strangely-shaped slabs and blocks and debris of coral, from which the sea may have but lately retreated; yet prolific in all the spontaneous wealth of its own locality, and in the imported and naturalized products of the volcanic isles.

It is beautiful beyond thought to the eye of the longing mariner, as it first rises in the distance a blue hummock from the Pacific wave; and it is grateful beyond sense when, with a day's liberty of the shore, he can quaff the nectar of its young cocoa-nuts, and regale himself with a banquet of its sugary bananas and *niaa*, and lie along under its palms, and *kukuis*, and *kamanis*, repeating, perhaps, the lines which another has said for him, as he lists to the mighty knocking of the ocean's great battering-ram against the impregnable ramparts of coral that have mysteriously built for him this fair knoll:

Turrets of stone, though huge and gray,
Have crumbled and pass'd in dust away,

Cities that sank in the sea of yore
Have turn'd to slime by the fetid shore;
But when shall crumble the coral wall
That parts the billows so bright and tall?
Ho! who can fashion a work like me?
The mason of God in the boundless sea.

But the inhabitants of these divers island-paradises, who are they? and whence did they come? As the whole world knows, they were vicious savages and cannibals, and their condition and character almost the furthest possible from paradisiacal. The researches of both English and American missionaries, and the later investigations of the scientific corps of the United States Exploring Squadron, especially in the department of ethnography and languages, together with the vague traditions of the islanders themselves, concur in the conclusion that they are of Malayan origin, and that the islands have all been peopled in one way, and from the same quarter, either by accident or emigration, or both, at a period of time indefinitely far back.

Numerous facts showing what long voyages may be performed with safety in native canoes, and how liable they are to be swept by boisterous winds from their intended courses; certain marked physiological resemblances; coincidences of manners, customs, usages, living, and arts; and, more than all, a common Polynesian family tongue having strong affinities with the Malay, of which every different group of islands has its peculiar dialect, intelligible after a little intercourse to every other: these considerations establish conclusively a common paternity to the divers families of Polynesia.

Double Canoe of the Tonga Islands.

Radack Island Canoe.

Ancient songs and genealogies of Hawaiian kings, preserved by tradition, give two thousand and ten years as the time elapsed since their settlement, allowing thirty years to a reign, which the linguist of the Exploring Squadron thinks allowable. These genealogies, however, can not be relied upon as accurate; but significant facts in connection with both the Sandwich, Society, and Friendly Islands show that the periods of commencing depopulation in each of these groups nearly synchronize with the times of their discovery by Europeans, or but a little precede it.

This melancholy decay has, doubtless, been hastened by contact with a new race, but it has by no means been caused by it. The accumulating vices of the Polynesian races, from bad to worse, had been slowly digging their graves for several generations prior to their discovery; and the crisis of their fate, when the natural laws they had been violating by their unnatural vices and crimes began to enforce their penalty, seems to have arrived coetaneously with, perhaps was precipitated by, their intercourse with foreigners.

Mr. Ellis says,* in respect to the Society and other neighboring islands, that, although no ancient monuments are found indicating that they were ever inhabited by a race much further advanced in civilization than those found on their shores by Wallis, Cook, and Bougainville, yet that race has evidently, at no very remote period, been much more numerous than it was when discovered by Europeans. "In the bottom of ev-

* Polynesian Researches, vol. i., p. 103.

ery valley, even to the recesses in the mountains, on the sides of the inferior hills, and on the brows of almost every promontory in each of the islands, monuments of former generations are still met with in great abundance. Stone pavements of their dwellings and court-yards, foundations of houses, and ruins of family temples, are numerous. All these relics are of the same kind as those observed among the natives at the time of their discovery, evidently proving that they belong to the same race, though to a more populous era of their history."

At the time when the nation renounced idolatry, the population was so much reduced that many of the more observant natives thought an old prophecy of a priest was about to be literally fulfilled, which said, The *feau* (hibiscus) shall grow, the *farero* (coral) shall spread or stretch out its branches, but man shall cease. Tati, the chief of Papara, talking with Mr. Davies on this subject in 1815, said with great emphasis, that "if God had not sent his word at the time he did, wars, infant murder, human sacrifices, &c., would have made an end of the small remnant of the nation."

A similar declaration was pathetically made by Pomare soon after, when some visitors from England waited upon him at his residence. He addressed them to this effect: "You have come to see us under circumstances very different from those under which your countrymen formerly visited our ancestors. They came in the era of men, when the islands were inhabited, but you are come to behold just the remnant of the people."

Monuments of Easter Island.

Man of Tanna Island

Mr. Ellis adds to this that he had often heard the chiefs speak of themselves as only a small *toea*, remainder, left after the extermination of Satani, or the evil spirit; comparing themselves to a fire-brand unconsumed among the smouldering embers of a recent conflagration. These figures, and others equally affecting and impressive, were but too appropriate as emblems of the actual state to which they were reduced. Under the depopulating influence of vicious habits, the dreadful devastation of diseases that followed their first intercourse with Europeans, and the early destruction of health thereby; the prevalence of infanticide; the frequency of war, rendered more fatal by fire-arms and the barbarous principles on which it was prosecuted; and the increase of human sacrifices, it does not appear possible that they could have existed as a nation for many generations longer.

Another cause more potent, perhaps, than all others in the destruction of the Polynesian races, until recently checked, was the introduction of the art of distilling, and the extensive use, in consequence, of ardent spirits. It has been to the Polynesians like fire-water to the North American Indians. Before they were visited by ships they had only one kind of intoxicating beverage, called *awa*, and the deleterious effects of that were confined to a small portion of the inhabitants. The growth of the *awa* plant was slow; its culture required much care, and it was kept by tabu for the chiefs alone, being as much prohibited to the common people as game is to the peasantry in England. Its effects, too, are more sedative and stupefying than narcotic or inebriating.

But after those native islanders had been taught to distill spirits from various indigenous roots by demoralizing deserters from foreign ships and fugitives from Botany Bay ; and when rum was brought to the islands in abundance as an article of barter, brutal intoxication became almost universal. The aggravated crime, misery, and mortality that have been always consequent upon strong drink among savages, now added fearfully to the already accumulated sorrows and wasting scourges of the aborigines. Drunkenness put new fuel to licentiousness, provoked to unnatural wars, bred discord among families and friends, increased the unutterable abominations of the Areoi Society, and made indolence and infanticide still more common and pernicious. The idol priests were in the habit of drinking to intoxication before going to the temples to offer human sacrifices to their gods, in order that they might be the more insensible to the outcry which we can not but think outraged nature must have made in them against that horrid work.

All these causes, brought to bear upon a people whose simple food and habits of living, and climatic temperament laid them fatally open to violent impressions, satisfactorily account for the rapid depopulation that has been going on throughout Polynesia for the two last generations. Neither a genial climate in which the wants of nature were few, nor the fitness and abundance of their natural products, making but a slight demand upon human labor for their support, nor all the beauty and salubrity of their island abode, as of the garden of the Hesperides, could long retard their extermination by the vices of heathenism, when

War Canoe of the Island World.

once those vices had reached their acme, as it is clear they did just before their discovery by white men, and were then re-enforced for the work of destruction by all the vices of civilization.

Since that period almost every islet, and bay, and sand-bank, and coral reef throughout Polynesia has been the scene of some thrilling disaster or romantic adventure by shipwreck, or massacre, or capture, or cut-off, or rescue, or conflict, or mutiny, with the harrowing narratives of which in detail, as they have come to my knowledge, we could fill volumes. For many years the track of whale ships, merchant ships, and men-of-war, from island to island, was marked by unbridled license, treachery, butchery, bloodshed, murder, and almost every conceivable crime and outrage; the latter often found to be instigated by monsters in the shape of men, those convict vagrants from New Holland, who in some cases made themselves very giants in iniquity, obtaining a fatal ascendency over the natives by their superior intelligence and resources, and teaching them to practice all conceivable wickedness with greediness.

It was just in this crisis of their fate, tutored into all the vices of civilization without its virtues by runaway sailors and transported refugees from English justice, that missionaries found them from England and America—the mother and daughter—and effected a peaceable settlement. The fame of their successful experiment is now world-wide, and it is recorded with exultation in the annals of humanity, to the praise of God's glorious grace.

In the succeeding chapters of this work I propose

to give the true aspect of an important part of this island world of the Pacific, as it appears now to the traveler after a little more than a quarter of a century's trial of Christianity. Various threads of personal adventure, anecdote, and illustration will be freely interwoven with the warp of our narrative; and though the fabric come out in consequence *party-colored*, it is hoped, nevertheless, that it will not fail of curious interest and acceptance with all *parties*. Let us then initiate our readers into this ISLAND WORLD with a few appropriate stanzas from Dana's poem of The Buccaneer, that may serve to exemplify our plan, and be prophetic of the result we arrive at by means of this book:

Inland now rests the green, warm dell;
The brook comes tinkling down its side;
From out the trees the Sabbath bell
Rings cheerful far and wide,
Mingling its sound with bleatings of the flocks,
That feed about the vale among the rocks.

Nor holy bell, nor pastoral bleat,
In former days within the vale;
Flapped in the bay the pirate's sheet;
Curses were on the gale:
Rich goods lay on the sand, and murder'd men
Pirate and wrecker kept their revels then.

But calm, low voices, words of grace,
Now slowly fall upon the ear;
A quiet look is in each face,
Subdued and holy fear:
Each motion gentle—all is kindly done:
Come listen, how from crime these isles were won!

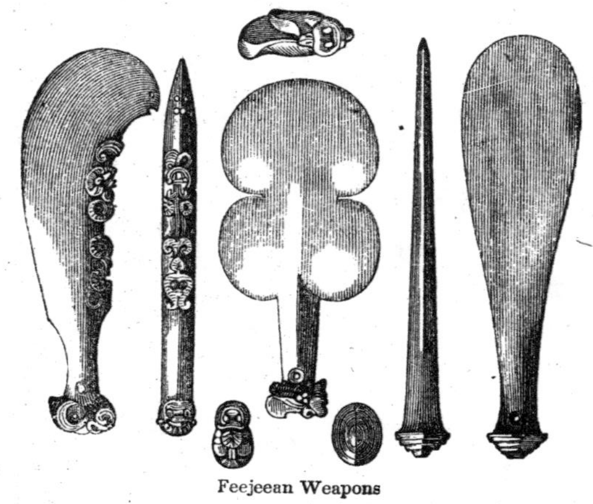

Feejeean Weapons

A Feejee Islander.

CHAPTER II.

PENGUIN ROOSTS AND ALBATROSSES OF CAPE HORN AND THE PACIFIC.

At length did cross an albatross:
  Thorough the fog it came;
As if it had been a Christian soul,
  We hail'd it in God's name.
It ate the food it ne'er had eat,
  And round and round it flew:
The ice did split with a thunder-fit;
  The helmsman steer'd us through!
And a good south wind sprung up behind;
  The albatross did follow,
And every day, for food or play,
  Came to the mariner's hollo.

Rime of the Ancient Mariner.

THE first introduction of my readers to the good ship Wales, whereby we pass to the Pacific, is as she is lying off and on in Berkley's Sound, at the islands called Foul Weather Group, otherwise named Falkland, after an English lord. Cape Horn weather here begins, and the ship and her company put on their Cape Horn suit; which, so far as some of our men are concerned, is quite as unique and nondescript as the notable "White Jacket."

This group is so near to the gate of the Pacific, though belonging to the Atlantic side, that an account of a ramble over the moss-covered rocks and penguin roosts of the uninhabited land, off which we now lie, is no inappropriate introduction to the island world we are just entering. In the language of seamen, this is our first *land-fall* after seventy-six day's sailing from New York; and one can easily guess at the pleasure we have had in making it, when for eleven weeks the eye has been looking upon nothing but sky and water, with now and then a passing sail. As Maximilian feelingly says, in the Piccolomini,

> Whate'er in the inland dales the land conceals
> Of fair and exquisite, O! nothing, nothing
> Do we behold of that in our rude voyage.

Floating kelp-weed, ducks, and albatrosses, the discoloration of the sea, and a peculiar fishy odor, like that exhaled from salt flats and spawn, had for several days warned us of our proximity to land. It was dimly discovered this morning about three o'clock, near the time of summer sun-rising in this high southern latitude. As the wind headed us off from our course to Cape Horn, and was fair either to enter or leave this Sound, the captain was persuaded to put in for a few hours, and send the boat ashore: a favor he was not unwilling to grant, the harbor being accurately surveyed and laid down on the chart, and the depth of water and the boldness of the shore such, that a ship can safely *lie-to*, and be ready at once for departure without the detention of weighing anchor. We doubled Cape St. Vincent, the easternmost point of this group of islands, about twelve; and after dinner the boat was lowered, and nine of us in all put off for the cliffs, which had seemed in the distance, and through the spy-glass, studded with white stones. Ducks, geese, and various other birds, hovered over, and flew close to us, all unaware of the fatal instruments that were leveled with such cruel precision by some of our number, that eight or ten were shot on the wing, and many more on the water.

Selecting a small indentation or bight in the cliff as a landing-place, what was our surprise to find what we had thought a facing of white stones to be innumerable penguins, standing erect, in the rank and file of battle array, upon the declivity of the rocks, and occupying at least two acres, in dense columns, away back to the moss and grass. Where the rock was nearly perpendicular, or its face jagged and broken, on every out-jutting angle or hollow, there was a duck's nest, with the bird sitting upon it, and so unacquainted with man, that we could climb up and lay hands upon them before they would move.

The limestone cliffs were in many places perforated with caves, one of which we explored two or three hundred feet, and found it dripping with dissolved carbonate of lime, and giving evidence of being broken in upon by the sea in easterly winds. It was upward of fifty feet high at the mouth, and singularly groined, like the architecture of the Goths; its roof as if some vast force from beneath had lifted up and ruptured in the middle the superincumbent strata.

With a basket on arm, to hold flowers and mineralogical specimens, it was no easy task to clamber up the steep precipice. But the height once gained, the verdant knolls, hillocks of moss, and various wild flowers that met the eye, more than repaid the toil of ascent. There were tufts of grass and wild daisies in every cleft where mold could form; and higher up, when the precipice was fairly gained, there was a large area of many acres thickly covered with mosses and flowers, in a loose black soil of two feet depth. There were wild honeysuckles and geraniums, a kind of dwarf cranberry, numerous flowers of sweet perfume, with leaves like the globe-flower, and several kinds of white and yellow heath-flowers and liverworts, of which we now have a graceful bouquet on the cabin table.

Grateful to tread once more the soft greensward, and glad to be alone under the canopy of heaven, after so many weeks' confinement on shipboard among men, I experienced a gush of joyful emotion never before known. Leaving a basket of specimens by a large white rock at the edge of the cliff, while the rest of the party were intent only upon game, I proceeded alone inland to a high rocky ridge that commanded a view of the sea, the islands, some fresh-water lakes, and a distant sand-beach. It was good to be again by one's self. Christ's closet was once the mountain, and here, where prayer, perhaps, was never before made, it was a privilege to pour out the heart's pent-up emotions, which flow more readily in the channel of articulate expression than when limited to an internal utterance which God only can know. Home, friends, health, Christian firmness, and the wisdom that is from above, and, more than all, spiritual renovation and healing for companions of the voyage, were the subjects of that prayer. May it be presented with Christ's prevalent intercession before the mercy-seat on high! A surprisal by some of our ramblers interrupted a communion that, short as it was, shall make that rugged island more verdant in memory than the gardens of the Hesperides. One short half hour in which the soul lives and has intercourse with its Maker is worth more than years in which every thing is enjoyed but God. It was after such happy experience that the gentle Cowper wrote those lines:

> There, if thy Spirit touch the soul,
> And grace her mean abode,
> Oh! with what peace, and joy, and love,
> She communes with her God.

After a visit to the penguin quarters, we reassembled at the boat with much spoil, and reached the ship safely, in time enough to allow the rest of the ship's company and passengers the same excursion, there being light enough to read in this latitude until ten o'clock in the afternoon.

To those who have never seen a picture of the penguin, it would be impossible to convey an idea by description of this odd amphibious creature. It has the head, bill, and two web-feet of a bird, and stands erect on land, sometimes two and a half and three feet in height. They have no wings, nor proper feathers, but a covering intermediate between fin and feather, and two fins or flippers like the seal. Their motion on land is by successive hops, in the most awkward manner conceivable. When going down a declivity, the center of gravity is often thrown too far forward, and away they tumble and scramble, and roll over till they get to the sea, in which they dive and swim with great swiftness. They are often seen singly, or two and three together, far out at sea. Their cry or bark is like the inarticulate human voice; and when it is clear and calm, and no object can be seen all around the horizon, their cry will sometimes startle and appal one, sounding as it does from the surface of the ocean, like the cry of a man in distress. Near the penguin quarters of this island were thousands of ducks sitting upon their eggs, which sailors and passengers destroyed with remorseless cruelty, shooting and knocking down the birds by hundreds, in barbarous sport. Some of the game was prepared for the table, but it was found too strong and fishy by those who ate of them to be relished more than once.

The largest species of the Patagonian penguin is said to weigh about forty pounds, and is four feet and a quarter in length. The bill measures four inches and a half, but is slender. The head, throat, and hind parts of the neck are brown, the back of a deep ash color, and all the under parts white. When sitting or attempting to walk, they have been compared to a dog that has been taught to sit up or to move a minuet. Their short legs drive the body in progression from side to side; and were they not assisted by their flipper-like wings, they could scarcely move faster than a tortoise. This awkward make of the legs, which so disqualifies them for living upon the land, admirably adapts them for life in the water, inasmuch as they serve for propellers, and, being placed so far behind the moving body, and worked the more swiftly for being short, they push it forward with great velocity.

The Magellanic penguin is about the size of a goose, the upper parts of its plumage, so called, being black,

Patagonian Penguins.

and the under white. Thus, with their heads erect, and their fin-like wings hanging down as half arms, they look like so many children with white aprons. Hence they are not improperly said "to unite in themselves the qualities of men, fowls, and fishes. Like men, they are upright; like fowls, they are feathered; and, like fish, they have fin-like instruments that beat the water before, and serve for all the purposes of swimming rather than flying. They are also covered more warmly all over the body with feathers than any other bird, so that the sea seems entirely their element."

These penguin islands lie between 51 and 53 degrees S. lat. and 57 and 63 degrees W. long. They are at present claimed by the English, they having a government colony at Port Egmont, on an island seventy or eighty miles to the westward of Berkley's Sound, where American whaling ships frequently put in for supplies and vegetable antiscorbutics. Eighty years ago there was a French settlement twenty miles up the Berkley Sound, but it was long since abandoned by them, and is now occupied by another colony of English. A troop of wild horses, seen by us above the cliffs while we were standing into the Sound, must have originated from that colony, the only natural quadrupeds being wolves and foxes. Seals and sea-elephants are abundant in the waters. The island on which we landed is expressively called by the Spaniards Isla de la Solidad, or the Island of Solitude. The weather there is said to be uniformly cold and stormy, and all the islands, indeed, have been sometimes denominated Foul Weather Group. They produce no trees, and only a dwarfish shrubbery, but there are

The Wales off Cape Horn

were sold for the benefit of the underwriters, and the voyage abandoned. The frigate Brandywine was once fifty days off the Cape, and it is not uncommon for vessels to make the Cape once, and after four or five weeks' sailing, to make it again. Hope is predominant that our tempestuous weather is over, and that a fortnight, at the utmost, will bring us to port. While the inmates of the cabin, like birds after a storm, are sunning themselves on deck, let my readers that purpose traversing with me the ISLAND WORLD, take a leisurely survey of our first fortnight in the Pacific.

We little thought that doubling Cape Horn in summer would have been so full of difficulty. Now we doubt whether it would be worse in mid-winter. It would seem as if the genii of storms ruled the realm. The ancients, had they known it, would have located the cave of Æolus at the end of Tierra del Fuego, in the side of one of those burning mountains. Auster and Eurus, and Boreas and Euroclydon, and all the intermediate winds of the thirty-two points of the compass, seem to have arranged their forces from the Falkland Islands to 60 degrees S. on the east of the Cape, and from 60 to 48 on the west, so as most advantageously to dispute every inch of the way with the bold navigator. The Dutch adventurer, from whom the Cape is named, that first doubled this formidable barrier, was not less a hero than he of fabulous story who loosed the dove and boldly ventured between the rocks of the Symplegades, that were fated to close upon and crush all who should attempt it, till the perilous passage, once safely made, should fix them forever apart. The Latin proverb was our consolation: *Quod fuit actum potest fieri*—what has been done can be done. We knew the difficulties of the passage had been surmounted, both in mid-summer and mid-winter. Four other ships which we caught sight of at different times were contesting the passage in like manner with ourselves, through cold, and sleet, and opposing seas. All of us, we argued, could not be baffled, and our own chance is as good as any. Patience held out with most. At every abatement of the gales and interval of sunshine, the sailors would cheerfully hang up their sea-soaked clothes, joke over the perils of the storm, and equip themselves anew for reefing and tacking. It was truly pitiful sometimes, at the hours for changing watches, to see the top of a sea break over the bow or quarter and wet them all while pulling at the ropes, so that the watch just called must stay wet their four hours of duty, and the watch going below must turn in dripping. A landsman could hardly help trembling for their safety, when ordered aloft to furl, while the ship was rolling so violently, and the wind blowing in such gusts of fury, that it would seem almost impossible for the topmasts and yards to sustain the shocks.

For several days we were reduced to close-reefed fore and main-topsails, the ship meantime rolling so tremendously that a man incurred no small risk of breaking bones who should attempt to cross the deck, or stand for a moment any where without being firmly braced or having a rope to hold to. Even in the cabin, when sitting on a firm chest, the lurch of the ship will often be such that a man will be raised from his feet and thrown with most dangerous rapidity and force to the opposite side. I saw this in one instance, when the individual plunged with such suddenness and stunning violence, head first, against the opposite side of the cabin, that we feared for a moment he was dead. There was hardly a man of us that did not learn, by some woeful bruise or wrench, with what prodigious force the body is brought up against the bulwarks or bulkheads, when once started from its place on the deck of a ship that is making an angle of forty-five degrees with the plane of her upright natural position. Putting out the arms to break the blow only throws the center of gravity further forward, and increases one's momentum.

It was amusing sometimes to see the steward, who has been several times round here in a whaleman, and whose body seems to have learned the trick of bending the other way—it was amusing sometimes to see him navigate between the galley and cabin. If caught half way by a bad lurch of the ship, he would either fall upon his knees, and do his best to hold on to himself and his dish, or else, if so fortunate as to get his foot against the capstan, he would throw his body so far forward the opposite way that on one side his person would make an obtuse angle with the deck of one hundred and thirty-five degrees or more, and on the other an acute angle of forty-five degrees or less.

We did not get sight of the redoubtable Cape (which is in 56 degrees S. lat. and 67 degrees W. long.), but were driven off to the parallel of sixty, near the South Shetlands, and afterward made the land of Cape Desolation, on the western side of Tierra del Fuego. Discoverers have rightly named it, for we thought land never seemed so bleak and desolate, snow lying between the hills and in the hollows of the mountains in this July of the South. I used to think, when studying geography at school, and bounding the continent of South America by that unexplored Island of Tierra del Fuego, or the Land of Fire, that its soil was brimstone, and the fiery materials volcanoes are made of, "a burning marl," like that which held the unblessed feet of Milton's angel when risen from off the lake of hell:

> A land that ever burn'd
> With solid, as the lake with liquid fire;
> And such appear'd in hue, as when the force
> Of subterranean wind transports a hill
> Torn from Pelorus, or the shatter'd side
> Of thundering Ætna, whose combustible
> And fueled entrails thence conceiving fire,
> Sublimed with mineral fury, aid the winds,
> And leave a singed bottom all involved
> With stench and smoke.

The German name Feuerland, or Fire Land, a German passenger tells me, had made him conceive the same idea. We were closer to it than we would like to be again as a lee shore, but saw none of its volcanoes in action, nor any traces of volcanic fire, unless it be the blackened aspect of those ugly rocks.

While off the coast of Patagonia, what time the weather would permit, some of the passengers, and the watch on duty, occupied themselves in fishing for albatrosses. They are caught by baiting a hook with pork or blubber, fastening a piece of wood near the bait, so that it may be kept floating, and letting it tow astern. The noble birds would wheel and hover over it, and at length alight on the water like a swan, and

South Pacific Albatross.

often succeed in getting all the bait without being hooked. But six or seven times they were taken and hauled aboard, the unsuspected hook catching within their long bills. They measure nine and ten feet across the wings. The first one was killed and stuffed, to be carried home for some museum. The rest were sacrificed for their long bills, wings, and large web feet. This bird is uncommonly beautiful and majestic, whether soaring sublimely upon the wing, or seen as a prisoner upon a ship's deck, from which we found they are unable to rise. Their motion through space is the easiest and most graceful conceivable. In storm or calm, once raised upon their broad pinions, you never see them flutter, but away they sail, self-propelled as naturally as we breathe; a motion of the head, or the slight curl of a wing serving to turn them, as the course of a rapid skater will be ruled at pleasure by an almost imperceptible inclination to right or left. It is the reality of that motion through space, which we sometimes conceive of in dreams, when we are borne along without conscious effort on our part, or any means of propulsion but our own free will.

If the eagle be the king of birds, the albatross ought to be called the queen, so queen-like and stately is her course on the wing, and so dignified, mild, and unfearing is her expression when captured. Her eye is full, bright, and expressive, like that of a gazelle; the head and neck large, but admirably proportioned; the feathers either a pure white or delicately penciled and speckled, except on the upper side of the wings, which are mostly black. There was an expression of pathos and intelligence about the eye of the first one captured that made it seem to me like a sin to take its life. Could I have had my way, that look should have given it liberty.

A poor Peruvian, who is working his passage home, ascribed all our bad weather and high winds afterward to having killed the albatrosses; and he and the superstitious cook, in the height of the gale, prevailed upon a young passenger who had taken one the day previous, and was keeping it alive in the long-boat, to let the noble bird go free. Like the mariners in Coleridge's Rime, they said,

We had done a hellish thing,
And it would work us woe:
Stout they averr'd we had kill'd the bird
That made the breeze to blow.
Ah, wretch! said they, the bird to slay,
That made the breeze to blow!

If superstition always made men thus humane, we might almost mourn that its dominion is passing away; but our cheerful belief is that in the good time coming it will soon be succeeded by an intelligent and pure faith, that shall make men humane from principle and inbred humanity, and gentle from unaffected love toward all the creatures of God. The lesson the Ancient Mariner learned from his strange experience, and told to the Wedding Guest, is the true one:

He prayeth best, who loveth best
All things both great and small;
For the dear God who loveth us,
He made and loveth all.
Farewell, farewell! but this I tell
To thee, thou Wedding Guest!
He prayeth well, who loveth well
Both man, and bird, and beast

Some one says of himself, what is true of humanity at large, that when the mind is fair and open, and the soul right, there is not a bird or flower I see that does not move my heart to feel toward it as a child of God; and it is a maxim of conduct I take from the poet Wordsworth,

> Never to blend my pleasure or my pride
> With sorrow of the meanest thing that lives.

This glorious bird, the albatross, is the most beautiful and lovable object of the animate world which the adventurer meets with in all the South Pacific. Philosophers might take a lesson of it in æsthetics, for when on the wing it is the very beau ideal of beauty and grace. Seamen ought to love and prize it dearly, for the drear monotony of life at sea is often relieved by its always welcome appearance, and by watching with admiration, almost envy, its glorious gyrations and curves, and swoops in the elastic ocean of air, a free race-ground, where it has no competitor.

The capture of a whale, especially on the New Zealand whaling ground, and still further south, when eight hundred or a thousand miles from land, will bring them trooping from afar, as a carcass in Mexico or Louisiana will the turkey-buzzards. I have watched them singly keeping company with our ship for days together; the last living thing, without us, to be seen at nightfall, and the first the eye recognized again and saluted in the morning. Again, I have seen them gathered by hundreds when the cutting-in of a whale alongside allured them from a circuit of five hundred miles.

In some whale ships they make a practice of catching them after the manner described above, and plucking their feathers for use, and many a whaleman's head is pillowed on them. Not unfrequently they measure eleven feet from tip to tip of the outspread wings, and they weigh from seventeen to eighteen pounds. In the Antarctic Exploring Voyage, Doctor M'Cormick met with one weighing twenty pounds, and having twelve feet stretch of wings.

It sits upon the water light and graceful as a swan, and I have often seen it dive under like a hawk or pelican for something discovered by its keen eye beneath the surface. When it wishes to rise on the wing, it has to tread water a long way, like a running ostrich, before it can attain its due momentum and soar aloft; but once fairly up, and its pinions free, it cleaves the air with exceeding swiftness, and skims the waves, like the smallest swallow, with inconceivable ease and grace.

An anonymous writer, who must have seen the bird in its native seas, says that it flies against, as well as before, the wind, and hovers around a ship at sea, never outstripped by its speed. "It enjoys the calm, and sports in the sunbeams on the glassy wave; but it revels in the storm, and darts its arrowy way before the fury of the gale. It seems to be then in its element. Mocking the surges of the mighty sea, and breasting the tempest's blast, its flight has not less sublimity, perhaps, than that of the eagle darting upward to the skies. It is a beautiful sight to behold this noble bird sailing in the air in light and graceful movements. After the first muscular exertion which gives impulse to its flight, its wings are always expanded, like the sails of a ship, and show no motion, as if it were wafted on by some invisible power. It is from this cause that it sustains untired its long and distant flight across the sea. It feeds on small marine animals, mucilaginous zoophytes, the spawn of fish, and blubber."

Notwithstanding its large size, the albatross does not appear to be a quarrelsome bird, but when attacked by its enemy, the skua gull, seeks safety in flight. It is easily captured, and was used in quantities, boiled and roasted, by Captain Cook and his crew, who gladly regaled themselves on it after being confined for a length of time at sea to salt food. When breeding, the female flies to some inaccessible rock or lonely spot of ground, lays, it is said, but one egg, and makes a nest around it. The male watches with tender anxiety while she is on the nest; and ever on the wing, brings her the daintiest food from his piratical wanderings on the deep.

In the classification of Linnæus, the albatross is the Diomedea exulans, a genus which is described as having the bill very long, stout, edged, compressed, straight, suddenly curved; upper mandible channeled on the sides, and much hooked at the point; the under smooth, and truncated at the extremity; nostrils lateral, remote from the base, tubular, covered on the sides, and open in front; legs short, with only three very long toes entirely webbed; the lateral ones are margined; wings very long and narrow, with the primary quills short, and the secondaries long.

From its often choosing the same places for breeding with the penguin, the albatross is thought to have a peculiar affection for that singular amphibious creature, and a pleasure in its society. Their nests are to be seen together on uninhabited islands, where the ground slants to the sea, the penguin not being formed either for flying or crying. As if for mutual protection, the albatross raises its nest on a hillock of heath, sticks, and long grass, about two feet high; and round this the penguins, in a circle, make their lower settlements in burrowed holes in the ground, commonly, it is said, eight penguins to one albatross.

Sailors generally, but especially right-whalemen, have many yarns to tell of this noble bird, which they call by the unclassical name of *gony*. They have a partiality, which is not to be wondered at, for this superb specimen of oceanic ornithology, although coarser ones among them are too apt to show it in a way not so pleasing to humanity, and which I have often tried to dissuade them from, that is, capturing them so cruelly by hook and line. When so taken, knowing ones often carve little billets of wood with inscriptions, which they tie to their necks, and then set them loose again. These birds in repeated instances have afterward been captured in different and distant latitudes by other ships, and curious information has been so communicated.

The albatross has often served poor Jack a good turn for grub when his larder has run low, or when he has been cast upon some desolate sea-bird island; and many anonymous anecdotes are told in the forecastle respecting them. But the most remarkable I have ever heard, bordering indeed upon the marvelous and incredible, if not itself a providential miracle, is the following, contained for substance in a letter from an officer in the eighty-third regiment of the English army to his friends in Montreal. While the division to which the writer belonged was on its way to the Orient, being at the time a short distance eastward of the Cape, one of the men was severely flogged for some slight offense. Maddened at the punishment, the poor fellow was no sooner released, than, in the sight of all his comrades and the ship's crew, he sprang overboard. There was a high sea running at the time, and, as the man swept on astern, all hope of saving him seemed to vanish. Relief, however, came from a quarter where no one ever dreamed of looking for it before. During the delay incident on lowering a boat, and while the crowd on deck were watching the form of the soldier struggling with the boiling waves, and growing every moment less distinct, a large albatross, such as are always found in those latitudes, coming like magic, with an almost imperceptible motion, approached and made a swoop at the man, who, in the agonies of the death-struggle, seized it and held it firmly in his grasp, and by this means kept afloat until assistance was rendered from the vessel!

Incredible as this story seems, the name and position of the writer of the letter, who was an eye-witness of the scene, places its authenticity beyond a doubt. But for the assistance thus afforded, no power on earth could have saved the soldier, as, in consequence of the tremendous sea running, a long time elapsed before the boat could be manned and got down, all this time the man clinging to the bird, whose flutterings and struggles to escape bore him up. Who, after this, should despair? A raging sea—a drowning man—an albatross; what eye could see safety under such circumstances? or who will dare to call this chance? Is it not rather a lesson intended to stimulate Faith and Hope, and teach us never to despair, since, in the darkest moment, when the waves dash, and the winds roar, and a gulf seems closing over our heads, *there may be an albatross at hand*, with a commission to save us from Him, of whom it is said, *As birds flying, so will the Lord of Hosts defend Jerusalem; defending also, he will deliver it, and passing over, he will preserve it.*

There is another lesson taught me by this most majestic and beautiful of birds, for which I think I am a wiser man than before. We observe that when captured and set at liberty in the ship, it can never of itself rise from the even surface of the deck, though outwardly unconstrained and free; but we must toss the noble bird overboard, or lift him quite clear of the ship's rail, before he can use his glorious pinions and mount aloft into the air. Then he will stretch those ample wings, and sail away through space in the very poetry of motion, as if the elastic element of air and the bird were one, making the gazer wonder and fairly long to be taking the same aerial flight.

Even so is it sometimes with the Christian. He is brought by Providence into straits and perplexities, whence he can not rise and extricate himself alone, where the wings of faith and love seem to be of no avail to him, until a friendly hand lifts him up and throws him out upon the deep, where he must say, with Peter, "Lord, save; I perish." Then at once he loses despair; he surmounts the difficulty; he breaks his prison; he mounts up as on eagles' wings; now the pinions of Faith and Love nobly sustain him, and bear him away aloft; and he wonders at the nightmare of doubt and fear that kept him from using them before. He is ashamed of the wrong thoughts of God that had begun to gather and darken in his mind. He sees that God was infinitely wise and good in appointing the discipline to which he has been subjected, and he flies all the higher and better for it in holiness now. Like the Ancient Mariner, who has served us for illustration once before,

> He goes like one that hath been stunn'd,
> And is of sense forlorn;
> A better and a wiser man
> He'll rise to-morrow morn.

CHAPTER III.

HONOLULU AND ITS ENVIRONS.

The constant sun
Had run his faithful round, and duly sunk
Beneath the crystal wave of this calm sea;
And centuries had fill'd their measure up
With quiet morns and peaceful eventides:
An unclad tawny race, age after age,
Had roved the woods and waters, all unchanged.
But men of other lip from a far land
Had brought religion, enterprise, and law.
The merchant's eye, with expectation large,
As oft it scann'd the far-outstretching point
Of this most charming isle, with anxious gaze,
Was often feasted with returning bark,
From coast barbaric, or from unknown isle,
Freighted with ocean's wealth, those pearly drops,
A growth indigenous beneath the flood;
Or laden with the spoil of mammoth brutes,
That roam the vast Pacific's liquid fields.—*Anon.*

Thirty-five mornings and evenings from Callao, and our anchor is scratching the outer reef round the island heart of the Pacific. This is a sailing distance of more than five thousand miles. Including the time in which we were becalmed in the *Doldrums*, the seamen's name for those parts of the sea directly under the Equator, where they have neither northeast nor southeast trades, but baffling winds and calms, we have averaged more than one thousand miles a week; a rate of progress which before, when we were so crank and heavy at the head with those ill-stowed naval stores, none of us would believe the snail-paced Wales could ever make.

At times the trades have been so strong that we could not carry top-gallant sails. It was luxurious sailing for our disabled seamen, with symptoms of the scurvy,* who could sleep on deck all the while, the temperature of the air for three successive weeks being indicated by the thermometer at eighty-three or eighty-four, while that of the ocean was seventy-seven or seventy-eight.

The aspect of Oahu, at first approach, is hardly more inviting to the mariner than purgatory was to Dante and Beatrice in the Inferno. For aught your eye can see of verdure, you would think, if there be

* It seems to have been discovered of late that the true source of scorbutic disease, as it shows itself in our ships and prisons, is the want of potash in the blood; that salted meat contains little more than half the potash in fresh meats; and that, while an ounce of rice contains only five grains of potash, an ounce of potato contains one thousand eight hundred and seventy-five grains, which accounts for the great increase of the disease since the scarcity of the potato. In patients under this disease, the blood is found to be deficient in potash; and it has been ascertained by repeated experiments that whatever be the diet, such patients speedily recover if a few grains (from twelve to twenty) of some salt of potash be given daily. Lime-juice is regularly ordered in the navy as a specific for the disease, and the reason of its efficacy is not the acid, but the amount of potash, being eight hundred and forty-six grains in an ounce. On these facts it seems possible to found a slight, but very salutary, improvement in the navy. Let a portion of tartrate of potash be ordered regularly to be mixed with the lime-juice that is given out for use, and let arrangements be adopted for boiling the salt meat in steam. A large portion of the salt would thus be eliminated, and the food made more wholesome. A similar course might be adopted in work-houses and prisons.

inhabitants, that the azure ocean which laves their coast must be also the garden that yields their food, did there not blow ever and anon, from off shore, grateful odors like the heliotrope,

"That tell you whence their fragrance is supplied.'

Huge waves are ever breaking over the coral reef that incloses the harbor of Honolulu, and rolling along both sides of the channel till they are lost in deep water inside, but not without infusing a stranger who may be rowing in from a ship outside with the sedative fear of being capsized as he mounts the ridges of those broad-backed rollers.

To the right, and directly in front as you enter the harbor, rise the frowning craters of Leahi and Puawai, now called—my readers may say whether more euphoniously or not—Punch-bowl Hill and Diamond Point. These once vomited their combustible and fueled entrails upon the plains and into the sea; but they have long since gone to sleep, and "green grow the rushes O" in their concave and smooth basins, where it is to be taken for granted almost every classic visitor at Honolulu has taken lessons as we have in stone-rolling, and scanning Virgil to the sound,

Quadrupedante putrem sonitu quatit ungula campum.

On the flats at their base are the extensive cocoa and palm groves of Waikiki, and the beautiful valleys of Nuuanu and Manoa, verdant with patches of kalo, and other creations of the tropics—terrace upon terrace, and sparkling all along with squares and diamonds of the flowing brook by which they are irrigated.

A stranger coming into port, however, sees nothing of all this, but only a dusty, arid plain, lying four or five miles along the shore, and from one to two miles inland, occupied in its western extremity, for about three quarters of a mile, with a singularly promiscuous array of low hay-stack houses for seven or eight thousand people, to whose dry grass-thatching one thinks he has only to hold a torch in order to wrap the whole village in smoke and flame. It is the wonder of every new observer that a town built of such fire-inviting materials, and the houses often so close together, is not daily consumed in a general conflagration.

The fort, which the French, under Admiral Tromelin, have recently dismantled, is built upon a small, low promontory in front of the town, and furnished with fifty-two guns that command the channel and inner harbor. It is itself again commanded in the rear by a battery of fourteen guns on Punch-bowl Hill, at an elevation of five hundred and fifty feet above the sea. Some of the government offices, the custom-house, a large four-story edifice, the Romish Cathedral, and a few of the warehouses, stores, and dwellings of the foreigners, are well-made structures of coral, either shingled or covered with zinc, and furnished with lookouts on the top for descrying approaching sails and vessels in the outer roadstead.

The greater part of the habitations of foreigners and of natives that are looking up in the world are constructed after the style of building prevalent on the coast of Spanish America. The common soil, pulverized and wet like clay for brick-making, is then mixed up with dry grass and put into molds of a large size, usually eighteen inches or two feet long, a foot wide, and from six to eight inches thick. These are dried in the sun, and then laid up into walls. They are called *adobes* or *adobies*, from the old Egyptian word *adaub*, derived in Spain from the Moors. There being no frost to heave the ground, nor long-continued rains to crumble these sun-dried bricks, walls made of them are durable enough for common purposes in the first stages of civilization. When plastered with lime and white-washed, they are commendably neat and comfortable.

Among them the sailor's chapel is agreeably conspicuous; from whose chaplain, the Rev. Samuel C. Damon, a warm reception and hospitable induction into the chaplaincy-house induced that comfortable feeling of being cordially made at home, and elicited at once those pleasurable emotions of confidence and love which it is necessary for a man to be a valetudinarian wanderer on the sea, and to find abroad such true Christian hospitality, in order rightly to appreciate.

It must be gratifying to the friends of seamen (and I begin to find their name is legion), as well as to the numerous whalemen themselves that touch at Honolulu, to know of the acceptableness and wide sphere of usefulness daily opening to this chaplain, and to the one also at Lahaina. Though installed only as seamen's chaplain, and supported by the society at home, yet as pastor of the Bethel church, and the only Christian minister for the increasing body of American and English residents, his influence and field of usefulness are by no means limited to the sea-faring class.

While it is an enviable post for the opportunities it gives for doing good, it is also one of difficulty and temptation, and far from desirable, except by a man of Christian firmness and independence, resolved upon the performance of duty,

> As ever in his great Taskmaster's eye,

and regardless alike of the smiles and frowns of a self-approving, haughty world.

In such a community as that at Honolulu, to a wayfarer a few years ago, every body seemed to have every body else by the ears, and an excessive eagerness for gain, gossiping, and news created a state of mind, as in California now, by no means favorable to the general inculcation of truth, or to individual growth in intellect or godliness. The truths that are the most wholesome, medicinal, and specific in such a case are far from being the most liked, and unless they be sugared and oiled, and fitted for the stomachs of worldly-wise men, and tuned for ears polite, they rather seem to disorder digestion, to generate acidities and flatulence, and put fleas in the ear.

If a man, also, will use the moral probe and lancet in the case aforesaid, it is required that he put on gloves and magnetize his subjects, or administer chloroform, so that they shall not feel or writhe. And he must be very careful not to operate too far or too long at a time, lest there ensue so much constitutional irritation as seriously to affect the patient's prognosis.

The seamen, however, in whose behalf the chaplain at Honolulu is to labor every way in his power, need no such management or mesmeric manipulating or etherization. The plainer Gospel truths are shot at them the better, though it be at point-blank aim, and with ball-cartridges. They will testify always that pungent words of warning and counsel, affectionately but fearlessly spoken, to suit individual sins and states of minds, without circumlocution or disguise, is the preacher's best way of doing good, whether it be at Oahu, or San Francisco, or New York.

If faithful to his trust, the chaplain at Honolulu will be a ministering friend that shall never be forgotten, to thousands of transient mariners. And may he be enabled also (which perhaps needs the greater grace) rightly to divide the word of truth to residents there; *to reprove, rebuke, and exhort with all long-suffering and doctrine; to charge them that are rich in the world that they be not high-minded, nor trust in uncertain riches, but in the living God, who giveth us richly all things to enjoy; that they do good, that they be rich in good works, ready to distribute, willing to communicate, laying up in store for themselves a good foundation against the time to come, that they may lay hold on eternal life.*

The location of " The Mission," so called, at Honolulu, is in the upper or southeastern part of the town, about half a mile from most of the houses of other foreign residents. Here are seven dwelling-houses, occupied by the families of the pastor of the First Church, the book-binder, printer, teacher, general superintendent, and two secular agents. Besides these there are a stone building for the printing-press and bindery, another for the depository, a large school-house or conference room, in which are held the general meetings, and the capacious stone church, together with several small *adobe* or dirt buildings, for housing the families from out-stations, and excellent for fleas, cockroaches, scorpions, centipedes, and tarantulas.

The coral edifice for the Honolulu First Church is a spacious building, one hundred feet long and seventy-eight wide, with an unfinished basement for schools and prayer-meetings; and in its construction galleries are allowed for, but not yet made. It was planned and got under way by Rev. Mr. Bingham, and most of the materials collected at the expense of the chiefs and people. It was completed under Rev. Mr. Armstrong, at an estimated expense, in voluntary Hawaiian labor and contributions, of $30,000. It shows conspicuous through the spy-glass far out to sea, and is the first object of art the eye rests upon in coming into port; and it will stand, we trust, for ages, a pleasing monument to the stranger of the regard paid by this nation of emerging heathen to the institutions of the Gospel. May it never want a congregation of Christianized Hawaiians to fill its ample courts!

In this vicinity, also, are the Oahu charity school-house, a neat structure of stone, thirty-six feet long by twenty-six wide, for the mixed children of foreigners and natives, and the buildings appropriated for the school of the chiefs. This latter is under the care of Mr. and Mrs. Cook; and by common consent it is a most interesting and admirably managed family school. It consists of fourteen chief boys and girls, whose education and habits of living are strictly American or English.

They live and study together very happily, and ride daily on horseback, or make *adobes*, for punishment and exercise together, if refractory. While under suitable wholesome restraint, which the children of chiefs were never subject to before, they have every thing around them made so agreeable that restrictions are hardly felt; and there is, perhaps, hardly one of the number, much as they may sometimes hanker after the indulgences of heathenism, that would be willing to return to former barbarous liberties and ways. They are pleasing in appearance and deportment, and some of the girls are not wanting in personal charms, which, along with their appanage, have already won husbands to some of them among respectable foreigners.

The salaries of the teachers of this school, while they were missionaries of the American Board, and all its other expenses, were paid by the chiefs. As containing the future educated rulers of the Hawaiian nation, it is full of promise and hope, and should have the fervent prayers of God's people, that the noble youth there gathered may have their minds savingly acquainted with the Gospel, as well as properly disciplined and furnished with useful knowledge.

A mile and a half or two miles further along the plain in this direction is the pleasant site of the Punahou school for the children of the mission, under the care of Rev. Mr. and Mrs. Dole, and their associates, Mr. Rice and wife. The valuable lands connected with it were given by the chiefs to Mr. Bingham, and he first broke ground there by putting up some adobe buildings, which, after his departure for America in 1840, were added to and turned to their present use. The average number of pupils there is twenty-five;

of boarding scholars, seventeen. Boys can be fitted there for college; probably it will be found to be itself a Polynesian University in miniature, when hereafter graduates shall issue thence with academic degrees, and doctorates in the republic of letters be conferred upon mission-sprung or native-born Hawaiians.

I believe the boys and girls now there to be as happy and innocent a company of youth as ever were brought together, and they are in a fair way of being well disciplined and taught. None can question the propriety and needfulness of such an institution to a mission which has multiplied itself already, through God's blessing, by upward of one hundred and fifty living children. Its location at the Hawaiian metropolis is judicious—far enough from town to be out of the way of its scandal and noise, but near enough for the boys to have the benefit of one religious service at the Bethel every Sabbath.

In the rear of Punahou is the delightful Valley of Manoa, where, hidden by the trees and flowering shrubs, and velvet hill-sides that catch the rain, and lulled by the music of birds and purling brooks, a man may almost forget that a tropical sun is shining, and the stern cares and strife of life are passing upon the plain below. It was here that the strong-minded Elizabethan queen, Kaahumanu, retired to die in the faith of Christ. I have been once in the beautiful bamboo house where she breathed her last, and often since in my dreams have I gone back to that charming valley, when oceans have intervened.

It were well that the boys of the school, and the sunburned, adobe-walled residents often resorted there:

'twould smooth the furrowed brow of business, and cool the fervid blood of youth, and quicken the jaded spirits of the too studious boy or laborious man. It is a saying of Wordsworth:

> One impulse from a vernal wood may teach you more of man,
> Of human nature and of good, than all the sages can.
> Nor less I deem that there are powers
> Which of themselves our minds impress;
> And we can feed this mind of ours
> In a wise passiveness.

The valley itself, to one secluded in it, is one of the loveliest that Nature has imbosomed in these romantic isles; the scenery bold and beautiful; the volcanic hills on either side crowned with the rich and deep-green verdure; a sparkling brook making its way in a cascade over a precipice at the head of the vale, and, meandering along through it, creating beauty in its course; birds singing up among those bowers of verdure; watered kalo-patches, and *kukui* trees, with their silvery sheen, and now and then a glimpse of the azure sea.

Still away to the right, past the palm-groves of Waikiki, and at the foot of one of the extinct volcanoes, with a broad out-look on the ocean, are the remains of an ancient *heiau*, or heathen temple, its walls one hundred and thirty feet in length by seventy in breadth. Unless told that they were part of the sacred inclosure, called in Cook's voyages a *morai*, the visitor might suppose them to be the remains of some metropolitan hog-pen, like the suburban receptacles of that sort which have graced and perfumed the city of New York. Heathenism, hogs, and devils have gone together since the time that the latter, when cast out of the possessed, entered into the whole herd of swine feeding. Good will it be for humanity when this triple alliance shall be broken the world over, as it seems to have been at the Sandwich Islands.

Within the memory of some persons now living, the heads of slain warriors in the battle of Nuuanu were seen impaled on the walls of this *heiau*, and human blood and bones for unknown ages have manured the crumbling lava all around it. "Hecatombs of victims," says the historian, "have perished within its precincts, and it will remain for generations the dark and repulsive type to the Hawaiian of what this nation once was; while the dreary and frowning crest of Leahi, rising above, alike recalls the mind to that period when the fires and heavings of the earth beneath spread terror and destruction among the affrighted inhabitants. They stand well beside each other; one, the puny and desolate monument of man's apostasy; and the volcano, the wrathful sign that Nature shared the curse of Adam's crime."

CHAPTER IV.

HAWAIIAN HISTORY AND ETHNOLOGY.

Even the favor'd isles
So lately found, although the constant sun
Cheer all their seasons with a grateful smile,
Can boast but little virtue, and, inert
Through plenty, lose in morals what they gain
In climate—victims of luxurious ease.
These, therefore, I can pity; placed remote
From all that science traces, art invents,
Or inspiration teaches; and inclosed
In boundless oceans never to be pass'd
By navigators uninform'd as they,
Or plow'd, perhaps, by British bark again.
COWPER.

THE muse of the gentle poet that indited these lines, in the last century, was then all inadequate to project the important position on the map of the world, and on the highway of human progress, which those remote isles, whereof he doubted if they would ever be visited again, have now assumed. Those Hawaiian, or Sandwich Islands, so called by the English in honor of Lord Sandwich, were first made known to the rest of the world, at least to the commercial part, through their discovery of it by Captain Cook in the month of January, 1778. On the authority of Humboldt, in the late work entitled "Cosmos," Gaetano, a Spaniard, discovered one of the Sandwich Islands in the year 1542. But the discovery was not prosecuted, and little or nothing was known of it till the voyage of Cook.

> Placed far amid the melancholy main,

and lying on the direct route to India from the modern, perhaps the ancient Ophir, this island cluster, having eight summits, properly forms the Ararat of the North Pacific. They lie between the meridians of 155 and 160½ west longitude, and between the parallels of 19 and 22½ north latitude; about eighteen hundred miles from California, northeast; five thousand from China, west; five thousand from South America, southeast; twenty-seven hundred from the Society Islands on the south. The names of those inhabited, taken as they lie in order from southeast to northwest, are Hawaii, Maui, Kahoolawe, Lanai, Molokai, Oahu, Kauai, Niihau, embracing an area of about six thousand one hundred square miles. They extend in a curved line four hundred miles, and would appear to be the summits of two parallel ranges of mountains or volcanic centers, of which the volcanoes Mauna Loa and Mauna Kea, in Hawaii, are the southeastern extremities. These mountains are of nearly equal heights; Loa, according to the measurements of the United States Exploring Expedition, is thirteen thousand seven hundred and sixty feet above half tide; Kea, thirteen thousand nine hundred and fifty; Mount Hualalai, on the same island, is about ten thousand. On Maui, the next of the group westward, Mount Haleakala, is ten thousand two hundred and seventeen feet high, and Eeka six thousand one hundred and thirty. Oahu has two ranges four thousand feet high, and the highest point of Kauai is eight thousand feet.

The origin of all the islands is purely volcanic. They were evidently formed by repeated eruptions from the bed of the ocean, depositing layer upon layer of volcanic matter, until, by this process and the gradual retirement of the sea, they have attained their present elevation. That process may still be seen going on in the largest of these islands (Hawaii), the interior of which would seem to be a vast reservoir or chamber of pent-up mineral fire, that lets off now and then some of its redundant elements by violent emission, as the lancet does from the arm of a man threatened with apoplexy. Kauai, the northwesternmost of the group, is the oldest made, as proved by the lava there being most disintegrated and frequently formed into basalt, like that of the Giant's Causeway in Ireland. Hawaii, which Captain Cook naturally enough miscalled Owyhee, is the southeasternmost and latest formed, being the only one where there is an active volcano, and that in the southern portion of this large island. Volcanic fire seems to be working to the south and east, toward the great furnaces in the range of the Andes, on the continent of South America.

When these islands first came to be inhabited can not be conjectured: whence is probable. Tradition reaches not to their origin, although curious fables of Hawaiian cosmogony do. But the natives preserve the genealogy of seventy-three kings, have the names of some of the South Pacific islands, knew the direction of the Society Islands, the nearest inhabited group, and have tales of their ancestors' coming thence; and their language is a dialect of the one great family of Polynesian tongues.

When but a few years ago a Japanese junk came ashore at Waialua, on the Island of Oahu, and the natives saw the few survivors, men looking much like themselves, who had been drifting out of their course for nearly a year, and were five thousand miles from their homes, the missionary there told me that the first inference and talk of the natives was, "Now we know whence our fathers came from." A number of well-authenticated facts like this point to the way in which all the islands of the Pacific may have been populated, and indicate, too, how the highly-civilized aborigines of South America may have had their beginning directly in a pair of Japanese blown off by a typhoon from the shores of Eastern Asia, instead of our having to trace them down from Behring's Straits through the length of North America.

The temperature of the Hawaiian Islands is equable, and the climate in every way salubrious. The Northeast Trades fan them perpetually on the windward side, and there is a regularly alternating, gentle land and sea breeze on the leeward side. The heat experienced is at no place in the group so great as at New Orleans in the summer time, or often at New York. For the year round there is always the purest ocean air, and a variety of climate can be commanded by change of situation that is not to be had elsewhere in the world within the same area. American constitutions, debilitated by the uniform heat of a leeward residence, find repair and health by moving to a station where they can be fanned by the trades; and persons constitutionally inclined to pulmonary disease when living at the sea-side, are benefited by recourse to the mountains.

The highest elevation of the mercury observed in ten years at Lahaina (the port on the leeward side of Maui, where most of the whale ships recruit) was 86 degrees of Fahrenheit; the lowest, 54 degrees; greatest difference in any one day, 19 degrees, a diurnal range which is of very rare occurrence, the difference between noon and morning, or noon and night, being seldom more than 10 degrees. The highest range observed is in June, the lowest in January. The greatest heat noted at Honolulu for twelve years was 90 degrees; greatest cold, 53 degrees; yearly mean, 75 degrees. Sudden weather-changes are unknown, nor are there storms of long continuance; and in every view the Sandwich Islands may be deemed one of the most healthful countries in the world. Families are reared in great safety, as the remarkable increase of the missionaries shows. Children there do not yet have to run the gauntlet of those formidable diseases that invade families in climes less favored with genial skies and perpetual summer.

The human constitution, it is evident, had attained to great perfection at the Sandwich Islands, and, their barbarism and sensuality to the contrary notwithstanding, there was high physical health and beauty before it was poisoned and marred by the mixture of abandoned foreigners, and the fresh provocatives to profligacy thereby given. The reverse is now painfully true, for disease is rife, and there is evidence of fatal, we fear irremediable, detriment having been done to the native constitution. Still, the physical aspect of Hawaiians, as a race, is pleasing. Their complexion is a clear olive brown, like that of the Spanish gipsy, or as near in color to the kernel of an English walnut as any thing we are familiar with. They call themselves KA-ULU, the red skin, in contrast with the KEOKEO race, or white skin.

Their features would make them to be classed by physiologists with the Malay division of the human family, from which, doubtless, they have sprung. They have generally thick lips and large nostrils, but the nose is not flat, nor the hair woolly, but uniformly strait and black. They have rather high cheek bones, like the North American Indian, and the erect European forehead, certainly not depressed or retreating, as one of the Sandwich Island histories erroneously characterizes it.

The national Hawaiian head is of a good size, and phrenologically well shaped, though it has a rather unduly large base,* and is flattened and straight at the back. This unnatural flatness of the occiput is thought to be owing to the way the mother holds her babe, which is by the left hand, supporting the back of its head. Frequently, too, they lay its little head in a hard gourd-shell on purpose to flatten it; and the way of all Hawaiians, when sleeping, is to lie upon the back, which tends to keep the skull of the form given it in childhood. It is deemed becoming to a man to have his hair very short behind; and manly beauty, in their view, depends more upon the *plane figure*

* Of three Polynesian skulls compared in the tables of Dr. Morton, the largest capacity of brain was eighty-four cubic inches. Whether either of the skulls was Hawaiian, does not appear — probably not. We think the average capacity of the Hawaiian head would be found larger, and to come much nearer to the mean of the modern Teutonic family, which is, by the same table, ninety-two cubic inches.

and breadth of the occiput than upon the height and fullness of the forehead. We have often heard them wonder at what they deem the fondness of foreigners for round heads.

In person the Hawaiians are well formed, large limbed, and somewhat taller than the average of Americans. The race of the high chiefs especially was large, athletic, and finely proportioned. We have seen among the few that survive specimens of muscular power and manly beauty that might be the archetypes of Jupiter Tonans or Apollo Belvidere. The chief women are enormously big and unwieldly; but the impression of their greatness, as of the size of unclad savages generally, and of all people that dress loosely, like the Moors and Turks, is apt to be exaggerated and deceptive in the view of those that are not used to the sight of the human form in flowing robes or the state of nature. This consideration alone may account, in great part, for the tales of early voyagers as to the giant size of Patagonians and certain tribes of South Sea islanders; and it has had much to do in originating the idea so generally prevalent of the peculiar handsomeness of Persians, Greeks, and Turks. Let them be seen in the close coat, or strait jacket, or fashionable corset-boards of the occidental dress, and the illusion will straightly vanish.

Ethnologically considered, the Hawaiian race must rank high, both in its *physique* and *morale*. The forehead, as we have intimated, rises after the European model, and the common facial angle is nearer to the Caucasian than the Malayan type. I have had in possession a skull with all the teeth, which I picked up from among many others near an old battle-ground at Wailuku, on the Island of Maui; and it is judged superior, both for size and conformation, to the average of Anglo-Saxon heads. The native mind is docile, quick to learn, and more than ordinarily retentive. To arithmetic, and the arts of writing and drawing, the youth have a special aptitude. Our American school-book, called Colburn's First Lessons, may be said to be a national study. Their own language they acquire with more facility from books than boys with us do the English, and the volubility of almost all natives is immense. It is now a statute of the land that no young persons are to be married unless they can read; the want of this accomplishment is, therefore, very rare. Their language affords a fair field for ethnological inquiry, in the new department which the Germans have opened under the appellation of "Sprachenkunde," or "Glottology."

Now that it is reduced to writing, the language bids fair to last longer than the race. The stock of high chiefs has already nearly run out; their rapid decay being the more noticeable than that of ordinary natives, because they formed a large body by themselves, more distinct from the vulgar by peculiar and time-honored privilege and custom, than the nobility of any other land of which we have clear historic record.

Captain Cook estimated the entire population of the islands, at the time of their discovery, as four hundred thousand. But this was probably exaggerated, since the wonder-stricken natives flocked from every quarter whithersoever he landed, in order to see the *haole moku*, the foreign island, as they called the ship, and to lay eyes upon their returned God Lono, as they uniformly designated Captain Cook. In this way the same persons were often likely to be reckoned twice in his rough computation of numbers. But from other sources we have reason to believe that the population was at least three times what it is at present, a little rising of one hundred thousand. Wide-wasting disease, as in the case of every Pacific island yet visited by unrestrained foreigners, followed upon the first contact of the European with the native race: so far as can be gathered from the dim recollections of surviving old men, it was much like the "wonderful plague" that so providentially depopulated New England of its savage warriors, just before the settlement of the Pilgrims.

It is a singular fact, which the sagacious Mr. Williams, the martyr-missionary of Eromanga, takes notice of, that ravaging pestilence, in some form or other, has always ensued upon the first intercourse of foreigners with the different islanders of the South Sea. That the depopulation of the Sandwich Islands, in particular, has been considerable, is manifest, aside from the testimony of aged natives, by the traces to be often seen of extensive cultivation where now there are few or no inhabitants. This is especially true in the north part of the great Island of Hawaii, in the district occupied as a missionary by Rev. Elias Bond. There is a vast *heiau* or idol temple there, which we surveyed and measured; and in all the region about there are lines of low stone fences and inclosures for hogs, and the dividing marks of potato and *kalo* patches, where now there is scarcely an inhabitant.

It is a common saying on Hawaii, that Captain Cook's mark was deep and deadly. In the providence of God, he met his death by his own rashness and self-confidence, at the very hands of the incensed barbarians whom he had wrongly allowed to worship him, and who were restrained from injuring him when they felt themselves wronged, by the belief that he was a god, until a chief, whom he struck with his sword, instinctively grasped and held him in his powerful arms, at which Captain Cook uttered a cry of distress. The dread charm of his divinity was at once broken by that cry, and the chiefs and people fell upon him in anger and instantly slew him, exclaiming, He groans —he is not a god. The Hawaiian authors of a little text-book of history called *Moolelo Hawaii*, collated by Rev. Mr. Dibble, quote, in their simplicity, and apply to this event, that passage of God's word wherein it is said of Herod, when he received acclamation as a god, that he gave not God the glory, and was eaten of worms. Their inference is that God's hand was in his death; in thinking of which, at this late day, our most painful reflection is that the great navigator did not direct the rude natives to the God who made heaven and earth, instead of receiving divine homage himself. But we are willing to believe that he was not aware to what extent they honored and served him as a god.

The influence of Vancouver's visit, fourteen years after this melancholy event, was more benign. He endeavored to turn the thoughts of Kamehameha the Great to the true God, left him a pair of cattle under a promise that none should be killed for fifteen years, and several useful seeds. The intercourse of his men, however, and that of the whale-ships which now began to anchor in their waters, was sadly disastrous to the native constitution and morals, poisoning the fountains of health, and inducing premature decay and barrenness. Details, too, might be given which have come to my knowledge, of treacherous cruelty and wickedness, and that on the part of some of our own countrymen, so shocking to humanity and decency that they can hardly be named.

The vicious teachings of wicked sailors that now and then stopped among them, and of escaped Botany Bay convicts that strayed there, and of almost all transient foreign visitors that were glad to be able to revel uncurbed in the sensual sty of heathenism, were all the while digging the grave of the nation, and burying in it their victims, hideous and loathsome with disease. The first missionaries have things to tell a visitor of early heathenism, and of the habits of foreigners in those days, "to make both the ears of those who hear thereof to tingle." In the providence of God, however, the looseness, the utter abandonment, and practical infidelity of those who stopped among them had one good effect. It was to undermine the power of the idol-priesthood, and to loosen the oppression of the *tabus*. They, the foreigners, were seen to eat forbidden food on tabu-days, to pay no sacrifices to the gods, and habitually to break the tabus with impunity. The natives naturally reasoned upon this—it can not be so fatal as the priests tell us to violate the tabus: the foreigners do not die when they break them; why should we?

Those tabus were many of them horribly oppressive and harassing, and it is matter of astonishment, as well as of careful philosophic inquiry, how their despotism could have possibly obtained such a desperate death-hold, like a permanent nightmare, upon the imagination of the people. But the history of the world elsewhere than in those imbosomed isles of the Pacific, shows that nothing is impossible in the way of plebeian enslavement and degradation when king, priest, and nobility combine. The tabus at the Sandwich Islands would have been but a bugbear, had not the powerful idol-priesthood and the chiefs that played into their hands united to enforce them. They made it death to be found in a canoe on a tabu day (*La Tabu*). If any one made a noise on a tabu day, or while prayers were saying, he must die; if he were found with his wife on a tabu day, it was death; if a woman on the tabu day ate pork, cocoa-nuts, bananas even, and certain kinds of fish, she must die.

It is the statement of David Malo, one of the most sensible and pious Hawaiians living, counselor to the king, as was his father before him, and now a minister of the Gospel—it is his written declaration in the Hawaiian Spectator, that "when two persons entered the marriage state, the man must build an eating-house for himself, another for his wife to eat in, another for his god, another for sleeping, and another for his wife to beat kapa in, that is, to manufacture the native cloth from bark, which was formerly almost the sole employment of the women. In addition to this burden of building many houses, there was also another in providing food. He first heated the oven and baked for his wife;

then he heated another and baked for himself; then he opened the oven containing his wife's kalo, and pounded it; then he performed the same operation on his own. The husband ate in his house, and the wife in hers. They did not eat together, lest they should be slain for violating the tabu."

In accordance with the genius of the Hawaiian system of idolatry, birds, beasts, and trees were the adopted gods of different individuals. If one, then, made his idol of the native apple-tree (*ohia*), it was ever after tabu to him, so that he could not eat of it but on pain of death. If his god were *kalo*, the chief staple for food, then he could not eat *kalo*. If a hen, then such fowls were interdicted food. If a hog, then the hog was sacred. Stones, even, were objects of worship, and became tabu, so that one might not sit on them. Fish, in like manner, were idolized, and could not then be eaten; and so of specific things too numerous to be mentioned. Mr. Dibble justly remarks, that in this instance, at least, a state of heathenism was a state of bondage, not only moral and mental, but that also which toucheth the skin and bones of men, which wears out their sinews and cuts short their lives: a state of deep degradation and ruin, from which, even to the present day, they are but slowly recovering.

Now an incidental good effect of the very profligacy, so depraving, of abandoned foreigners at the Hawaiian Islands, undoubtedly was to induce the nation to abandon the system of idolatry and tabus; and it is at the present time a notable and world-known fact, as it was then so strangely providential, that while the first American missionaries were upon the high seas on their way to the islands in 1819, to try what scoffers called a novel experiment of knight-errant humanity, the idol gods were disowned, their temples burned, the great wall of tabus broken down, and the way prepared, so far as that went, for the reception of the true God.

A merchant of Boston, at that time an opposer of what is called the orthodox view of religion, upon hearing that the missionaries were about to embark, offered to send out gratuitously for them the frame of a dwelling, being the house in which the family of one of those very missionaries now reside at Kailua, whose cordial hospitality we have shared. When the merchant was asked his motives for this, he replied that it shocked him to think of civilized men leading so miserable a life as that of the missionaries must be if no such provision were made for them. And he added that he had given orders to all his captains to offer the missionaries a gratuitous passage back to this country when they were ready to return, as they would all be glad to do before six months.

In this he was, happily, disappointed; for although the first missionaries, when they landed at Kailua in 1820, were without furniture, other than they made out of their own boxes, without flour or food, except what they could procure from the natives, and without a tithe of the comforts missionaries now have, yet, being received with friendliness, they heroically held on by faith and prayer. It seemed to be thought then in America—such was the novelty of the missionary enterprise, the poverty of its resources, and the ignorance of what was needed by a missionary family—that they were to live much like the natives, and, consequently, the stores provided for them were exceedingly scanty and inadequate. Tender women, in those primitive days of the mission, and delicate young mothers, had to endure trials and hardships that would have either overborne or quite vitiated persons less sanguine and hopeful in God than they. It was that they were chosen of God, like their ancestral Pilgrims of New England, to be "a restorer of paths to dwell in, to raise up the foundations of many generations." And doubtless, that which excited and supported them was the same holy fire that burned in the breasts of their Puritan forefathers, whose experience, it is well said, was a prophecy of the missionary spirit that should come—"an inward zeal and great hope," in the language of Governor Bradford, "of laying some good foundation, or, at least, to make some way thereunto for the propagating and advancing the Gospel of the kingdom of Christ in those remote parts of the world; yea, though they should be as stepping-stones unto others for the performing of so great a work."

We have heard one of the missionary ladies detail with deep interest their early trials in a native floorless grass house, when ignorant of the language, and subject to the constant visits of curious, unclad natives. Their cooking utensils were a kettle and something else given them by their captain, wherein she must prepare food by a fire out of doors, surrounded by brawny savages, who evinced the same undisciplined eagerness as Robinson Crusoe's man Friday did when he thrust his arm into the boiling pot to catch the animal that was making the bubbling below. Yet were they happy then, and missionary families at the Sandwich Islands now, in the absence of some things elsewhere deemed necessary to contentment, but not wanting any of the solid comforts of life, are some of the happiest in the world. And were we called upon to point out where, in our estimate, there was a fuller measure than elsewhere of family felicity, peace of conscience, religious enjoyment, and true content in doing good, we should not hesitate to assign it to the honored missionary circles unostentatiously fulfilling their round of duties in those remote isles of the Pacific.

They were received at first by sufferance on good behavior, the chiefs replying to the insinuation of certain malicious foreigners that the missionaries had come to dispossess them of their lands and make war upon them, "If they had come to make war, would they have brought with them their delicate wives?" They were allowed to settle at Kailua and Lahaina, among a people who had just snapped the yoke of the tabus and the blood-stained system of idolatry. The king, Liholiho, and his chiefs, together with the common people, were just getting up from the universal debauch in which they indulged at the death of Kamehameha, the accession of his son, and the demolition of idol temples. It was a favorable time for the Gospel to enter, like that in the life of a profligate, when the edge of appetite for riotous indulgence has been somewhat blunted by satiety and exhaustion, and he feels the utter unsatisfyingness of sensual pleasure, which the poet Burns, alas! too well experienced, so aptly compared

To snow-flakes falling on a river,
One moment white, then gone forever.

But the surfeit they had taken did not operate like surfeits of some articles of food, as honey, to give a distaste for the repetition of those intoxicating draughts and licentious saturnalia. Depraved nature, stronger in the human animal than in all others, soon recovered; vicious propensities said give, give, louder than ever; and their deliverance from the restraint of tabus, the example of a profligate king, and intercourse with abandoned foreigners, all conspired to make the Hawaiian nation more besotted, beastly, and miserable in the early years of the reign of Kamehameha II. than probably it had ever been before. "Those were dark days, indeed (say the Hawaiian authors of the Moolelo Hawaii), and calling for commiseration, when even the death of rulers most venerated and beloved, instead of producing any salutary impression, was regarded as an urgent call to the indulgence of gross sensuality and debasement. The conduct of chiefs and people was like mad men and beasts, such as to forbid description. When they put an end to the ancient tabus and foolish rites, they did so with a view merely to their own interest, that they might be relieved of a burden, and that the path of pleasure and sensual indulgence might be less obstructed."

Intemperance and lust in those days may be said to have run riot. Almost every ship that anchored in their waters was made a floating brothel; and it was a fashion set by the highest chief women to hire themselves out for iniquity; and every where they *practiced all uncleanness with greediness.* We have heard it related by a resident missionary how at Kailua, on moonlight nights, they used to form rings in the open air, and shamelessly prosecute their abominable orgies with shouts and dancing. Modesty was a feeling quite unknown, or, if it ever had existed, the sex at that time seemed utterly devoid of it. Soon after the settlement together of the families of Messrs. Thurston and Bishop, at Kailua, two of the highest chief women in the nation, in order to show their friendship, called one day at the missionary house by the sea-side, after bathing, utterly unclad.

Where there was no female modesty, and licentiousness was quite unbridled, it is no wonder there was infanticide. Strange as it seems to parents within the pale of Christian civilization, this dreadful crime was notoriously common. Perhaps it had a parallel in no other country. Mothers destroyed their own offspring, both before and after they were born; they regarded the care of children as a burden that contracted their pleasures and impaired their personal beauty. In some cases an additional motive to infanticide was found in the illegitimacy of those children, and the consequent jealousy of their husbands. Hence, with a strange hardness of heart, as if destitute of all natural affection, their babes were often born only to die at the hands of the mother. There is a woman now living at Kailua (or was when we left the islands), a reputable member of the Church, who, when a child, was rescued by another after being buried alive by her own mother.

Their slight care of infants, also, almost amounted o infanticide, when that crime was not intended. We met with an elderly woman in Kohala who was said to have borne twenty-five children, not one of whom was living. "It is not uncommon," says Dr. Andrews, "to find females who have lost families of ten or twelve children in infancy. I know one woman who says she has borne twenty-one children, but one of whom is living, the others having all perished in infancy. The younger class of women could always tell me how many children they had borne; but from the aged, those who had become mothers in the days of darkness, I could seldom obtain any correct account. If they had any living, they could tell their number. If they had none, they could tell that. But ask them how many had died, and the reply was, *Ua nalowali, ua uni loa*—a great many, I have forgotten; so feeble was the impression made by the death of a child in those dark days."

There were other evil customs prevalent in those bad times, saying nothing of their wars, which rendered life uncertain and dreadful. There were various games of chance, at which they gambled deeply, and wherein they frequently lost their lives. There were others which had impure associations, and were practiced only in the night; and, not to enter into painful detail of particulars, which might easily be done, to show the horrid state of Hawaiian society, there were unnatural crimes, as well as polygamy, polyandry, robbery, murder, burying the aged alive, killing offenders without trial, and various other savage usages that rendered the state of society, mauger all the sickly stuff ever told of island innocence and bliss imbosomed in the Pacific, more like a community of devils let loose on a vacation from hell, and eager for all the pleasure of sense they could get before being cast out again into the deep, than a society of immortal men. "That time was very different from the present. Now the aged men and women walk safely, and sleep in the path. Reader, you know the customs of this country in days past. The land was full of darkness, folly, iniquity, oppression, pain, and death. A pit of destruction, dark, polluted, deadly, and ever-burning, was the dwelling of the Hawaiians in ancient times."*

There is a Welshman living at Hilo, Hawaii, who stopped at the islands in the days of Kamehameha the Great, and has been there ever since. He told me that nothing was more common in those days than for a whole village to get drunk all together and go to fighting; and for any spite they would set fire to each other's houses, burn their canoes, and pull up their growing food, and steal from each other as they could. Killing men (*pepehi kanaka*) was an art into which they were schooled; and there were those among them who taught how to strangle, and break men's bones, and how to dispatch a man at one blow of the fist without bruising him.†

* Translated from Moolelo Hawaii.

† "In former times, among this people, no man knew when he was safe. At any and every moment he was liable to be murdered, and that, too, by his supposed friends. Often, in standing together in familiar conversation, the first warning a man would have of any evil would be to see his own bowels falling to the earth. As they wore no clothing, or only the *kihei*, the operation was instantly performed by an instrument made of a hog's tusk, which the murderer concealed under his *kapa*."—Rev. L. Andrews, Hawaiian Spectator, vol. ii., p. 125.

This Welshman was himself once passing through a ravine, where he met a company of men who spoke to him peaceably; but he had no sooner passed them by a few feet, when a rolled *kapa* fell over his breast and enveloped his head; two of the men at once pulled him down and were about to kill him, when a friendly chief appeared in sight, on the opposite *pali* or ridge of the ravine, and forbade his death.

Those robbers by trade were usually men of great physical prowess, and their way was to lie in wait at a pass near the trodden path, and have a child stationed on some eminence near by, instructed to call out carelessly, as if in sport, *kaikoo* (heavy surf), if there were several in company, so that it would be unsafe to venture an attack; or *kai make* (low tide), if there were but one or two, so that he could venture. A robber in Puna, the southern country of Hawaii, had in this way killed the brother of a man living in Kohala, the northern section of the same island, who was determined to have revenge. He therefore came all the way round through Kona and Kau, and when he had arrived near the spot in Puna where the robber was supposed to lurk, he shaved his head close, and smeared his arms and whole body with some oil of old *kukui* nuts, so as to make his person slippery as an eel. Then taking a staff, and slinging something upon it after the fashion of the Hawaiians, he arranged his *kapa* so that it could be slipped off in a moment, and went limping along like a sick and lame man.

As he reached the place of ambush, the robber suddenly appeared and hailed him, "Sick, eh?" "*Ay!*"

was the answer, with a cough, and one hand placed, as if in pain, on his stomach. So he passed on until he had got a little beyond the robber, with an eye over his shoulder on the look-out; and when the robber stepped up from behind to grasp him and break his bones, he suddenly dropped his *kapa*, turned, and grappled with his foe. The slipperiness of his arms and whole body made it impossible for this notable villain so to keep hold of him as to break his bones in the professional way. They struggled and rolled, neither successful, until, both alike weary, they paused and couched upon their haunches opposite each other like tired tigers.

The robber pointed to his wife on the hill, and said, "You may have her, and we'll be quit." But not so thought the brother of the dead, and again began the mortal strife, till the avenger at length forced the head of the robber into a fissure of the rock, which the natives, who tell the story, point out to the traveler and sailors, and there trampled upon him until he was dead.

At the present time the perpetrators of deeds like these, and even the memory of them, are fast dying away; but here and there is a man to tell you tales of the times of *Naaupo* (darkness). There is a member of Mr. Coan's church who confesses to have killed two men with his own hands; and the grandfather of one of the school-girls at that station of Hilo was the murderer of nine.

Now we say, without the possibility of contradiction, that the agency which could so soon transform such a race of savages into the inoffensive, quiet people they are now, must be no less than divine; and the benevolence of Americans is richly paid back in the improvement effected in society, and the amelioration of man's temporal condition there, to say nothing of the souls we believe to have been saved, and the revenue of glory to God and the Lamb, from thousands of ransomed Hawaiians. History, in all its annals, shows nothing like this; compared with all other progressive improvements, it is A NATION BORN IN A DAY.

Thus when Religion bids her spirit breathe,
And opens bliss above and woe beneath;
When God reveals his march through Nature's night,
His steps are beauty, and his presence light:
His voice is life—the dead in conscience start;
They feel a new creation in the heart.
And then, Humanity, thy hopes, thy fears,
How changed, how wond'rous! On this tide of years,
Though the frail barks in which thine offspring sail,
Their day, their hour, their moment with the gale,
Must perish, shipwreck only sets them free.
With joys unmeasured as eternity,
They ply on seas of glass their golden oars,
And pluck immortal fruits along the shores:
Nor shall THEIR cables fail, THEIR anchors rust,
Who wait the resurrection of the just.
Moor'd on the Rock of Ages, though decay
Molder the weak terrestrial frame away,
The trumpet sounds, and lo! wherever spread,
Earth, air, and ocean render back their dead;
And souls with bodies, spiritual and divine,
In the new heavens, like stars, forever shine.
TAWNY HAWAIIANS THEN THE IMAGE WEAR
OF HIM WHO ALL THEIR SINS ON HIS OWN CROSS DID BEAR.

CHAPTER V.

NATURAL PRODUCTIONS AND PHYSICAL PHENOMENA.

In placid indolence supinely bless'd,
A feeble race these beauteous isles possess'd;
Untamed, untaught, in arts and arms unskill'd,
Their patrimonial soil they rudely till'd,
Chased the free rovers of the savage wood,
Ensnared the wild bird, swam the scaly flood:
Or when the halcyon sported on the breeze,
In light canoes they skimm'd the rippling seas.
The passing moment all their bliss or care,
Such as their sires had been the children were:
From age to age, as waves upon the tide
Of stormless time, they calmly lived and died.

MONTGOMERY.

THE nutrimental products indigenous to the Sandwich Islands are simple and few in number; but the list of naturalized exotics is large, and constantly increasing by fresh imports from other lands, inasmuch as there is scarcely a plant of the torrid or temperate zones that will not readily make its home on the Hawaiian soil. The *kalo*, of several species, sweet potato, yam, brake-root, *pia* or arrow-root, and a plant which the natives call *ki*, were the only edible roots of consequence to be found at the time of their discovery. The two former, kalo and sweet potato, still constitute the Hawaiian staple for food. The natives, indeed, do not allow the name of *ai*, or food, to

any thing but kalo, of which they are extravagantly fond.

This root is the Arum esculentum of botanists, or the plant commonly known as the wild Indian turnip. As found and cultivated at the Sandwich Islands, it is highly nutritious, mealy, and wholesome. It is of two kinds, the wet and dry kalo; the former grown always under water, which, when there is a brook, is let into a series of square beds or plats, sunk two or four feet below their borders, and let out again at one corner, when it has risen so as to cover all the plants, thus keeping a run of water through all the patches. It is estimated that forty square feet so cultivated wil. support a man. The root is eleven months gaining its full size. The natives then pull it, cut off the tops, and reserve them for planting, and bake the root in stone ovens made in the ground. They then peel it with a shell, and pound it with a stone pestle in large, flat, wooden trays, that may correspond to the kneading-troughs of the ancient Israelites as an article of household furniture.

If it is to be kept some time or carried away, it is then done up very neatly in bundles of forty and fifty pounds, made of the long leaves of a species of the aloe, and called *holoai*. If to be immediately used for food, it is mixed with a little water in a calabash, or large gourd, from the size of a bushel to that of a peck, and set away to ferment. By that process it becomes a slightly acid and pasty food, of a bluish white color, called *poi*, which no Hawaiian would exchange for the best turtle soup or macaroni. You will see a party squatting around a calabash and dipping success-

ively their forefingers into the pasty mass, and then with certain dexterous maneuvers, which a Hawaiian only knows, bring the poi-laden finger to a junction with the lips, with a smack of hearty satisfaction, such as no gourmand or toper could equal after a dram of Rhenish or best Madeira.

Foreigners make use of the root, boiled or baked, like a potato. The first missionaries had to subsist upon it almost entirely for some time, and it is now generally seen upon their tables, with or without the potato. Tolerable bread can be made of the poi and arrow-root mixed, which has to be resorted to sometimes at the out-stations of missionaries, when flour, brought round Cape Horn, is so hard that it has to be cut out with an ax, or so sour that saleratus can not cure it. The only indigenous fruits to be named are bananas of a very superior quality, the bread-fruit, cocoa-nuts, a kind of native apple, called ohia, the wild strawberry, and a species of whortle-berry, called ohelo, formerly sacred to the goddess of the volcano, the Cape gooseberry or *poha*, and the sugar cane.

A list of plants and fruits introduced from abroad, comprise wheat and barley (cultivated, as yet, but slightly), rice, raised by parties of Chinese settlers, Indian corn, and the Irish potato; the lime-tree, orange, lemon, fig, pomegranate, papaya, custard-apple, mango-tree, tamarind, guava, mulberry; anetto, pride of China; then the peach-tree, coffee-tree, cotton, tobacco, and indigo plants, delicious melons of every kind, the grape-vine, and a great variety of flowers and shrubs, all of which, except the peach-tree, attain to great perfection.

Forest-trees are the *ko-a* and *ko-u;* the first being the proper Hawaiian mahogany-tree, out of which the natives used to excavate their canoes, and which is now worked up into very beautiful furniture. Next are the *ohia*, a very hard and superior wood for fuel and timber; the fragrant sandal-wood, now almost extinct; the *kukui* or candle-nut-tree, from which there is made a very good paint-oil; the *hau*-tree; different species of acacia and mimosa, the *kamana*, *laauhala*, *wiliwili*, and other *sui generis* trees that have no English common name.

The ko-u is very ample and superb as a shade-tree, found chiefly by the sea-side. The ko-a belongs to the mountains, where it attains to great size and longevity; when young, it is a tree of rare beauty, with laurel-green, moon-shaped leaves, and sweet mimosa-like blossoms. I have seen war canoes made of this tree in the canoe-house of Kuakini, alias John Adams, late governor of Hawaii, that were seventy feet long, and more than three feet deep, and would carry seventy men. They came down from Kamehameha the Great, and were those in which he passed with his warriors from island to island, when this Napoleon of the Pacific made the conquest of the entire Hawaiian Group, and meditated an expedition to the Society Islands also, twenty-seven hundred miles off.

Groves of the cocoa-nut palm-tree, one of the characteristic symbols of the tropics, are every where to be found growing in the sands by the sea-side, and in clefts of the grizzly lava, where nothing else will thrive. When young, no vegetable product in the whole range of nature can exceed the beauty of such a grove; each stem supporting an endogenous growth of fan-like glossy branches, that grow out of the central bud, as if in a Louisiana forest the top of every cypress-tree should be plumed with verdure.

Destroy this plume or tuft of verdure, and you destroy the tree, because it is of the class of plants called endogenous, whose stems increase by internal growth, without distinction of pith, wood, or bark. Removing its crown, therefore, is like laying bare the entire brain of an animal, and death at once ensues, the trunk speedily rotting downward. It is not easy to calculate how benign a gift of Providence this single tree has been to the Pacific islanders. All that has been said of it at Tahiti and the Marquesas was true of it also on Hawaii, until now that many-fingered civilization, with its million substitutes, bids fair to supersede it.

"Year after year the islander reposes beneath its shade, both eating and drinking of its fruit; he thatches his hut with its boughs, and weaves them into baskets to carry his food; he cools himself with a fan platted from the young leaflets, and shields his head from the sun by a bonnet of the leaves; sometimes he clothes himself with the cloth-like substance which wraps round the base of the stalks, whose elastic rods, strung with filberts, are used as a taper: the larger nuts, thinned and polished, furnish him with a beautiful goblet; the smaller ones with bowls for his pipes; the dry husks kindle his fires; their fibers are twisted into fishing-lines and cords for his canoes; he heals his wounds with a balsam compounded from the juice of the nut; and with the oil extracted from its meat anoints his own limbs and embalms the bodies of the dead. The noble trunk itself is far from being valueless. Sawn into posts, it upholds the islander's dwelling; converted into charcoal, it cooks his food; and, supported on blocks of stone, rails in his lands. He impels his canoes through the water with a paddle of the wood, and goes to battle with clubs and spears of the same hard material."

The fruit-bearing powers of the cocoa palm are not surpassed by any tree of the kind in the kingdom of nature. An Englishman at Kealia, Hawaii, by the name of Thornton, who had lived there sixteen years, told me he had taken four hundred nuts, full grown, from one tree in a single year. Two hundred of them, besides innumerable white blossoms of others, have been counted upon the same tree at one time, and no two of them at precisely the same stage of growth.

The location where it best flourishes is right upon the sea-shore, as at Lahaina, Maui, and Hilo, Hawaii, where its roots, if not actually washed, are watered by the sea. It never grows large or vigorously inland, where other trees will thrive; but, like the prison-benevolence of Howard, it is congenial with, and it loves to beautify and enrich those arid spots which nothing else blesses.

The method of planting it is thus described by an observer: Selecting a suitable place, you drop into the ground a fully-ripe nut, and leave it. In a few days a thin, lance-like shoot forces itself through a minute hole in the shell, pierces the husk, and soon unfolds three pale-green leaves in the air; while, originating in the same soft, white sponge which now completely fills the nut, a pair of fibrous roots, pushing away the stoppers that close two holes in an opposite direction, penetrate the shell, and strike vertically into the ground. A day or two more, and the shell and husk, which, in the last and germinating stage of the nut, are so hard that a knife will scarcely make any impression, spontaneously bursts by some force within; and henceforth the hardy young plant thrives apace, and, needing no culture, pruning, or attention of any sort, rapidly advances to maturity. In four or five years it bears; in twice as many more it begins to lift its head among the groves, where, waxing strong, it flourishes for near a century.

Of the animal kingdom, the kinds found at the Sandwich Islands at the time of their discovery were few, the only ones then known having been the dog, hog, domestic fowl, mouse, and lizzard, and the usual variety of sea-birds. The dog was, and still is, the favorite animal food of the natives, although its use is discountenanced by the missionaries. Now they have the cat, sheep, goat, cattle, horses, asses, mules, and all the varieties of poultry. Not a noxious beast, reptile, or insect existed on the islands when first made known to Europeans. Now they have musquitoes, fleas, centipedes, and scorpions.

The snake, toad, bee, and all stinging insects of the latter sort are still unknown. One would think the flea certainly indigenous, where now it is found so much at home both with man and beast; but the natives have an amusing story of the first time they got ashore from a ship, through the trick of a sailor, which is better to be imagined than told.

Whether that be true or not, the name by which they call the flea is pretty convincing evidence that it has not been known as long as some other things. It is called *uku lele*, or the jumping louse, the *uku* being an old settler from time immemorial, and nothing else they knew so much like the imported flea. So they named the stranger the jumping *uku:* it is one of the first aboriginals a traveler becomes acquainted with in going about among Hawaiians and sleeping in native houses, and it is the last he is so glad to bid good-by to when he comes away, though it is ten chances to one if they do not insist upon keeping him company and making themselves familiar half the voyage home.

The mineral products of the islands are of course few, where igneous volcanic fusion has melted all elements into almost a homogeneous mass. There are crystals of olivine, obsidian, and augite often to be met with in the lava, and quartz has been found in the path of mountain torrents.

Salt is obtained in large quantities from a salt lake in the vicinity of Honolulu, and by evaporation from sea water. Chalk is also found on Oahu, and there are hills of sandstone, evidently made by sand blown from the sea-shore, and cemented by lime. It does not, however, answer well for building, not being compact or hard enough. A very good building material consists in blocks cut from the coral reef, which is found on the leeward side of most of the islands. The palace of the king, and other government buildings, as well as many of the stores and dwellings of foreigners on Oahu, are formed of this substance.

The great Bingham native church at Honolulu is

also made of it, a noble monument to the energy of the missionary, and the industry, perseverance, and piety of the people and chiefs. It is the first object that comes in sight, aside from the battlemented and fire-worn, frowning old craters that tower above it, as you approach Honolulu; a massive temple to worship God in, being chiefly the free-will product of a people that were only thirty years ago a most miserable and idolatrous race of savages, utterly ignorant of the true God.

The most beautiful product of the islands, or, rather, of the sea that laves them, is coral; not the coral of the reef, but that which the little coral insect makes *upon* the reef into so many curious and beautiful forms. As found at the Sandwich Islands, that which is called brain coral is in clumps or bunches, from a few inches to a foot or more in diameter at the top, the stalk being sometimes longer, sometimes shorter. The little coral polype begins his tree on solid lava, or on what is called a coral reef, or on a separate stone cemented by lime to the bottom. In the latter case the whole may be disengaged together, like a tree taken up with its roots and a portion of the soil and stones adhering. On this foundation he builds up sometimes a single trunk, sometimes more; this spreads and grows large at the top, so as to bear some resemblance in its divisions and sinuses to the lobes of the human brain; and the trunk or stalk bears just about the same proportion to the top as the human neck does to the head.

Horned coral, on the contrary, springs up in forms very closely resembling the sprigs of evergreen which New England boys get in the woods in spring-time, and sometimes dig out from under the snow. Other still comes out from its foundation like a deer's antlers, or in separate shoots that intertwine, and grow smaller at the top like the curious roots of the pandanus; or, to compare great things with small, so as to remind one of the celebrated tree of the East, that lets fall its off-shoots to the ground,

> Whose bended twigs take root, and daughters grow
> About the mother tree, a pillar'd shade
> High overarch'd, and echoing walks between.

Hawaiians will dive for coral to burn into lime, where the water is twenty or twenty-five feet deep, and so clear that you can see them below dislodging the coral, or indistinctly creeping along upon all fours like a great marine quadruped. Their surprising skill in the water amounts almost to a new faculty of living in another element, and exploring the unknown bed of ocean, where, dimly seen by rays of refracted light, there is nothing, real or imagined,

> But doth suffer a sea change
> Into something rich and strange.

Hawaiians are said to have been known to bring up small articles lost overboard from a ship in ninety feet of water, and a woman who was capsized in a canoe three miles from the shore is related to have swam the whole distance safe to land with a shark behind her in full pursuit.

With some natural allowance for the painting of imagination, which I found to have given a tallness and grove-like density to coraline vegetation hardly real, the poet Percival's description is as true as it is beautiful.

There, far below in the peaceful sea,
  The purple mullet and gold-fish rove;
There the waters murmur tranquilly,
  Through the bending twigs of the coral grove;
There, with its waving blade of green,
  The sea-flag streams through the silent water,
And the crimson leaf of the dulse is seen
  To blush like a banner bathed in slaughter.
There, with a light and easy motion,
  The fan coral sweeps through the clear deep sea;
And the yellow and scarlet tufts of ocean
  Are bending like corn on the upland lea.
And life, in rare and beautiful forms,
  Is sporting amid those bowers of stone,
And is safe when the wrathful spirit of storms
  Has made the top of the wave his own.

The general physical aspect and volcanic phenomena of the Hawaiian isles are such, that if a seaman's fancy has painted those gems of the Pacific in hues borrowed from the West Indies of the Atlantic, or from vague descriptions he may have seen, making them the loveliest ocean paradise, he is sure to be at first greatly disappointed. Blackened and bare lava rocks, steep volcanic ridges, gorges, and canyons, and irregular, truncated cones, the work of old out-breaking fires; these with abrupt, jagged precipices, grizzly or grass-grown, facing the sea and running inland; and directly on the shore, perhaps, a few lank cocoa-nut-trees, with their crowns of scanty, fan-like branches, are the characteristic features that first arrest and by no means satisfy the longing mariner.

The utter absence of trees to the sailor's eager eye-glance, and the apparent destitution of that vegetative luxuriance which he has learned from childhood to associate with the perpetual summer of the tropics, make the first approach to these islands on the leeward any thing but inviting. The rightly-named Cape Desolation, on the coast of Patagonia, which the eye may last have seen and dreaded as a lee shore, does not look any more desolate and barren than the island of Lanai, off which ships are commonly becalmed in approaching the Sandwich Islands. You may possibly discover something that may be taken for human habitations, from their resemblance to gray-grown hay-stacks that have weathered a New England winter. But how the inmates can get their meat and drink off those fire-caused and sun-burned arid rocks and steeps, is more than you can tell.

The fertile vales and dewy meads, now and then hidden between the black volcanic ridges, you do not see, where a purling brook from the mountains is made to meander through long successive ranges of kalo patches, until quite spent upon the verdure it has created. This aspect of country belongs especially to the leeward side of the islands, where it seldom rains. On that part of the great Island of Hawaii there is not a brook that runs into the sea for more than a hundred miles of coast. At Kealakekua ships can hardly get a cask of genuine fresh water for fear, love, or money.

The great navigator who met so untimely a death there procured a small supply by natives bringing it in calabashes from the mountains, four miles inland. The missionaries at the station have to be supplied, for the most part, in the same way. The natives themselves drink of brackish springs by the sea-side, the water of which is almost as nauseous and purgative, with a stranger, as a dose of salts.

When we proceed from Kealakekua to the southern and middle section of this island, where the active volcano lies, traces of recent eruption become more frequent; and, whether coasting along in a canoe or traveling on foot ashore, you pass great rugged cones and oven-like blisters, deep-mouthed caves and fissures, enormous gaps and ravines, overhanging arches and natural bridges, great tunnels and blow-holes, up which the water of the sea rushes with every return wave, through emboweled galleries, and spouts up its froth and gravel into the air a quarter of a mile inland, with a ringing sound like the blowing of a huge fin-back whale.

On the opposite or windward side of the islands, where there is frequent rain, you may see cataracts leaping a precipice of a thousand feet, directly into the sea, and waterfalls hanging like ribbons fluttering in the air. In making a circuit of the islands, you are compelled to go a large part of the way by canoe, the precipices being so steep, where ejected and running lava has stiffened almost in a perpendicular before its thick, molten mass found a level, that you can not scale them without the most painful labor.

The pedestrian and canoe traveler on Hawaii, in his way to the most stupendous and awful volcano in the known world, has the best opportunity for observing the unique and remarkable features of Hawaiian scenery, as well as the character and habits of the Hawaiian people; and if a missionary or a missionary's friend, and known to be such, he soon learns that he can trust himself and his goods into their hands with more confidence of impunity than into the hands of any other people the world over. He is surprised at the practical, every-day influence of the religious truths they have imbibed, and finds himself forced to the conclusion that there is not in all the world at the present time, nor in its whole past history, such another instance of a purely moral ascendency gained over a people by religious teachers as at the Sandwich Islands.

This is seen and proved in a thousand nameless ways, that can only be known to the observant and candid traveler. He will hear the voice of prayer in the lowly cabins where he is a wayfarer, morning and evening; and when there is a cluster of houses together, he will hear a conch-shell blown at the matin hour to summon the dwellers to the rude school-house for social worship and thanksgiving to the Giver of all Good.

On board the native schooner or canoe in which he may be traveling, he will hear the Hawaiian captain call to devotions every morn and even, E PULE KAKOU, and either himself lead in an appropriate extempore prayer, or call upon another. When sitting around their calabash of *poi*, he will hear them invoke the blessing of Jehovah—E KO MAKOU MAKUA MA KA LANI. On the Sabbath he will find a scrupulous external regard to the sacredness of the day, wherever he may be, far above what he has been used to in lands long Christianized; and often, perhaps, he will find his own practical irreligion, and that of his more civilized countrymen, signally rebuked by conscientious Hawaiians; as in the instance of the native governor of Oahu, Kekuanaoa, who, when waited upon once on the Sabbath morning by the lieutenant of a United States ship-of-war just arrived, in order to make arrangements for a salute to the fort, promptly answered that he was just going to the House of God (A KA HALE PULE), and would attend to that business on Monday.

Now we say this was both pious, manly, and honorable. May the race of Nehemiah-like governors of Oahu never run out! And if this official reverence for the Sabbath, which closes our present catalogue of Hawaiian productions, be the peculiar growth of those favored isles, who does not say, Let it be planted and propagated as soon as possible in all lands, whether trans-Pacific or trans-Atlantic? God grant that the future sons of Hawaii, whether born of missionaries or scions of the natural stock, may be able to sing of their native isle, as a patriotic Briton did of his:

> I love thee—when thy SABBATH DAWNS
> O'er woods and mountains, dales and lawns,
> And streams, that sparkle while they run,
> As if their fountain were the sun:
> When, hand in hand, thy tribes repair,
> Each to their chosen house of prayer,
> And all in peace and pardon call
> On Him who is the Lord of all.
> Can words, can numbers count the price
> Paid for this little Paradise?
> Never, oh! never be it lost;
> The land is WORTH the price it cost.

CHAPTER VI.

HAWAIIAN RIGHTS AND WRONGS, POLITICS AND RELIGION

Who swerves from innocence, who makes divorce
Of that serene companion, a good name,
Recovers not his loss; but walks with shame,
With doubt, with fear, and haply with remorse.
* * * * *
As star that shines dependent upon star
Is to the sky while we look up in love;
As to the deep fair ships which, though they move,
Seem fix'd to eyes that watch them from afar;
As to the sandy desert fountains are,
With palm-groves, shaded at wide intervals,
Whose fruit around the sun-burn'd native falls,
Of roving tired, or desultory war:
Such to "HAWAIIAN ISLES" her Christian fanes.

WORDSWORTH.

THE liberties and rights of the Sandwich Islands seem to be a ball for the bigger nations of the earth to play with, and it is batted violently about by one and another at the whim of rear-admirals and post-captains. Hardly does it gain equilibrium and rest from one shock before it is rudely struck by another. The latest blow has been given in the name of that once generous people, whose ambition now seems to be, as represented in its misnamed Republican President and Assembly, to keep foremost among the nations in meanness. This last outrage is the game over again which they played so long at Tahiti; but it is to be hoped, this time, they will *get out* much sooner than there.

The facts of the recent French outrage upon Hawaiian independence are these: By an article of the treaty formed between France and the Sandwich Islands in the year 1846, French merchandise, or goods recognized as coming from the French dominions, shall not be prohibited, nor shall they be subject to an import duty higher than five per cent. *ad valorem. Wines, brandies, and other spirituous liquors, are, however, excepted from this stipulation, and shall be liable to such reasonable duty as the Hawaiian government may think fit to lay upon them; provided always, that the amount of duty shall not be so high as absolutely to prohibit the importation of the said articles.*

As an act of self-protection, without contravening the letter of this treaty, the Hawaiian government imposed a duty of $5 a gallon on brandy. The French consul Dillon and Admiral Tromelin demanded the repeal of this, and the reduction of duty to fifty per cent. *ad valorem* upon all brandies and spirituous liquors of French origin, together with eight or nine other obnoxious stipulations degrading to any nation's independence to submit to, or the alternative of a formal abrogation of the treaty between the two nations, and the substitution of the La Place Convention of 1839. Three days were allowed for the Hawaiian government to comply with or refuse those conditions.

The king being absent from Honolulu, the admiral waited until his return, when, the government refusing to comply with the demands, the French troops landed and took possession of the fort. No resistance being offered, they spiked and threw from the ramparts the guns of the fort, destroyed the ammunition and public stores, and took all the Hawaiian vessels that were in port. The Hawaiian flag was lowered, and the French flag hoisted. After the quiet possession of the fort for three days, the French abandoned it, and retired on board their vessels. The king's yacht, Kamehameha III., was manned with Frenchmen, and dispatched, it is supposed, to Valparaiso; the steamer sailed for Tahiti; and the Poursuivante, with M. Dillon and family, sailed for San Francisco. The American consul and the British Consul General both protested against the action of the French forces; and the latter offered his services as mediator, but was refused.

It remains to be seen whether the United States and Great Britain will quietly see the guarantee of Hawaiian independence—which these powers have mutually entered into—virtually abrogated, and a solemn treaty declared a nullity. It can not be that the Republic of France, in 1850, will justify and endorse such a clear breach of a solemn treaty on the part of its agents, and thereby make it the injustice and perjury of the whole nation, any more than England did the similar outrage of Paulet in 1843. Significant facts, however, in late French-Italian history, give body and basis to the fear, that if France persist, and no other nation interpose between the wolf and his trembling prey, submission must be the only alternative for the Hawaiians. Unless God forbid, the roaring lion and ranging bear of Frenchism and Romanism, which have nearly devoured the Society Islands, may disastrously ravage the Sandwich. And this when the French in terests vested there are, in comparison with the English and American, so trifling, that the whole number of Frenchmen (not including the French priests) residing on the islands is *twelve!* Of these one is a merchant, and probably transacts about the *one thousandth* part of the commercial business of the islands; one is a hotel-keeper, and has about the same proportion in that line of business. The remainder (with the exception of one clerk) are in the employ of Englishmen and Americans.

At least ninety-nine one hundredths of the spirituous liquors imported into the country have been imported by English and American merchants; and Englishmen and Americans have consumed them, and of course paid the duty.

There has never been but *one* cargo of goods imported from France; and there has not been, for the last five years, a French merchant ship at these islands. A few French schooners, brigantines, &c., there have been, but they have been mostly freighted by English and American merchants. And while the number of American and English whale ships that touch at the islands, either in the spring or fall, is from two to four hundred, the number of French whalers in the two seasons is only from five to nine.

The attitude maintained by the Hawaiian government in its late conflict with the French has been a noble one. The king has peacefully thrown himself upon the laws of nations, without armed resistance, and boldly asserted the inalienable rights of his kingdom, while its public property was being destroyed, and the sovereignty of his Majesty, guarantied by

France herself, was being trampled under foot by a military force, armed, as against a belligerent opponent. It is a remarkable fact, and one that reflects high credit both upon the good government and character of the people of Honolulu, that during the landing of the French troops and the taking military possession, on the 25th of August, 1849, of the fort and other government buildings, not the least tumult occurred.

Notwithstanding that the streets were filled with foreign residents, seamen, and natives, who had congregated from motives of curiosity to witness the proceedings, and notwithstanding the unanimous feeling of indignation that pervaded every breast, the known wishes of the king, that not the slightest opposition should be made to any act the French troops were commissioned to perform, were so highly respected that not even a shout was raised, or the least effort made to create a disturbance; and since the outrage, and subsequent abandonment of the island by the military, French property and persons are as secure as ever from molestation, although, as may be naturally supposed, the obnoxious French name there is like vinegar upon nitre, and as odious as eggs that have "outlived their usefulness."

The public property in the fort was destroyed; magazines were broken open, and their contents thrown into the sea; the government yacht seized; seven private vessels detained; and the business of Honolulu temporarily thrown into confusion. But, conscious of having justice and the law of nations on his side, the king did not swerve from his position, but bore the wrong without even a feint of opposition, which the French so much courted. The result, we trust, will demonstrate the wisdom of this masterly inactivity. The jury in the Court of Nations will acquit the Hawaiian king, and bring in *guilty* the French admiral of a plain breach of treaty; for the laughing of native boys at *papal mummeries*, and the *constable's* entering a *priest's* domicil to arrest a fugitive, appear to have been the "head and front" of Hawaiian offending. To force *brandy* and *Catholicism* on the islanders, at the mouth of cannon and point of the bayonet, was the real object of the enterprise.

Outraged liberty and justice have spoken for the oppressed, and the indignant voice of Christendom has condemned, as they have deserved, the high-handed piracies that have been perpetrated from time to time upon the sovereignty and liberties of these islands. The names of French La Place, and English Paulet, and Tromelin de la Belle Republique, will henceforth go down to infamy together on the page of history.

> "What can ennoble fools, or knaves, or cowards?
> Alas! not all the blood of all the Howards."

Neither titled ancestry, nor noble name, nor the shield of government, nor the interposing providence of God, bringing good out of evil, can save them from the united reproach and shame to which, by the acclamation of the Protestant world, their career at these islands has consigned them.

Particulars might be given of their course, and of the humiliating dilemma to which the Hawaiian king was reduced, which the world does not know; and circumstances in detail might be exhibited, going to show the extreme injustice of the claims, both of the

Frenchman and of the Briton, which preclude all shadow of excuse for the lawless policy they pursued. But it is hardly magnanimous, still less necessary, to strike a man when he is down; nor is it important that the world should know more than is already known of affairs here transacted.

It is seldom, of late years, that there is not trouble either a brewing or breaking out among the foreign Honolulites. It takes but little wind to make a breeze there. In the intervals between the piracies of Paulet and La Place, and when there is no foreign man-of-war in port to divert the attention, they set-to on one another, and make game of each others' reputations, as they used to of the poor missionaries. The latter has got to be rather too stale and tough a kind of scandal to swallow well. So now, like jealousy, they make their own apples of discord, breed slanders, and hatch cockatrice's eggs between themselves, and make what capital they can of the unnatural offspring.

Something's always to pay among the five or six hundred foreigners at Honolulu. The chorus to the witches' song might be sung all the year round:

> Double, double, toil and trouble;
> Fire burn, and caldron bubble:
> Black spirits and white,
> Red spirits and gray;
> Mingle, mingle, mingle,
> You that mingle may.

But all this is but the scum and smoke rising to the top, and necessarily consequent upon the agitation of the elements of society before settling, in a community where there is so much that is fermentative and heterogeneous. The troubled sea of society here, working like a beer-barrel on the dregs of heathenism, and the refuse of civilization washed ashore on these islands like drift-wood, must, of course, cast up a good deal of mire and dirt before getting its equilibrium; but in due time it will work itself clear.

Society is in the transition state, and the Hawaiian nation itself, as one of its missionaries has well observed, is just emerging from darkness, just opening its eyes in the twilight. The elements of old Chaos have been thoroughly agitated; shadowy forms and the misty outlines of Order are slowly appearing, and the indistinct voices of Harmony are faintly falling on the ear. Social regeneration will duly follow the religious, though, from the nature of things, it can not be in a flash. This conflict of parties, and all the smoke and din of controversy and steam of effervescence, do not alarm us, nor need we stop to tell of them.

It is better to dwell upon the all-wise and beneficent providence of God, through which the piratical capture of these islands by the English, in 1843, was probably made to prevent a worse conquest, at that time, by the French; and was found, in the end, to be the necessary means of securing the guaranty of independence from England and France, for which Messrs. Richards and Haalilio *might* otherwise have waited in vain upon cabinets and courts.

God determined that their embassy to Europe and America, undertaken not without much self-denial and a surrender of private interests and feelings to public duty, should not be in vain; and, therefore, these islands were suffered to be taken by the commander of one nation, acting without the instructions of his government to that effect, that both the rival powers might be convinced of the importance of these islands maintaining an independent neutrality; and that the French king, especially, might be induced to come into the mutual bond for their independence with the English, when he saw them already within the clutches of the latter; thus securing that they should not be the possession of a rival, while reluctantly brought to the necessity of abandoning them as a part of the French conquests in the Pacific.

The annals of diplomacy show it were vain to expect magnanimity in the policy of a great power, like that of England or France, toward a weaker, as the king of the Sandwich Islands, unless such magnanimity be plainly in a line with her self-interest. Governments, like selfish individuals, are always for getting, if they can, the best of a bargain. How far this appears or not, in the treaty effected by the British Consul General, Miller, with the government of the Sandwich Islands, an examination of facts will show.

In the fall of 1842, Messrs. Richards and Haalilio left Oahu for the United States and Europe, as accredited ministers plenipotentiary of his Hawaiian majesty, Kamehameha III., to procure an acknowledgment and guaranty of independence to these islands, and with full power to form treaties in the name of his Majesty. In the February following was the forced cession of these islands to the British, through Paulet, the news of which reached England at the time Messrs. Richards and Haalilio were prosecuting their embassy at the Court of St. James. An officer was immediately appointed by government to repair to these islands, to examine into and settle all difficulties, and to form a convention on the most advantageous terms; the draft of which he carries with him. Mr. Richards, in the mean while, is kept in ignorance of the fact that General Miller goes to make a treaty, being himself and Haalilio the proper agents through whom such business should be transacted.

After much vexatious delay, especially on the part of France, to sign the bond guarantying to the islands an unmolested independence, this important end is at length secured, and the way opened to review and settle treaties. But, in the mean while, a treaty was made at the islands without the concurrence of the king's best counselors, which, while it is generally equitable, contains a provision in the third article which *may* be highly adverse to the interests of justice. The following is a copy of the convention prepared in England, while Mr. Richards was there, though without his knowledge, which the Consul General said "he was authorized by his sovereign to prepare and sign in the name of her majesty."

CONVENTION BETWEEN GREAT BRITAIN AND THE SANDWICH ISLANDS.

The differences which existed between the governments of Great Britain and the Sandwich Islands having been happily settled, the following articles of agreement have been mutually entered into between the King of the Sandwich Islands, on the one part, and William Miller, Esq., her Britannic Majesty's Consul General for the Sandwich and other islands in the Pacific, in the name and on the behalf of her Britannic majesty, on the other part, for the preservation of harmony, and the prevention of future misunderstanding between the two parties.

ARTICLE I. There shall be perpetual peace and amity between her Majesty the Queen of the United Kingdom of Great Britain and Ireland, and the King of the Sandwich Islands, their heirs and successors.

ART. II. The subjects of her Britannic Majesty shall be protected in an efficient manner in their person and properties by the King of the Sandwich Islands, who shall cause them to enjoy impartially, in all cases in which their interest is concerned, the same rights and privileges as natives, or as are enjoyed by any other foreigners.

ART. III. No British subject accused of any crime whatever shall be judged otherwise than by a jury composed of foreign residents, proposed by the British consul, and accepted by the government of the Sandwich Islands.

ART. IV. The protection of the King of the Sandwich Islands shall be extended to all British vessels, their officers and crews. In case of shipwreck, the chiefs and inhabitants of the different parts of the Sandwich Islands shall succor them and secure them from plunder. The salvage dues shall be regulated, in case of difficulties, by arbitrators freely chosen by both parties.

ART. V. The desertion of seamen embarked on board of British vessels shall be severely repressed by the local authorities, who shall employ all the means at their disposal to arrest deserters; and all reasonable expenses of capture shall be defrayed by the captains or owners of the said vessels.

ART. VI. British merchandise, or goods recognized as coming from the British dominions, shall not be prohibited, nor shall they be *subject to an import duty higher than five per cent. ad valorem.*

ART. VII. No tonnage, import, or other duties shall be levied on British vessels or goods, or on goods imported in British vessels, beyond what are levied on the vessels or goods of the most favored nation.

ART. VIII. The subjects of the King of the Sandwich Islands shall, in their commercial and other relations with Great Britain, be treated on the footing of the most favored nation.

Done at Lahaina, the twelfth day of February, one thousand eight hundred and forty-four.

(Signed), KAMEHAMEHA III.
(Signed), KEKAULUOHI.
(Signed), WM. MILLER.

Signed in the presence of
G. P. JUDD, *Secretary for Foreign Affairs.*
ROBERT C. WYLLIE, *Secretary to Gen. Miller.*

A similar treaty has lately been negotiated, in the month of November, 1849, between the Hawaiian minister, G. P. Judd, and the United States commissioner, Charles E. Eames, meeting at San Francisco. These will secure reciprocal justice between the nations that are parties thereto, and the French will be forced in honor to conclude a similar arrangement, and to indemnify the Hawaiian government for recent losses by the unauthorized acts of Admiral Tromelin.

With the aid derived from competent foreigners who have taken the oath of allegiance, and the wise counsel his Hawaiian Majesty can command, this government is now more competent to try and punish crimes in all cases than are most of the republics of South America. Why, then, should it not be permitted to administer its laws like other independent nations, without the arrogance of protests on the part of foreign consuls and commissioners, or the interference of navy captains? It has a written code of laws, which are singularly simple and direct: they are translated into English, and all foreigners may know them. Why, then, should they not be tried and dealt with for crimes committed, according to the laws of the land?

Foreigners have helped each other out of scrapes (as the phrase is) too long; profligacy in them has gone unpunished hundreds of times, when, in natives, it would have been visited with condign penalty, as the law directs. It is high time that these distinctions should be abolished, and that Hawaiian justice should be meted out to all who choose to visit or live in Hawaii nei. And let Christian states and their agents resident there, as well as the men-of-war that from time to time appear in the Pacific seas as the guardians of their commerce and rights, see to it that they put no obstacles in the way of broad Hawaiian justice.

God's providences have been too marked and many toward this rising nation and its band of missionaries to allow a doubt that His banner will still be held over it, and that the Gospel shall be allowed to try its efficacy to elevate and preserve this so recently idolatrous and miserable race. Is it too much to hope that the causes of national extinction and decay may yet be arrested, and that the people of Hawaii nei may yet become the joy and pride of the earth? a glorious example to all the world of a regenerated race of heathen: forming an illustrious exception to that melancholy rule of destiny by which all the races of savages seem melting away before the arts, and vices, and enterprise of the white man. Whether or not it be true, as some assert, that "commerce is digging the grave of this nation," we do not pretend to decide. It is quite certain that most of those who go there *to deal in commerce* little care, provided only that a race of intelligent, enterprising Anglo-Saxons supplant them, and occupy the soil in which the Hawaiians are quietly entombed.

If such shall ever be the melancholy fact, let those remember whose contact with the race has been demoralizing and deadly, "Be sure your sin will find you out." The injured shades of Hawaiians will meet their destroyers in another world with stern and terrible recrimination. Your ships and your men, will they say, brought the vice and disease that have been our ruin. You *foreigners lent your whole influence to make the Hawaiian Islands one great brothel!* You opposed and slandered our teachers, and did all you could to nullify the force of their instructions. If "Christian merchants" came among us, what did they more than others but make us hewers of wood and drawers of water to themselves? When and how were they known to help our teachers? or to consecrate the gains made among us to the Christian work of saving our souls? Whether, intent only upon gain, it was in your heart to do so or not, ye did but help the process of our extermination and decay. "The Christian's God that paid the debt,"* whom many of us rejoiced to find, now taketh vengeance, and pays in eternity the wrongs of time.

In the history of the world since the Christian era, the settlement of foreigners for the mere purposes of gain among nations of savages, so far from being beneficial, has been found detrimental to *their* growth and prosperity. The new-comers have gradually overrun and dispossessed the native races, or they have become the mere serfs and menials of those that were first received on bare sufferance.

It remains to be seen whether the Hawaiians will form an exception to this rule. What is eminently needed is, that devoted laymen of the different professions and trades go and settle there on purpose to do good, not with the selfish design of merely enriching themselves, but with the disinterested intention of benefiting the nation by teaching the useful arts, industrious habits, and ways of developing the physical resources of civilized life. Such men, with the virtues of economy, prudence, and thrift, could any

* Anecdote of the poor African, who, anxious for his soul, and vainly seeking for help, was at length told by a wicked sailor who had been cast upon his shores, Why don't you go where somebody will tell you about the Christian's God that paid the debt? He went all the way to London, and, sitting down in one of its streets, besought the passers-by to tell him of the Christian's God that paid the debt.

where get a livelihood, and they could every where do great good.

In a little work, called A Voice from Abroad, by Rev. Sheldon Dibble, the author justly remarks, in the chapter entitled Laymen called to the Field of Missions, that not only is a reform in government necessary, but an introduction of the useful arts also, to raise up the people from their indolence and filthy habits, and to promote thrift, order, neatness, and consistency. "Look at a heathen family, as before described. They are almost naked; have a mere apology for clothing. They live together in one little hut, without table or chairs; gather around one calabash, eat with their fingers, and sleep on one mat. How can you expect from them refinement or elevation of soul? How can you expect from them the proprieties and consistencies of a Christian life? Even though they may attend the sanctuary, and be instructed in schools; and even though the government be reformed, and hold out motives to industry, yet will not something else be wanting? Unless the various useful arts and occupations be introduced, how is the land to be filled with fruitful fields, pleasant dwellings, and neatly-clad inhabitants?"

"To introduce these improvements, *men must go forth for the purpose.* They should be men who cheerfully throw themselves and their property on the altar of *entire consecration*, and go forth to labor and toil, so long as the Savior pleases to employ them, with the lofty design of doing good to the bodies and souls of their perishing fellow-men. Going forth with such a spirit, and allowing *no other* to intrude, they could do much in raising up the nation from their deep degradation. By exhibiting in their dealings an example of uprightness, honesty, and conscientious regard to justice and truth; by showing practically the only proper use of wealth, the good of men and the glory of God; by conversing daily with individuals, at their houses and by the way side, on the great subject of the soul's salvation; and by presenting, in themselves and in their families, examples of a prayerful and godly life, and habits of industry and strict economy, they might exert a very powerful influence, and perform a very important part in Christianizing the world."

But while the help of such good men, who would go there, and keep there purposely to do good, is so much a desideratum and a duty, we can not but question the boasted usefulness of mercantile firms and individuals whose sole object is to make money. They may talk loudly and largely of the benefit their operations are to the Hawaiian nation; and let it be granted that a small moiety of good has flowed off indirectly in by-streams from their selfishness. But when they come, vain-gloriously, to compare the unmeant good they have done with the substantial results of missionary labors, we are not alone in being either so blind that we can not see it, or so justly skeptical as to say,

> That optics sharp it needs, I ween,
> To see what is not to be seen.

Timeo Danaos et dona ferentes—which is, being interpreted,

> I fear these money-loving Greeks,
> Whose purse-strings pelf, not conscience, keeps.

Above all, we think, is to be deprecated the influence of any large company of mere money-making foreigners for agricultural operations. If successful, instead of giving to the nation industry, enterprise, and wealth, we fear it would but monopolize the best lands and the most productive modes of enterprise, and end in making the people, through the utter inability of independent competition, mere tools and unambitious helpers to foreign acquisitiveness. To teach the people to do their own government, to make and execute their own laws, to develop their own resources, is the policy of enlightened benevolence toward a nation of emerging savages, the end of which will be thwarted if foreigners are introduced to fill all the offices of government, and to improve for their own advantage all the available facilities for enterprise and acquisition.

It was amusing, we are told, in the reign of Paulet and the British commission, to witness the *patriotic* grief and distress of certain foreigners whose influence and pecuniary interests were then put in jeopardy. The pious fever of sympathy with the king and chiefs was thought by some to be owing more to the dread of failure to certain favorite schemes of pecuniary aggrandizement than to any deep-felt, disinterested desire for the preservation of Hawaiian independence, or the perpetuity of the Hawaiian race.

So physicians, in their inquiries into the etiology of disease, often ascribe more to causes that are occult and indirect than to the more apparent and proximate. Perhaps an intelligent physician, who had felt the pulse and noticed the symptoms of some of the foreign Honolulites, both at the time of the cession and restoration, would have cast about him for some other cause than the alleged and apparent one for the phenomena then exhibited.

The California fever has proved both a counter-irritant and sedative to the totality of these symptoms, most of the subjects of them being swept off to San Francisco, to the great relief of the body politic. This, and the quickening of trade by opening a new maret to Sandwich Island products, and making Honolulu a depôt and place of transit for the Pacific, perhaps of residence for the families of Californian merchants, have cleared the coast for native improvement, and for the more unobstructed action of the missionaries on the Hawaiian mind, which their teachings may almost be said to have created.

The months of May and June, when members of the mission from the eighteen stations on the different islands are usually together in what is called General Meeting, afford the most favorable time for a Christian stranger or mariner, touching at this port, to become acquainted with the very worthy body of missionaries. I say *Christian* visitor, because it is impossible for any man who has not with them a bond of Christian sympathy, and who does not possess a Christian character congenial with theirs, to become sufficiently acquainted to know and estimate their worth. According to Sallust, *Idem velle atque nolle, ea demum firma amicitia est*—To have the same moral tastes and distastes, this, indeed, is firm friendship. A community of feelings and great principles is the only basis of thorough acquaintance and friendship. The necessity of morals or religion in one's self, in order to be a competent judge or friend of the religious, is like the necessity in chemistry of a mutual solvent, in order to bring into play the powerful affinities of any two substances.

True Christians and men of the world may live side by side together; they may have much to do with each other, and considerable knowledge of each other's affairs, but they can not combine; their natural affinities will not act, and the latter can not judge the former until they have a common ground of religious motives, hopes, and fears. Hence the judgment which non-religious travelers and book-makers pass upon missionaries and their work is of no more worth than the judgment of the world upon the Church generally, *whose life is hid with Christ in God;* that is, of about the same account as the criticisms of other birds in fable upon the ingenious *sui generis* nest of the magpie.

It is getting, indeed, to be fashionable and politic now for travelers to speak well of missionaries and their work, for their characters are at this time so generally known, and the valuable results of their labors are so prominent before the world, as to give the point-blank lie to misrepresentations of this sort that were once made, and that used to pass current. A book of travels now in missionary lands, that did not testify favorably to missionary work and character, would not perhaps sell. Missionaries at these islands begin to feel that they may be in danger from this very cause, now that the tables are turned, and governments and book-makers are commending them. They remember the words of their Master, Woe unto you when all men shall speak well of you.

However, this shall not prevent my paying an honest testimony, drawn from intimate personal acquaintance with most of them at their several stations, to the ability, devotion, and eminent usefulness of the missionary band at these islands. We do not believe there could be found any where in England or America a more pure, conscientious, laborious, or consistent association of ministers than the body of missionaries there. It is not too much to say (and may it always be equally true), that they are generally men of strong sense, high, stern principles, patient of labor, and sincerely devoted to God's work; zealous lovers of humanity generally, but especially of this island race.

By patient continuance in well-doing, and the signal blessing of God, making the results of their labors known to all the world, they have lived down opposition, stopped the mouths of slanderers, and put to silence the ignorance of foolish men. Intercourse with them is profitable, especially after a long seclusion from Christian society on the sea, not because they are persons of uncommon gifts or information, but because they are generally plain, natural, well-educated, warm-hearted Christian men and women; at the out-stations especially, cordial, hospitable, unostentatious; saying what they think, and letting you do the same, and performing their duties from principle, in doors and out, in a quiet, orderly way, without having to stop and consider what people will say of them, or to cut and trim for others' eyes so much as at home; discarding generally, certainly away from the metropolis, the gossip, and fashion, and unsatisfying things of heartless foreign society, and dealing mainly in the substantial realities and practical duties of happy domestic life within doors, and active usefulness abroad.

Becoming missionaries has not made them saints, nor procured them exemption from the ordinary infirmities and peccability of men; nor has it placed them on the high vantage-ground which some imagine for the cultivation of piety. Nor do we find the odor of sanctity, nor that imaginary halo of holiness with which certain memoirs, and some other things that have been written, have surrounded the missionary's person and office. The process of mind through which, probably, most of them went in deciding to become missionaries, and the habits then formed, have made, or naturally would make, them better Christians than the mass. But as to outward helps in the cultivation of piety and a holy life, there are by no means so many on missionary ground as at home.

If a man has not obtained a devout mind and habits of holy living before he enters upon the work of a missionary, he will be little likely to alter amid the numerous distractions, versatile pursuits, miscellaneous duties, and rapid wear and tear of a missionary life. A missionary, if he will be faithful, can rarely be a closet man, for he has far more to do in his own household, and more to do abroad, than the pastor at home. His must be a life of action, not of contemplation or study, from the time he enters the foreign field till his bones are laid in an honored missionary's grave; or, disabled and broken in health, he is compelled to withdraw with reluctance from the most honorable service that a man can be devoted to this side of heaven.

As fulfilled by American missionaries, I can testify from close observation, it is a service that is no sinecure, and admits of little intermission of patient toil. Even the time of General Meeting is no vacation. This is convened once every year, or two years, at Honolulu, for necessary business. After the choice of a moderator, and the formation of the various committees, on overtures, for writing the general letter to the Board, &c., &c., a day is generally appointed for religious exercises. Then follows reading of reports from the several stations, which occupy some days; then come up for discussion the various matters presented in the reports of committees, in which all the interests of the mission, and the modes of operating advantageously upon the race of Hawaiians, are freely canvassed, and the thoughts of each member elicited.

Meetings for religious conference and prayer are frequently interspersed, and the children are gathered in a meeting every morning at nine o'clock, at which time the brethren preside by turns. They form an interesting company, and not a few of them are children of great promise.

Maternal meetings are also frequent, and more or less of the ladies are present with their children at all the daily sessions. A ministerial association has been also formed, which has its appropriate exercises in the evening. Annual meetings of the Hawaiian Bible and Tract Societies are held at some time during the session. At the close is a day for thanksgiving and prayer, when the sacrament is administered to the mission church.

There is apparent much brotherly love, mutual confidence, and tender regard for each other through these meetings, which make them times of special religious and social improvement. While they differ often in opinion, and use toward each other great plainness of speech, it is not allowed to impair their Christian and friendly esteem. They may have spoken and written of each other in particular instances somewhat too freely; but, if I am not greatly mistaken, they are all mutual, confiding friends; eminently a united, consentaneous band. That may be said of them which is hardly true to such a degree of the less favored though older English Mission of the Society Islands, Behold how these Christians love one another.* May

* One of the first things which impressed the people favorably in regard to the missionaries was the union which prevailed among them. The expression was very common, and became a proverb: *Hookahi no ano o ka na missionari hana aoli ku e kekahi i kekahi.* (The missionaries have but one aim in all that they do: there is no division among them.) Then they noticed that the missionaries were industrious, toiling night and day, with no ostensible object but to confer blessings upon others. They especially marked the meek and unrevengeful character of the missionaries when provoked by enemies. A certain foreigner treated one of the missionaries with gross insult and abuse, but the missionary took no notice of his conduct. The foreigner was weak and staggering from intoxication. The crowd that was looking on remarked, "This man is weak; the missionary could easily punish him, but shows no disposition to be revenged." Others said, The word of God is verified, which speaks of meekness and forgiveness; for this drunken man insults the teacher, but he does not resent it. Instances of this kind had great influence. Even the heathen have their eyes open to the conduct of ministers, and are nice judges of consistency; and there is no jealousy that can not be *lived down* by a uniform and Christian deportment.—*Dibble's History of the Sandwich Islands.*

it ever be so in the future history of this Mission! and may God continue to bless all its members with entire devotion to their great and good work, until there shall be raised within the nation, and nursed at its own breasts, a native ministry adequate to the care of its churches, and able of itself to perpetuate the noble institutions planted here.

Angels unseen, as ministering spirits went,
When forth the chosen witnesses were sent,
With power from high to preach, where'er they trod,
The glorious Gospel of the blessed God.
Good angels still conduct, from age to age,
Salvation's heirs, on heavenly pilgrimage:
Bright angels through mid-heaven shall hold their flight,
Till all that sit in darkness see the light;
Still the good tidings of great joy proclaim,
Till every tongue confess a Savior's name.
Hearts, harps, and voices, in one choir shall raise
The new, the old, th' eternal song of praise.
May ye who read, with him who wrote this strain,
Join in that song, and worship in that train!

Montgomery.

CHAPTER VII.

VOYAGE TO HAWAII, AND A HOME WITH THE KUMU.

The wild waves are my nightly pillows,
Beneath me roll the ocean's billows;
And as I rest on my couch of brine,
I watch the eternal planets shine.
Ever I ride
On a harmless tide;
Fearing naught—enjoying all things;
Undisturb'd by great or small things.
C. MACKAY.

Ships are but boards, sailors are but men: there be land-rats, and water-rats; water-thieves, and land-thieves; and then there is the peril of waters, winds, and rocks. The *craft* is, notwithstanding, sufficient.—*Shylock: Merchant of Venice.*

I TOOK my departure rather more than a week ago from Honolulu, in a little schooner of thirty or forty tons burden, commanded by a Chinaman. There were ten of the missionaries returning from general meeting, and upward of eighty natives, stowed so close that one could not stretch himself without making a transverse section of several others. And as to navigating from stem to stern, it was impossible, without making stepping-stones of a dozen or more Kanaka-bodies, unless you chose to go round on the outside of the craft, as the sailors did, holding on by toes and fingers to keep you from falling into the mouths of hungry sharks, that glided noiselessly about in the blue waters a foot or two below, ready to act on the law of freebooters every where,

> That he may keep who has the power,
> And he may catch who can.

There was a good proportion of native women with infants at the breast; and when we had all got our postures on the deck for the night, or were taking food together after sea-sickness by day, or were instructing the monsters of the deep (in the way that sea-sick folks are wont to do) into the gastronomic changes and juices of animal chemistry, our deck was a rare field for the pencil of some Cruikshank designer.

We arrived the third evening at the roadstead of Lahaina. The signal of a white flag at the foremast head informed those ashore of the approach of missionaries, and brought off the station double canoe, in which we were all safely carried ashore through the surf, and hospitably disposed of for the night by Rev. Mr. Baldwin. We called the next day upon the king, Kamehameha III., and were introduced to him in a warm bath, which he was taking for the benefit of a rheumatic or gouty knee. He afterward appeared in the reception-room in a loose dress, and we could not help being pleased at the simplicity of his manners, and at the same time gentlemanly bearing, while one could hardly help laughing at the Oriental novelty of our first introduction to his Hawaiian Majesty.

John Young, the governor of Maui, a half-breed, was also present, and for grace and elegance of demeanor, and personal presence, he would have done honor to the court of Queen Victoria. There were

View of Diamond Head Crater, near Honolulu

also several huge giantess chief women in the room, whom pork and *poi* had made almost as unwieldy as Daniel Lambert. Officers and attendants passed through the room without parade or ceremony, or any seeming reference to the king. He sat upon a handsome sofa, and the room was furnished with an elegant large mahogany bureau and center-table, as well as convenient chairs. It was hung around with the portraits of his father, Kamehameha II., and his favorite queen, Kamamalu, who died in England, and of Prince Blucher and Frederic of Prussia. A large frame-house of stone is in process of erection for the king; but he will probably always prefer, as now, to live in a grass house. His signing the temperance pledge, and putting away all spirit, and the follies indulged with it, have made him a man whom frequent drunkenness was fast turning into a brute.

I had time but for a hasty bird's-eye view of the Mission seminary, printing-office, and three dwelling-houses of Lahainaluna. They make a pretty white-washed hamlet, six hundred and twenty-two feet above, and about two miles ride from Lahaina. The circle of missionary families there is a very pleasant one, forming sufficient society in itself, often, also, enlivened by the random visits of missionaries passing to other stations, and transient visitors making the tour of the islands. Mr. Dibble had a residence one thousand two hundred feet higher up the mountain, where there is enjoyed a climate of almost unrivaled salubrity, and an invalid may comfortably prolong his days, and make himself useful, whom another atmosphere would soon destroy.

Commended to God in prayer, and having experienced the warmest Christian hospitality, we set off again the fourth evening for Hawaii. The natives and missionary brethren that stopped at Lahaina left us the space they had occupied to recline in, so that we had each as much room as most men occupy when they come to die, but hardly more.

After two nights more under the open canopy of a dewless, star-lit, Pacific sky, we were landed on Sabbath, P.M., at Mahukona, Kohala, the northern county of the great Island of Hawaii. It is a barren, lava fishing village, with a little indentation between the jagged rocks just large enough for a boat to be thrust up. A school-house of mud and lava received us, the people having already gathered there to bid us *aloha*, and attend divine service, at the blowing of a conch. We were ushered at once into a half-naked, squatting assembly of eighty or one hundred persons, which was addressed by Messrs. Coan, Lyman, and Bond.

It were foolish to attempt to paint so grotesque and odd a scene as was offered in that school-house to the eyes of a man, a *novus homo* in these ends of the earth. To be imagined, it must be seen. After the native service was over, and the house at length cleared of the curious urchins and red-skinned, naked barbarians that lingered to observe us, we had a precious meeting, at which each prayed and gave thanks, and then ate of our frugal supper, sitting down all together upon the mats, around the Hingham bucket that held our food. We were hardly through before the natives again swarmed in upon us, and made one glad to leave and walk abroad in the twilight, to meditate upon the goodness of God, and the strangeness of our situation in a land of so recent, and but now half-weaned idolaters.

Sleep was slow to visit a frame to which the notable Hawaiian fleas now had their first introduction. They were so eager and clamorous for acquaintance, and prone, like the human *kamaainas*, to renew their friendly gripe and *aloha*, that I turned and tossed upon my gravel bed till dawn of day, and then arose, sorely bestead, weary, and hungry.

It was on the same track, by which we have thus gained safely our island home, that a swimming feat was performed, a few years ago, by a native woman in peril, which surpasses all other achievements of the kind on record. When about midway between the outmost points of Hawaii and Kahoolawe, or thirty miles from land on either side, a small island vessel, poorly managed, and leaky (as they generally are), suddenly shifted cargo in a strong wind, plunged bows under, and went down, there being on board between thirty and forty persons, and a part of them in the cabin. This was just after dinner, on Sunday. The natives that happened to be on deck were at once all together in the waves, with no means of escape but their skill in swimming. A Christian man, by the name of Mauae, who had conducted morning worship and a Sabbath service with the people in the forenoon, now called them round him in the water, and implored help from God for all. Then, as a strong current was setting to the north, making it impossible for them to get to Hawaii, whither they were bound, they all made in different ways for Maui and Kahoolawe.

The captain of the schooner, a foreigner, being unable to swim, was put by his Hawaiian wife on an oar, and they two struck out together for the distant shore; but on Monday morning, having survived the first night, the captain died; and in the afternoon of the same day his wife landed on Kahoolawe. A floating hatchway from the wreck gave a chance for life to a strong young man and his brother; but the latter perished before the daylight of Monday, while the elder reached the island in safety by eight or nine o'clock. A feeble boy, without any support, swam the same distance of nearly thirty miles, and arrived safe to land before any of the others. Mauae and his wife had each secured a covered bucket for a buoy, and three young men kept them company till evening; but all disappeared, one after another, during the night, either by exhaustion, or getting bewildered and turning another way, or by becoming the prey of sharks.

Monday morning the faithful pair were found alone; and the wife's bucket coming to pieces, she swam without any thing till afternoon, when Mauae became too weak to go on. The wife stopped and lomilomied him (a kind of shampooing common here), so that he was able to swim again until Kahoolawe was in full view. Soon, however, Mauae grew so weary that he could not even hold to the bucket; and his faithful wife, taking it from him, bade him cling to the long hair of her head, while she still hopefully held on, gradually nearing the shore! Her husband's hands, however, soon slipped from her hair, too weak to keep their hold, and she tried in vain to rouse him to further effort. She endeavored, according to the native expression, to *hoolana kona manao, to make his hope swim*, to inspire him with confidence by pointing to the land, and telling him to pray to Jesus; but he could only utter a few broken petitions. Putting his arms, therefore, around her own neck, she held them fast on her bosom with one hand, and still swam vigorously with the other until near nightfall, when herself and her now lifeless burden were within a quarter of a mile from the shore. She had now to contend with the raging surf; and finding the body of her husband, which she had borne so long, stone-dead, she reluctantly cast it off, and shortly after reached the land.

But there she was hardly better off than at sea, for long exposure to the brine had so blinded her eyes that it was some time before she could see; her strength was too much spent to travel, and the spot on which she landed was barren lava, on the opposite side of the island to any settlement. Food and water she must find, or die. Providentially she obtained the latter in a rain that had recently fallen, and that was standing for her in the cups of the rocks. Monday night, Tuesday, Wednesday, and Thursday came and went without relief, while she crept on gradually as she could toward the inhabited parts of the island. At last, on Friday morning, when her *manaolana*, her swimming hope that had held its head so long above the waves, was fast sinking with her failing strength, by a gracious providence she discovered a water-melon vine in fruit. Eating one, "her eyes were enlightened," like Jonathan's by the honey; soon after she was found by a party of fishermen, by them cared for and conducted to their village, and the next day transported by canoe to Lahaina, whence the foundered schooner had sailed just one week before.

Such fatal disasters have often occurred in these seas to the crazy and ill-furnished craft that navigate from island to island; but never before was there known such an instance of endurance and escape, in a woman, as that I have here narrated, derived from sources the most reliable and authentic. The like peril might have befallen us (and missionaries are especially exposed to it), but for that buoyant, great life-preserver which God is to those that commit themselves to him in the plain course of duty, whether on journies by sea or land. How cheering it is to feel and be sure of this, when traveling abroad for a worthy end, or toiling manfully and usefully at home for a competence! The all-seeing Eye that never sleeps is watching over us for good in all the paths of life, on ocean or earth, if we be but therein serving our Lord and Saviour. In the exercise of duty to God and man, and guided by providence and reason, we can venture any where safely, sure to be immortal till our work is done. The spirit with which one of the sweetest poetesses of America has written these lines, should animate us all in the different labors and callings of life:

Ye who in home's narrow circle dwell,
  Where Love's flame lights the household hearth,
Weave the silken bond, and frame the spell,
  Binding heart to heart throughout the earth;
Pleasant toil is yours: the light of day
On naught holier sheds its blessed ray.

Diverse though our paths in life may be,
  Each is sent some mission to fulfill;
Fellow-workers in the world are we,
  While we seek to do our Master's will;
But our doom is labor, while the day
Points us to our task, with blessed ray.

Fellow-workers are we; hour by hour
  Human tools are shaping Heaven's great schemes,
Till we see no limit to man's power,
  And reality outstrips old dreams.
Toil and struggle, therefore, work and weep,
In God's acre ye shall calmly sleep,
                When the Night cometh!

We encountered on the way, though at such a distance as to be beyond the reach of danger, one of those singular phenomena called water-spouts, which are of frequent occurrence in these seas. There was but little wind with us at the time, but we could perceive a squall, and showers falling at a distance; and directly over where the water-spout was observed, a dense cloud was whirling around, and forming its folds into a tube, trumpet-shaped, but bent to an angle of sixty degrees or more with the sea. The tube thus let down from the cloud, like a large engine hose, joined another more fully formed from the sea, whose position and appearance were that of a cone or a cypress-knee. At the point of junction of the two, I should not judge the diameter of the column to have been more than two or three feet, but six or eight times that at the end.

As thus formed, it seemed like a hollow cylinder of vapor and water, extending obliquely from the sea to the cloud, thin at the middle, and broad at the two extremities. A whirling motion, as of fluids in circulation from below upward, could be clearly seen within the tube, suggesting the idea that this water-spout was but a cloud-feeder, like the suction-pipe of a fire-engine, and, by some process or law in pneumatics not fully known, that water was pumped up by it into the region of clouds, and there or on its way converted into vapor. This idea was corroborated by the fact that, after being distinctly observed by us in motion three or four minutes, the pillar vanished from below, and the upper end only remained, entering the cloud in the position and at the usual angle of the first branch of a great oak-tree. Soon it disappeared entirely, and the surcharged clouds were rent under the vapors which we had observed circulating upward, and a deluge of dark rain was seen falling in that quarter where this great force-pump of Nature had been at work.

We were too distant to observe whether there was uncommon agitation of the sea at the bottom of this water-spout; but I have noticed it elsewhere on the ocean, when nearer to these phenomena, in cases where the origin of the water-spout was clearly in a whirlwind, and began below. In the present case its formation seemed to begin in the cloud, and a connection was gradually effected downward, whereby vapor was conveyed to the clouds in extraordinary quantity and quickness, which may or may not be immediately formed into a flood of rain. When, on the other hand, a water-spout begins in a whirlwind from below, there seems to be reason to think that it always bursts bodily, after being wafted along and striking against some object, or from having been fired into; or, because of the wind not acting with equal force upon its upper and lower extremities, the column is bent and speedily ruptured from the unequal velocity of its parts.

A water-spout of this latter sort once broke over the harbor of Honolulu. It was first observed moving along slowly, of about the thickness of a hogshead, accompanied with a violent ebullition of the water at its base. Upon touching the reef the column broke, causing a sudden rise of the sea of three feet on the beach.* Great numbers of fish were said to have been destroyed by the force of the falling water. Other water-spouts have at different times broken on the land here, and have washed away houses and drowned the inhabitants. They are experienced in the Atlantic, where I have myself observed them, as well as in the Pacific, and upon all maritime coasts. Trees are torn up by them, valleys flooded, eminences plowed away, deep pits excavated, and habitations, harvests, and cattle borne away. If a ship be struck by one, it is easy to see that destruction must be inevitable. Mariners, therefore, dread and avoid them. Hence the allusion to it of the philosophical Latin poet, Lucretius:

Like a vast column gradual from the skies,
Borne o'er the waves, descends it; the vex'd tide
Boiling amain beneath its mighty whirl,
And with *destruction sure the stoutest ship*
Threatening that dares the boisterous scene approach!

These dangers of the deep safely passed, the Sabbath over, and our first flea-memorable night at Mahukona ended, Messrs. Coan, Lyman, and Wilcox set off early on foot, Monday morning, for their long tramp

* Jarves's History of the Sandwich Islands, p. 23.

to Hilo. After our breakfast of roasted sweet potatoes, Mr. Bond began preparing for the exportation of his goods on the backs of natives, twelve miles up and down hill, to his house on the other or windward side of the island. His wife and child were carried on a Hawaiian *manele*, or long hurdle, like a Hindoo palanquin with its set of *booies*, made so as to recline in, lashed at the head and foot to a long pole running lengthwise, that was made to rest on the shoulders of natives, two carrying at a time. Other packages, weighing eighty pounds, were carried by single men on their backs, and lumber, and other heavy boxes of books, &c., were carried by companies of four and six. After all the goods were deposited in the school-house, or distributed upon the backs of the carriers, we mounted horse, and arrived at the rural mission-house about noon.

It is finely situated on a very gentle, verdant slope, adjacent to a cane plantation of ninety acres, belonging to some Chinamen. It stands in the center of an area of some five or six acres, inclosed with a neat stone wall, and having a part of it cultivated as a garden, adorned with flowering shrubs and trees, as the pine-apple, guava, acacia, mimosa, tamarind, kukui, mulberry, geranium, banana, Pride of China, sugar-cane, &c. The house is thatched with the long leaves of the *hala*-tree (Pandanus), and has a very pretty, neat appearance, in connection with the tasteful keeping of the walks and grounds, like the pictures we have of thatched cottages and rural scenes of Old England.

May it long be the cheerful abode of domestic peace,

and piety, and missionary faithfulness. And may a healthful moral radiance shine out from it into all the surrounding realms, as a center of religious light and civilization, till a thousand such pleasant cottages shall gem

> These russet lawns and fallows gray,

and smile out upon the Christian traveler from every verdant ravine of this lovely land.

> O! 'twas not thus in ages gone!
> These isles in Error's night lay dim:
> God's jewels, they in silence shone
> Most beautiful, yet not for Him!

My first Sabbath on Hawaii was, of course, one of especial interest. The church,* a grass house, somewhat more than one hundred feet long, and thirty or forty wide, was thronged with natives to the number of seven or eight hundred, sitting upon the unmatted,

* A framed and plastered church edifice, since erected at Kohala, with incredible pains on the part of the indefatigable missionary, Rev. Elias Bond, was overthrown by a hurricane on the 21st of December, 1849. The hard labor of years seemed swept away at a stroke, and the energy of the pastor was well-nigh broken. But a knowledge of the disaster speedily reaching New York, substantial sympathy was enlisted, and, beginning in the liberality of the Church of the Puritans, a plan is now being consummated, in May, 1850, to transport at once, from America to the Sandwich Islands, the entire materials of a new missionary meeting-house for Kohala. It is a charity the more becoming and necessary, now that the Hawaiian churches are made independent of the American Board; and it is but a suitable interchange of benevolence with the Church of Kohala, which has sent to the American Home Missionary Society, within two years, upward of $100, inclusive of $30 just received.

The tempestuous winds that have recently devastated the Sandwich Islands, and proved so destructive to plantations and shipping, are exceptive phenomena quite out of course from the hitherto observed equability of weather, and comparative immunity from destructive storms in that part of the Pacific.

grass-strewn floor. Three hundred and seventy-seven children were at the Sabbath school between the services They recited, with very pleasing effect, in a measured or chanting manner, by classes, the verses from Scripture that constituted the lesson for the day.

As you look at the bright-eyed boys and girls, and hear them chant their lesson, or say to you their merry *aloha*, you long to be able to talk with them; and, tawny as they are, you think there were never gathered finer looking or more animated children. Adults often look stupid, and incapable of, or averse to, close attention. The youth far excel them in intelligence and activity. The boys of Mr. Bond's boarding-school, fourteen in number, when they meet twice a week with the teachers from the several school districts, far outstrip them in arithmetic and other exercises; and the teachers say they can not at all stand with them for aptness and mental agility. The hope of the nation is there.

In the morning was a sermon by the pastor, from "*The wages of sin is death.*" In the afternoon the whole congregation, or, rather, all the members of the church, recited by divisions some verses of Scripture from the AO A KA LA, or Daily Food, on the verse-a-day system, and the pastor commented upon them. Many of the adults and children came from a distance of ten miles. We found them holding a prayer-meeting when we returned, after the intermission, at two o'clock P.M. Tolerable attention was given to the service, and the deportment of all was correct. All the women were dressed in loose gowns, and many of the men had pantaloons: all their *kapas*. Notwithstanding this, there were naked limbs enough, and the attitudes and costume of the audience were such as to make the scene truly barbaric.

After the Sabbath, one of the good deacons having furnished me with a powerful horse, I went, in company with the pastor, to attend meetings at four different school districts. The people were gathered on the grass floors of the rude school-houses in their every-day dress, or, rather, undress—men, women, boys, and girls, and nursing babes as they were born; young eyes sparkling, and their generally sleek and plump forms giving ample evidence of their full feeding, in this foodful region, upon pork and *poi*. It is painful, however, to see so many limbs and persons scaly and scarred with eruptions, and holes made, and features gnawed away by the scourge that came with licentious foreigners. Some of the men we saw are very giants in their dimensions, and immensely strong.

When we had exchanged the usual Hawaiian salutation of ALOHA OUKOU, or love to you, Mr. Bond opened the meeting with prayer, followed by a hymn and a portion of Scripture, and then proceeded to call over the names of all the church members in the district, and to ask them each questions in regard to their religious estate, and their friends who were absent. When this was through, he made a few general remarks, and the meeting was closed with singing and prayer. Then followed shaking of hands, and the parting *aloha*. The different groups, with so much that was peculiarly Hawaiian and barbaric, were to a stranger a novel and curious sight. No less strange, and romantic too, was the ride through glens, adown *palis* (precipices), along *kalo* patches, and the edge of precipitous ravines, that would make one friend almost shudder for another in riding over.

The face of the country is intersected by numerous deep ravines, that are richly shaded with the verdure of tropical trees, the bread-fruit, ohia, banana, hau, kou, kukui, and others; their sides, even when per pendicular, covered all over with the most gigantic brakes ever beheld, of which a scientific Scotch traveler and naturalist (the unfortunate Mr. Douglass) estimated that there were three hundred and sixty-five different species in Hawaii alone.

At one of the meetings there was accidentally present, being beckoned in as he was going by with a back-load of *laauhala*, a Catholic, or, as the natives say, one who had gone over from the Church to the Pope. Mr. Bond questioned him at some length, and took the occasion to give the people instruction on popery, make them repeat the second commandment, &c. He had learned from his priest the recent date of Protestantism; how Calvin burned Servetus; that Catholics only were to be saved; and that the proper name of Protestants was *Kaluina*, or Calvinists.

Mr. Bond thinks that every convert to popery in his field could be brought back by promising to let them into the Church. Men have sometimes come to him saying, If you don't let us into the Church, we will go off to the Pope; or we will dive into all manner of sin. One man who had gone to the Catholics was asked by Mr. Bond why he had done so. "Oh!" said he, "I tried three or four times, and you would not let me into the Church, and I would not wait any longer."

Christians,* in some places, are accustomed to pray to be kept from popery, as the thing brought in with the gun, *ka mea i lawe ia mai me ka pu.* The *Poe-Pope*, or popish party, is but another name for the adulterous and sin-loving *puhi-baka*, or smoking party, that practice all uncleanness with greediness. When a man is caught in adultery, he often turns Catholic; and going to the *Poe-Pope* is merely going to get a license to commit sin, *e hana hewa.* They will often give no other reason for some things than to say, Our side does so and so. Riding out once with another missionary, we met two men smoking, and the missionary entering into conversation with them, "Oh!" said the spokesman, as if that were enough, "our side smokes"—*He Poe puhi baka makou.*

It would be well if things were called by their right names every where as much as here. In the more southern groups of Polynesia, Williams tells us, Christians and idolaters were distinguished from each other as "Sons of the word" and "Sons of the devil." Here they are the *Poe-Pope* and *Poe-Hoahanau*, or fraternity of brothers. Popery came in here with the guns and brandy of La Place too popish-like, and its

* At a meeting of native assistant missionaries at one of the stations, one of them read an essay on popery, of which the following is an abstract: Popery. What has it proved to be? Has it proved to be food, or fish, or water, or tapa, or cloth, or wisdom? No. It has introduced confusion and disorder into the government and into the Church. It has led men astray, and disorganized families. There is no goodness about it, no humility, no love; but opposition and rebellion. It has extorted $20,000 from the rulers. Is this the blessedness of popery? Believe it not, follow it not. It is idolatry. Believe not that the Pope is a god; he is nothing but a man, whose dwelling-place is in Rome.

discordance with genuine Christianity is too glaring for it ever to attain great popularity or influence with the Hawaiians. The Bible was too long before it, and the names of blasphemy and deceit were stamped too deep on its brazen brow for it ever to get into reputation here. It is not too much to hope that the *Poe-Pope* and the *Poe-Hoomaloka*, that is, papists and unbelievers, will soon be merged in the overwhelming preponderance of the *Poe-Hoahanau.*

An old man, once a member of the Church in Kau, on this island, was excommunicated for some immorality from the Protestant Church, and united at once with the papists. The missionary called on him some time after, and asked him why he turned to images again. Do you not worship images and pray to Mary? He replied, "We do." Why? "The French priests came to me, and flattered me, and made every thing appear so smooth, that I thought I would consent to go to their worship, though I did not like it. I went, and they persuaded me to receive baptism, and told me I should see the kingdom of Heaven. I consented; but saw no other heaven than we all see, which I saw in the days of Kamehameha." Do you not see their religion is false? "Yes, it is false," was his emphatic reply. My advice to you is to turn to Christ, and repent truly, and renounce images. He replied, "I will not worship images any more; but you see me. I am just what I was when you excommunicated me; I have never repented." The next morning he came to the Protestant meeting, publicly renounced popery, and put down his name among the inquirers, saying, "The priests made me the arbiter of all the papists in this part of Kau."

Another fallen church member became awakened, returned to the missionary, and told that shortly after he was excommunicated a papist came to him and said, "Now they have put you out of the Church, I wish you to turn to my God." "To your God!" he replied; "what is your God?" The papist then held out his image—a small bronze crucifix—which he wore strung about his neck. The man took it, and looking at it, said, "This is your God, is it? I will not turn to your gods. This is the kind of gods we always had before we heard of the true God. I will not turn to that."

When the Jesuit missionaries first arrived, they used many arguments with the natives to show that their instructions and those of the Protestant missionaries were alike. It was on one of these occasions that an old man, who made no pretensions to religion, replied that the missionaries had taught him about God. "Oh yes," replied the priest, "Mr. Thurston taught about God, and that was right; you heard him, and now I wish you to hear me." The old man gravely answered, "But the Bible says I can not serve two masters." He further objected to their images, when the priest said, "Oh, we do not call this God, and do not pray to it. It is only a representation (shadow) of God." The old man replied, "Let me see it; that can not be any representation of God. It is made of brass. *If there be any shadow or representation of God, it must be in the heart, not in an image.*"

A wonderful answer, truly, for a heathen, and deserving to be set down with that saying of an ancient poet, and Paul's comment upon it—For we are

ALSO HIS OFFSPRING. *Forasmuch, then, as we are the offspring of God, we ought not to think that the god head is like unto gold, or silver, or stone, graven by art and man's device.*

This old man of Hawaii nei, taught thus by Nature and then by Nature's God, in the Bible, did he not utter more true philosophy and common sense in that saying, IF THERE BE ANY SHADOW OR REPRESENTATION OF GOD, IT MUST BE IN THE HEART, than many an educated and would-be-philosophic babbler of the schools, whether ancient or of our own day?

Abjuring thus the image graven by art and man's device, but awake to the echoes of his Maker's footsteps in the human soul and throughout the visible creation, methinks he would say with the poet, could he speak in our Christianized English,

God's spirit smiles in flowers,
And in soft summer showers
He sends his love.
Each dew-drop speaks His praise,
And bubbling fount displays,
In all their lucid rays,
Light from above.

The tiny vines that creep
Along the ravine steep
Obey his nod.
The golden orb of day,
And ocean's crested spray,
To him due homage pay—
Creation's God.

The correspondence these old men of Hawaii saw in the rites and the heaven of popery with the paganism they remembered of "the days of Kamehameha Nui," has its parallel in the identity between the scenes and the shows of Rome papal and Rome pagan, as observed by the classic Middleton, who says of himself when visiting modern Rome, that "nothing, I found, concurred so much with my original purpose of conversing with the ancients, or so much helped my imagination to fancy myself wandering about in old heathen Rome, as to observe and attend to their religious worship, all whose ceremonies appeared plainly to have been copied from the rituals of primitive paganism, as if handed down by an uninterrupted succession from the priests of old to the priests of new Rome; while each of them readily explained and called to my mind some passage of a classic author, where the same ceremony was described as transacted in the same form and manner, and in the same place where I now saw it executed before my eyes; so that as oft as I was present at any religious exercises in their churches, it was more natural to fancy myself looking on at some solemn act of idolatry in old Rome, than assisting at a worship instituted on the principles and formed upon the plan of Christianity."

We say, furthermore, that notable facts warrant the assertion that the history of Romanism at the Sandwich Islands, like what Victor Hugo has lately said of Jesuitism in Europe, is written in the history of human progress there, BUT IT IS WRITTEN ON THE BACK. Every step forward has been taken in spite of it. Had French popery had its way, a "civilized Satan" would now have been dominant there instead of the benign Christian Church; and French brandy and licentiousness would have wrought for the nation's destruction what American Protestantism and temperance have done for its salvation. God's providence be praised, which has made the difference!

It was New England missionaries, inspired by a wisdom not their own, that carried there, in the early opening of the island world of the North Pacific, and before Romanism had at all invaded it, New England religion, New England common schools, and New England freedom. And even as Wordsworth has described the early evangelization of the British Isles, so might it be said of the first apostles of civilization and Christianity to Hawaii nei:

> Rich conquest waits them: the tempestuous sea
> Of ignorance, that ran so rough and high,
> And heeded not the voice of clashing swords,
> These good men humble by a few bare words,
> And calm with fear of God's divinity.

The products of New England are too well naturalized in the island soil to be uprooted now by the arts, or the cannon, or the brandy of Rome; and what we have called the ISLAND HEART of the North Pacific bids fair to become such a centre of Protestantism to the realms beyond the seas on either side of it, as Great Britain has been to Europe and North America.

CHAPTER VIII.

ROMANCE OF TOURING AND PROSE OF WORKING.

Who is my Brother? 'Tis not merely he
  Who hung upon the same loved mother's breast;
But every one, whoever he may be,
  On whom the image of a man's impress'd.
True Christian sympathy was ne'er design'd
  To be shut up within a narrow bound;
But sweeps abroad, and in its search to find
  Objects of mercy, goes the whole world round.
'Tis like the sun, rejoicing east and west,
  Or beautiful rainbow, bright from south to north;
  It has an angel's pinion, mounting forth
O'er rocks, and hills, and seas, to make men bless'd.
  No matter what their color, name, or place,
  It blesses all alike, the universal race.

T. C. Upham

I am just resting from the fatigue of a tour recently made with the pastor of Kohala, for an examination preparatory to the sacrament of the Lord's Supper. The first day, after riding about eight miles up and down the sides of deep ravines, fertile with *kalo*, bananas, bread-fruit, and *ohias*, and over the fine arable lands between them, we arrived at the brow of a *pali*, or precipice, about one thousand feet high, and nearly perpendicular, down which we must go to be at the school-house in the beautiful valley at its base. Leaving our horses in charge of the last schoolmaster, at the rude seat of whose pedagogic sway a meeting had just been held, we let ourselves down by the zig-zag path as best we could.

The sight of the valley beneath was truly unique and beautiful; luxuriant *kalo* patches, irrigated by a crystal stream that here and there was made to form in ponds; native houses, and trees and men in miniature, from our overlooking, lofty position; a steep, twin *pali*, of the same height opposite, its almost rectangular sides verdant and blossoming with the *kukui* and convolvulus vine. At one end the ravine ran up for more than a mile, till the *palis* met where sprang the living fountain from the heart of the lava rock. Had it been in Scotland, it was a place which Sir Walter would have chosen for the appearance of the white Lady of Avenel; and Grecian imagination would have made it sacred to Nymphs and Naiads, and a recess for the sons of genius to implore the inspiration of the sacred Nine. But here in Hawaii nei, where there are no classic gods or goddesses, it is but a fountain of *wai maole*, as Nature and the after-throes of her volcanoes made it, to irrigate the food patches, and fill the *huewais* of common *kanakas*.

At the other end this magnificent avenue opened upon the deep, with a beach of the finest black writing sand, over which the sea rolled in immense hoary breakers, nearly up to a wall made to prevent its incursions upon the *kalo* patches. Boys and girls, and athletic men were sporting among the billows, diving through the huge rollers as they rushed in from the ocean, and sometimes riding in upon them clear up on the beach, the boys and girls on little surf-boards, the men by dint of their own muscles.

The meeting over in this romantic valley, it remained either to climb a precipice as high as that we had descended, or to pass round it by the sea, subject to be wet by the huge billows that beat, often to the perpendicular wall of the precipice. Choosing the latter, we had to disencumber ourselves of nether garments, and arranging our other apparel somewhat like a native *malo*, to watch the opportunity when the sea retreated, in order to get round a projecting point. *Sans culottes* as we were, we did not pass without a wetting to the waist by a violent wave, that came near to raising me from my feet. A company of natives attended us, one of whom waddled to my aid and held me by the arm, as a *haole* does his *wahine*, they said.

After passing thus the most difficult part, we coasted on over the wave-washed stones and masses of broken lava for more than a mile, the abrupt wall of cooled lava on one side five hundred feet high, the raging sea on the other, washing to its base. Here and there masses were broken off, which we would have to surmount. Now and then we could see holes in the face of the rock, where pent-up gases had burst out after the great mass was cooled, and left a space all around like a honeycomb. Sometimes the rock was completely vitrified; at other times we would meet with places whose solid rock seemed only cracked, not fused. Again it would be nothing but slag and scoria; in another place a formation plainly basaltic.

A mile of such walking brought us to another valley, where were gathered the inhabitants of that and of another valley, which we should have had to climb four *palis* to get to, and which neither Mr. Bond nor any missionary had ever visited but once. It was a valley yet more beautiful, if possible, than the other; the sides higher, and more densely covered with the *hau*-tree and other shrubs; the water more abundant, and the *kalo* more luxuriant. A native house—one of a thousand—gave us comfortable entertainment and rest for the night. We had an apartment to ourselves, and a part raised and covered with mats, called in Hawaiian *hikiee*, on which we lay with considerable comfort, after a supper of roasted *kalo* and *ha*, the latter being the butt end of *kalo* tops, and very much in taste like asparagus.

A good old man there, who *lomilomi*-ed my weary limbs with a surprisingly grateful sense of refreshment, and who seemed to regard our white feet with great admiration, kindly offered me his buxom daughter, and a *kalo* patch for a dowry, if I would stop with them as their *kumu*. Who knows but that some such liberal offer to one of the forthcoming celibates of the Mission will yet tempt them to abjure monastic vows, and yoke themselves here in Hawaii into the state they eschewed in America. *Nous verrons.*

The superiority of the white skin to the Hawaiian olive was matter of long conversation to the assembled natives, who came together, both young and old, and of both sexes, as many as could get into the house, to see the strangers, how they looked, and ate, and slept. In the morning, too, tawny faces were curiously peering in at our little window, and every motion was observed with an eager, savage interest. The man at whose house we stopped was one of uncom-

Kaipuaolo's Bread Fruit.

mon ingenuity and enterprise, by the name of Kaipuholo, or the Running Gourd. Growing up among the stones in his little inclosure, where one would think nothing could grow, he had coffee-trees, oranges, guavas, limes, broom corn, bananas, sugar-cane, &c. He was, too, a conscientious, good man, whom I shall love to remember. Long after prayers with the natives in Hawaiian, and in our room by ourselves, I heard the voice of our host, after all others were asleep, praying without in the open air. In the morning, as soon as light, the conch was blown for prayer-meeting, as in all the islands.

We started on our return by eight o'clock, but found the tide in, and the sea so high that we had to climb the steep *pali* which we had come round the previous day. It was a work like climbing the Hill Difficulty, in Pilgrim's Progress. Often was I compelled to stop for breath, and recline holding on, completely exhausted. But the scenery at every stage was so novel and beautiful, that mere turning to look was rest. After descending another *pali*, and climbing its mate, we found our horses at its brow, and reached a missionary's cheerful house by three o'clock

We stopped by the way in a beautiful cocoa-nut tree dell, and had two agile natives climb the trees, which they did by merely clasping hands around it and then stepping up, the feet pressing the trunk by the balls and great toe. A man never looked so much like a baboon as then. They went up thus the tall, branchless trunk quicker than we should climb a ladder, shook off ten or twelve, which the natives peeled of the tough, fibrous husk with their teeth; and we drank the bland milk of three or four with great relish and refreshment, wearied and hot as we were with scaling and descending *palis*.

The next day we set off anew on a tour to the leeward of the island, making a complete circuit of its northern end. At the village where we quartered for the night, we were met with a hearty *aloha*, and a cordial shake of the hands by young and old. With hospitable intent they had prepared potatoes, fish, and fowl for us; and there was a great scuttle-fish, with its hundred hands, for the natives that accompanied us.

Our riding was the dreariest opposite of the route before, over tracts of barren lava which seldom or never feel the rain, but which in summer and winter reflect and radiate the rays of the sun with fierce intensity. The inhabitants get their support by fishing, drink the brackish water found in springs at the edge of the sea, and exchange their fish for food with the inhabitants of the other side. There is an intermediate region between the leeward and windward, which was formerly populous, and produced yearly one large crop of potatoes.

An immense old heathen temple, or *heiau*, is standing there, which we measured, and found to be two hundred and ninety feet long, one hundred and twenty-five broad, and the walls at the base thirty feet thick and twenty feet high. The area so inclosed is now a tobacco-field. In one corner we found human bones, along with those of dogs and hogs, that were once offered in sacrifice.

They knelt to idols carved of stone;
To fish and fowl, to block and bone;

They enter'd hell to find a god
Worse than the rest, and gave him blood.

But the idol, the altar, and priest are gone, and there are few surviving who can give an intelligent answer to the question, What meaneth this great heap of stones? So perish and come to naught all the devices and remnants of cruel paganism! And soon may the dark lines it has written; the dreadful characters of pollution and death which it has been burning in for ages upon the heathen constitution be effaced, and the moral image of God be every where reenstamped upon the sons of the apostasy.

"Once, while the name, Jehovah, was a sound,
Within the circuit of this sea-girt isle,
Unheard, the savage nations bow'd their heads
To gods delighting in remorseless deeds;
Gods which themselves had fashion'd, to promote
Ill purposes, and flatter foul desires.
Amid impending rocks and gloomy woods,
To those inventions of corrupted man,
Mysterious rites were duly solemnized.
A few rude monuments of mountain-stone
Survive; all else is swept away. How changed
The existing worship, and, with those compared,
The worshipers how innocent and bless'd!"

The work of raising a people like this from the dire abyss of heathenism is a dead lift; it is no boy's work or child's play, and whoever looks for poetry in it is sure to be mistaken. I have learned something about it in the preparations that have been making here some weeks for the quarterly celebration of the Lord's Supper. These are plain, prose labors to the pastor of no ordinary magnitude. They consist in the examination of *Imis*, or inquirers, and candidates for the

Church; and disentanglement of cases of *hihia*, or difficulty and sin in the Church, and the administration of discipline; which, in a Church of ten or twelve hundred members, is a work of no small magnitude. Indeed, you will hear the pastors of this Mission say generally that the admission of new members, the hearing and adjustment of difficulties, and the exercise of discipline are the most perplexing and patience-trying things they have to do. It needs Briarean hands and Argus eyes, a constitution of iron, and a brain of more than Voltaic energy (to say nothing of the heart), in order to do this faithfully.

The common method pursued with inquirers is, to enter in a book the names of those whom the *lunas* (deacons) present as proper subjects of admission. With these they converse a little at every tour or meeting of the *Hooikaikas* (another name for the inquirers), giving them suitable instructions. At length, after having been upon the book for six months, or a year, or two years, as the case may be—having run well for that time, being well reported by the elders, and giving evidence of sincerity in seeking the *pono*, some are chosen from the list and presented by the pastor to the company of elders (numbering in this church upward of forty), and voted in. But it is often difficult for the pastor to satisfy himself, or give a reason to another why he should receive this man rather that; or to say of ten set aside or put off, that they are not as worthy of membership as ten admitted.

Among such an unlearned and simple, or, as they express it, *naaupo* people, it is impossible to fix a certain amount of knowledge to be possessed, or to establish any invariable criteria to be applied to all who are received to the table of the Lord. The great desire generally felt to be in the Church, its respectability, the secret belief, oftentimes, that being in the Church will somehow insure their salvation, will induce many a man to live correctly, wait carefully upon his teacher, and *hoomanawanui* (persevere), as the saying is, in the good way, until they get admitted into the sheep-fold.

Those who are successful will be often asked, How did you get in? and inquirers will get informed by others of the questions the missionary is likely to ask them, and of the proper answers to be given; and stereotyped forms of expressing their *manaos* will get in vogue among them, so that the missionary has to be racking his brain to vary the mode of examination, and in his questions is not, perhaps, half the time understood. The perplexity of the work to young missionaries, whose acquaintance with the native character and language is far from perfect, may be faintly conceived.

The forms of Church government and discipline are semi-Episcopal, Presbyterian, and Congregational, a mingling of the three. Members are admitted and discipline administered in (I believe) all the churches only by the votes of the company of deacons or elders. But while the pastor is much assisted by them, and is enabled by their means, in a certain sense, to multiply his own eyes and ears, the responsibility and weight of all rest upon him. And whether under the usages of Presbyterianism or Congregationalism, every pastor is by necessity an independent prelate, and his restraining hand has continually to be laid upon his deacons, who, in their charity, are eager to get many in whom he would longer keep out. However, they generally bow to his superior wisdom, and by the exercise of a little skill their *manaos* (thoughts) may be made always to coincide with his.

At this station, yesterday, fifty-eight children were baptized, and the names of forty were read as expelled or suspended, and the names of twenty-two couples published for marriage. In the afternoon was the sacrament. Kaipuholo, the man at whose house we slept, up in the romantic valley of Honokane, had previously come to Mr. Bond to know if his wife should come to the communion, she having the evening before, after the preparatory lecture, had a quarrel with another couple about her goats getting into their inclosure. As we entered the house in the afternoon, the husband of the other couple was confessing his sin before the whole congregation, and professing his repentance. His wife followed, in a style of great dignity and self-possession, and professed the same; but Kaipuholo's wife was silent. At the communion, when it was asked if any had been omitted in the distribution, the wife of Kaipuholo rose to confess her sin, and profess repentance. The pastor rather significantly nodded to her to stop; but in a few minutes she rose again and relieved her burdened mind by a few words of confession; and when the element was passed to her, with considerable hesitation she partook. The whole incident evinced a conscientiousness and sense of propriety, the more pleasing as it was entirely self-moved.

The elements of the Supper were little pieces of *kalo*, about the size of the elemental bread at home, and water. The communicants were all seated upon the ground; but many could not get within the house, and had to be in the frequent showers. There was perfect decorum and stillness, and a good degree of seriousness apparent; and it was both affecting and grateful to look around upon such a company of docile barbarians, and hope that so goodly a number of them were the disciples of Christ. One longs to tell them of his fervent desires for their improvement and progress in civilization and grace, and to exhort them, wayward and liable to fall as they are, to be steadfast, unmovable, always abounding in the work of the Lord. You can only hope with trembling for the best of them, so liable are they to yield to temptation, and fall into the Hawaiian sin.

Almost all the suspensions have been on account of adultery, and the illicit intercourse of the unmarried, some of them under circumstances painfully polluting. The people are yet but half-reclaimed savages; much further advanced in Christianity than civilization; perhaps, indeed, as far Christianized as they can be until their habits of living, sleeping, working, and dressing are more civilized. School instruction, such as it is, is general; the people are mild and docile in disposition, and can almost all read; the Bible, or a part of it, is, perhaps, in every dwelling; the forms of religion are established, and its saving power felt in a multitude of cases; an excellent system of laws is enforced; old abuses and oppression corrected. But it is plain that the people are not yet sufficiently disciplined and intellectual for the exhibition of a blameless, spiritual religion; and if a man comes here thinking to find in the recently converted, simple islanders the brightest trophies of the cross, he will be disappointed. Embracing the Gospel does not at once make barbarians spiritual, conscientious, or intelligent; nor does it at once release them from the vicious habits of body and mind to which they have been addicted for generations: it is only the necessary initial step of reform.

The English missionary, Williams, remarks of the South Sea savages, with whom he labored, "That until the people are brought under the influence of religion, they have no desire for the arts and usages of civilized life; but that invariably creates it. While the natives are under the influence of their superstitions, they evince an inanity and torpor from which no stimulus has proved powerful enough to arouse them but the new ideas and new principles imparted by Christianity." The same is true of Hawaiians. It is the Gospel that has begun their civilization, and that has done for them all the good that has been done; and to that be all the glory. It is church members that are foremost in quitting the ways of barbarism, and adopting the proprieties of the civilized state.

But they are not weaned at once; nor can they be in one generation. And living, as they generally do, on a highly nutritious, gross food, without habits of self-restraint; knowing no limit to the indulgence of any appetite but satiety; still going, when away from foreigners, half naked in the bronze of nature, or with the barest apology for clothing; generally without apartments in their houses; all sleeping together on mats, and not abashed at bathing, or the performance of the common offices of nature before each other, is it to be wondered at that adultery and illicit intercourse are frequent?

A people that live like Hawaiians can not be virtuous and pure, how far soever they may be Christianized. And yet, through the rigor of the laws, the vigilance of magistrates and constables, the discipline and restraints of the Church, it is probable that there is *no more* licentiousness than among the same number of inhabitants in cities of England, France, or America. And as to Hawaiian piety, it may as well be said now, once for all, that *both absolutely and relatively it is brighter, purer, and wears better than the most of that which is imported from around the Cape, or straggles across the Rocky Mountains.*

In the present transition state of society from barbarism to pure Christianity, it is often a perplexing question to ministers, What parties shall I marry? The law allows the clergy only to solemnize a marriage, but makes it obligatory on the parties to procure a certificate from the Lunakanawai that there is no legal barrier to their union. Any persons may get such a certificate who are fourteen years of age, who can read, and who are not known to have another husband or a wife living. The same magistrate grants divorces on the application of both parties, on proof rendered of adultery against either.

Among a people with whom the institution of Christian marriage is of so recent date, who held so lightly to the marriage vow, whose habits of intercourse were of old so indiscriminate, and whose hearts still have a leaning to former liberty and lusts, it would be strange if there should not occur frequent violations of the marriage covenant, or if it should not be felt as a yoke. As a matter of fact, so it is. Not a few of the people are adulterers and adulteresses. When, therefore, any of these present themselves to a minister with a legal certificate of marriage, he knowing both or either of them to have been guilty of adultery, shall he marry them, or shall he not?

The judgment of our Savior is, that *whosoever shall put away his wife, except it be for fornication, and shall marry another, committeth adultery; and whoso marrieth her that is put away, doth commit adultery.* Of course, then, in His view, he that should be accessory to the union of persons so disqualified is accessory to their sin and condemnation. *When a man shall leave his father and mother, and shall cleave to his wife, they twain shall be one flesh. What, therefore, God hath joined together, let not man put asunder.*

Nothing, in the judgment of Scripture, but adultery and death, can annul the marriage obligation. *The law hath dominion over a man as long as he liveth. The woman who hath a husband is bound by the law to her husband, so long as he liveth; but if the husband be dead, she is loosed from the law of her husband. So, then, if, while her husband liveth, she be married to another man, she shall be called an adulteress; but if her husband be dead, she is free from that law, so that she is no adulteress, though she be married to another man.* The death of one party sets the innocent free to marry again, but adultery in either, according to the divine law reasserted by Christ, divorces and forever precludes the guilty party from matrimony. And by the lawgiver of old to the Jews, it was expressly provided by God that *the adulterer and the adulteress shall surely be put to death.* In other words, to invest the marriage state with the utmost sacredness, and to keep it inviolate, the Almighty prescribed for adultery the solemn penalty of death under the Jewish law, and our Savior the prohibition to the adulterer of ever marrying again. This is the divine law: shall the Christian minister, who is set for its defense, and to maintain the purity of society, shall he solemnize the marriage of one that is proved an adulterer?

But it is argued that marriage is a civil as well as sacred institution, and whomsoever the civil magistrate declares marriageable the religious minister ought to marry, *asking no questions for conscience' sake.* To those who have conscientiously weighed the matter, and who think we *ought to obey God rather than man,* this argument is of no force. To those who have not, or who think it altogether safe and right to act as in ignorance, and on the presumption that the magistrate will not give a certificate to any who are unworthy of it, this reasoning will be valid, and doubtless is held so by many ministers both here and elsewhere. But we can not help thinking that the purity and well-being of society every where would be promoted by the oftener asking of questions for conscience' sake, and by a more careful inquiry on the part of ministers as to the worthiness and right of those who present themselves to be solemnly pronounced man and wife.

It is objected again, that if parties so disqualified by the divine law are not married, they will nevertheless live together as man and wife, and thus more sin will be incurred than there would be if they were legally united; or they will go elsewhere and get married. This argument will be efficacious with those who admit in morals the doctrine of expediency, who think we may do or allow evil that good may come, or a greater evil be avoided, and that we may break one law to save another. It is of a piece with the old reasoning of rum-sellers, If I don't sell, my neighbor will; the drunkard will still get his dram, and another will pocket all the money.

A more weighty argument in favor of solemnizing such marriages is that drawn from actual usage among the Jews. *Moses, for the hardness of their hearts, suffered them to put away their wives, and to give a bill of divorcement*, and parties so divorced married elsewhere. Why may not the same be allowed in Hawaii nei? where the people are not yet fully *used* to the restraints of the Gospel; where they are but two thirds reclaimed from the ways of old heathenism; and where a great many must spend the rest of their lives out of matrimony, unless an exception be made in their favor.

To this it may be replied, in the first place, that if the Protestant clergy make this exception, the people who have now the Bible will see it to be contrary to the New Testament law, and will very naturally argue that if it be right to give up or evade one statute, it may be also to pass by another. In the second place, there is a Catholic clergy in the land that are glad to solemnize any marriages, whose denomination is composed of adulterers and adulteresses, and upon whom it would be much better to let the odium rest of all marriages that are not strictly right and Christian. In the third place, it is of the utmost importance that the nation's religious teachers take the high vantage-ground of truth from the outset, and a position upon it that need not be departed from, but up to which society may be gradually lifted. A complete renovation of the family constitution, and a permanent establishment of the domestic system, which heathenism has left in ruins, can only thus be effected.

The practical effect of its being rendered easy for divorced persons to get married is (there can not be a doubt) deleterious. Who does not know that in the two first years of the French Revolution and Republic, when the flood-gates of iniquity were thrown wide open, the fountains of the great deep of human depravity broken up, and every lawless passion set afloat, there were more than six thousand divorces in the city of Paris alone; while in ancient Rome there was not a divorce for five hundred and twenty years.

But in the change that ensued in respect to the facility of divorce, when Rome had reached the apex of her power and grandeur, Gibbon discovers a principal cause of her swiftly succeeding corruption and decay; for he affirms that the sentiment of chastity, of female honor, one of the necessary clamps and safeguards of society, is necessarily loosened, and falls off by the allowance in a state of frequent divorces. The facility with which divorces are obtained from State Legislatures in America is a wide and dangerous departure from the good old Puritan and English usage; and it is an evil that ought to be steadfastly resisted by all the virtuous, both as proving, and itself provoking the depravation of public morals. The family compact is too important a bond of union to the State, for the State to render it unstable by a readiness in yielding to petitions for divorce. Marriage is made by it a loose cloak for lechery and grossness, instead of a permanent bond and mortgage for purity.

Facts enough have come to my knowledge while at these islands, to prove that the foreseen probability of being able to be married again has operated as a premium to crime. Persons discontented in their present marriage relations have actually committed crime in order that they might be released by divorce from a state that was grievous to them, and be free, after the lapse of time, more or less, to try married life again with a new partner.

It is a pity that the principles and customs of Protestant pastors in relation to this subject should not be uniform, as also in regard to all matters of Church discipline. While a few, as, for instance, the pastor at this station, will not marry a believer to an unbeliever, and will discipline his church members for planting or using *awa*, or tobacco, others will marry even the divorced, and retain in their connection both smokers of tobacco and drinkers of *awa*.

There ought to be a little treatise in the language

on marriage and on the family constitution. Hawaiians precipitate themselves into the state too early and too lightly. By the established Hawaiian custom and etiquette, the female is generally the suitor. I was not a little pleased by the honest reply given to a suit of this kind by a man at Kealakekua, employed n the family of one of the missionaries there. He was among the *hooikaikas*, earnestly seeking the *pono*, and was asked in marriage by a woman, one of the church members. His answer was, that he must first secure the salvation of his soul, and then he might be ready to think of her.

Another, of whom I once asked why he did not have a wife—a strange lack for a likely Hawaiian—replied to me, with all frankness, that none of the girls had yet asked him.

On the other hand, the accomplishments and good looks of some of the boarding-school girls at Hilo and Wailuku have made the tables turn, and have secured them suitors from the other sex, both from their own countrymen and foreigners. But they have hitherto rejected them, on the ground that they had not been long enough in school.

There occurred a case at a marriage scene, while I was at Kohala, so provokingly droll and amusing, that I can never narrate or call it to mind without laughter. At the Wednesday afternoon meeting, six or seven couples presented themselves together for marriage. Somewhat curious to witness the ceremony, I sat by the minister within the desk. They stood together, opposite, in a line; and when their names were called, and hands were to be locked for responding to the marriage vow, one was found without his mate; and on the pastor's naturally enough asking for her, Oh! said the *sans culottes* bridegroom, with a grave drollery all the more ludicrous for being unmeant, *E hookomo ana i kona kapa komo ma ka puka—She is at the door putting on her frock!* This to tell of his bride before a whole congregation, was more than the officiating minister or his friend could hear and keep their countenances. A few moments elapsed, and Mr. Bond and myself exchanged knowing glances as the just now gownless bride came in from her toilet by the meeting-house door.

It was no fair bevy of waiting-maids that accompanied her, but only her dutiful swain that had been out to hasten and help her in putting on her bridal attire. They were married duly and in order, but the ludicro-serio-comico of this original scene was long after food for fun, when we were disposed to be merry; nor will either the missionary or his friend soon forget the maid of Kohala that was making her toilet outside the church door, while her lover was standing up to be married within. Probably she had carried her dress and shoes under her arm for some miles. This is quite common, for the feet of Hawaiians have not yet grown to shoes, or become wonted to such confinement. When they are traveling, therefore, they take them off, and only put them on again when they have got to the church, or to the house of the missionary.

They have a special liking to shoes that are given to squeaking. This squeak, by-the-way, the natural creaking of new and dry leather, they seem to think a part of the shoe, and they are willing to pay for it extra; so that the shoemaker who can manufacture the most squeak will be likely to have the largest run of custom among Hawaiians. There was an escaped Botany Bay convict shoemaker in Mr. Bond's district, that married one of his church members, and the natives used to employ him for making squeak.

He was expected one day at Mr. Bond's, and a native who knew it left word to have a pair of shoes made with a squeak. Willing to see how far the man's fondness for squeak would carry him, Mr. Bond asked how much worth of squeak he would have put into his shoes, whether a *hapaha's* worth or a *hapalua*, a quarter of a dollar squeak or a half-dollar squeak. The man's love for squeak got the better, I believe, of his love for money, and he concluded to have the largest squeak that Crispin could manufacture, even if it cost as high as a dollar. Now,

> As rhyme the rudder is of verses,
> With which, like ships, they steer their courses,

we might say of this our Hawaiian knight of the squeak, with a slight accommodation, what Butler did of Sir Hudibras,

> A wight he was, whose very sight would
> Entitle him mirror of knighthood,
> That never bow'd his stubborn knee
> To any thing but chivalry.
> He was well stay'd, and in his gait
> Preserved a grave, majestic state;
> And yet so fiery, he would bound
> As if he grieved to touch the ground.
> Cæsar himself, who, as fame goes,
> Had corns upon his feet and toes,

Was not by half so tender-hoof'd,
Nor trod upon the ground so soft.
From out his soles a squeak did sound
That brought him gazers from around;
But being loth to wear it out,
He therefore bore it not about,
Unless on holidays or so,
As men their best apparel do.

CHAPTER IX.

THE POETRY OF TRAVELING, AND THE PHILOSOPHY OF LIVING AT A MISSIONARY'S.

From that lovely retreat though forever I part,
Where smile answer'd smile, and where heart beat to heart;
Yet how often and fondly, when far we may be,
Will we think, thou bless'd isle, of each other and thee.
I go from the haunts where the blue billows roll,
But that isle and those waters shall live in my soul.

Anon.

NOT without many regrets, I have cut adrift from the quiet missionary house of my boyhood's friend, that has been harboring me so hospitably for many weeks; and I am here at the Metropolis of the old Hawaiian conqueror, Kamehameha I., and at the station first occupied in 1820, just after the providential downfall of idolatry, by missionaries from the United States. The missionary pair that was left here then, poorly supplied, not *knowing what should befall them*, where all was rude and heathenish, and the grim idols of decaying paganism stood guarding the bay, are here still, in health and vigor, gathering the fruit of their labors, and blessing God for the change they behold in the people, and for the comforts of house, furniture, children, and friends with whom they are now surrounded.

I arrived two mornings ago, after half a day and

the livelong night upon the sea in a little open canoe. It was a tedious night, with but little wind, and the three natives had to paddle almost all the time, when so sleepy that they could scarcely keep open their eyes, and one of them was every now and then nodding into the water and against the sides of the canoe so amusingly as to provoke me to laughter, though it sometimes provoked his nose to bleed.

The boatmen, also, being too fearful of the *mumuku* (a blast that sometimes rushes down with irresistible fury from between the mountains, and capsizes or drives canoes out to sea) to venture far from land, I had a good opportunity to observe the rough lava shores of Hawaii, and to look into the ragged throats of some of those yawning caves that line the coast.

We passed in the afternoon the Bay of Kawaihae, and saw the huge *heiau* which Kamehameha II. went to consecrate at the death of his father, when he boldly broke the *tabus*, and in his revelry and intoxication brought idolatry to its end. I watched the stars come out one by one from their azure depths, kept vigil with them the livelong night, and saw them fade away again before the dawn, and the sun rise up in his glory from over Mauna Hualalai, in the rear of Kailua.

Here was the boundless ocean, there the sky
O'erarching, broad and blue,
Telling of God and heaven, how deep, how high,
How glorious and true.

It was new and grand also, "in the stilly night," to see the hoary breakers dashing and spurned against the giant rocks, to feel our little canoe lifted by the backward wave, and to hear the thunder-beat, and incessant roar of the surf.

> "Up through the cavernous rocks amain,
> With short, hoarse growl, they plunge and leap,
> Like an armed host, again and again,
> Battering some castellated steep.
> Great pulses of the ocean heart,
> Beating from out immensity,
> What mystic news would ye impart
> From the Great Spirit of the sea!"

Sights and sounds so unlike the din and dust of coaches, the booming of steam-engines, and the hissing and clatter of locomotives, have made me think a man must come out to Hawaii nei in order to know the romance of travel. They can never get here railroads and locomotives; but if Yankee enterprise has its way, steamers will soon come and take off all the shine from Hawaiian canoes and schooners.

The aspect of Kailua is sternly forbidding, and its radiated and reflected heat exceedingly oppressive, after living amid the verdure and grateful trades of Kohala. If caloric be visible, you can see it going up all over the Kailua lava, like heated air from a stove. The harbor is only a little bight in the lava, with a small beach, the rocks on each side covered with large and rich coral, which they burn into lime. The northern boundary was formed by an eruption, forty-five years ago, from one of the large craters on the top of Mauna Hualalai, which inundated with fire several villages, destroyed a number of plantations and extensive fish ponds, filled a deep bay twenty miles in length, and formed the present coast.

When the impetuous fire-stream had been running

for several days, unabated in its fury by the offering of hogs, &c., and was threatening to destroy every thing on this part of the island, it is said that Kamehameha the Great went to it with a company of chiefs and priests, and, as the most valuable offering he could make, cut off part of his own hair, which was always considered sacred, and threw it into the torrent. A day or two after the lava ceased to flow. The gods, it was thought, were satisfied; and the king acquired no small degree of influence over the minds of the people, who attributed their escape from destruction to his supposed interest with the deities of the volcano.

Several houses meet the eye as you enter the harbor, that at once give evidence of increasing wealth and civilization; and there is a range of tombs, and a fort built by Kamehameha the Great, in which there formerly stood a number of hideous idols. The church is a good structure of stone, one hundred and twenty feet long, and forty wide, built at the expense of Governor Adams, with an old-fashioned wooden belfry, pulpit, and gallery. Soon after its completion, he made an ordinance that no woman should enter it without a bonnet—a requisition that brought into use all the cane-blossom stalks in the country round, for the manufacture of an odd something which they called bonnets.

The Governor's house is a handsome two-story building of stone; the doors, window-stools, and all the wood-work of beautiful *koa*, the Hawaiian mahogany. An elegant *koa* center-table, the work of a German mechanic, veneered, finished, and jointed with great beauty, adorns the reception-room, or hall of entrance. Two large bed-rooms lead out of this, one of which the Governor occupies. But the handsome curtained bedstead he leaves to its own repose, and sleeps on a raised platform strewed with mats; on which I saw the luxurious appendage of a large back-scratcher, common, I am told, with chiefs.

There is a similar hall above, and two rooms used for stores. A tasteful Gothic window over the front door and balcony, and in the rear a pillared veranda, which shows to advantage in coming into the harbor. Within the same inclosure is a long native house, for the accommodation of attendants and other chiefs, in which some were making *poi*, women stretched out on their mats, a carpenter making a bureau, and children crawling about and squalling.

Near by, under the spreading shade of some fine *koa* trees, is a boat-house, where a little schooner is on the stocks; and not far is the house for canoes, where they may be seen of every size, from the length of fifteen feet to seventy. The Governor's wealth, it is said, is ample, and his greed as great, which does not relax in the prospect of death. All the chiefs have been here of late to see him die. But he is getting better again, and has his portly person drawn about in a little hand-wagon, several attendants being always by to *lomilomi* his limbs, which are stiff and useless. He learned English of Mr. Thurston; is a member of the Church, but has been under censure; and, though restored, his avarice and selfishness are so shameless, and his piety appears in "such a questionable shape," that many challenge it.

This relic of the olden line of high chiefs, called in native Kuakini, is a very remarkable man. Before he obtained admission into the Church, he used to wonder how it was that common people could get in, while he, who had been used to have his way and wish in every thing, was kept out. At length, on one occasion, when there was a church meeting, he was seen going too. His sister, the celebrated Queen Kaahumanu, had the door shut against him ; and it is said he went home, and read the Testament all night, till he found the secret of the *pono* in the first chapter of the Epistle of James.

When he was once under suspension from the Church, for some misdemeanor, along with quite a large company, he used to have them meet him for exhortation, reading, and prayer, until restored. When he was Governor of the Island of Kauai, some years ago, and it was proposed to him to sell rum, and make a monopoly of it, but only to foreigners and sailors, thereby addressing his well-known weak side, the love of gain, he replied nobly, "To horses, cattle, and hogs, you may sell rum, but to real men you must not on these shores."

In the character of this late barbarian, as in that of many men who have figured on a larger stage than he, there is a mingling of contrasted traits and habits, that leave even his pastor in doubt what to think of him as a Christian. But in God's mercy there is hope for him in that world, which it is clear he will soon enter, and solve for himself the great problem of life. The key to its solution we will believe he has found in Christ, which has opened the gate of a blessed eternity to many an evangelized barbarian before him.

> Hope below this consists not with belief
> In mercy, carried infinite degrees
> Beyond the tenderness of human hearts;
> Hope below this consists not with belief
> In perfect wisdom, guiding mightiest power,
> That finds no limits but its own pure will.
>
> WORDSWORTH.

Besides the residence of Kuakini, there is also a mission-house by the sea-side, now occupied by Dr. Andrews, an odd, planless dwelling, built in the early days of the mission, and added to and altered since to suit emergencies, till its original design or paternity it would be hard to tell. Dr. Andrews is the only physician for the six stations on Hawaii, the extremes more than one hundred miles apart. The demands of his profession necessarily keep him much from home. His missionary work here, other than as physician, is the care of schools, from which he has sent some of the most promising girls and boys that are known throughout the mission, to the seminaries at Wailuku and Lahainaluna.

Quarter of a mile up the hill, standing by itself, and inclosed by a stone wall six feet high from all sight or ingress of natives, except at the house door, is the residence of the missionary pastor, Rev. Asa Thurston. It is a wooden building, its material from America, two stories high, with a spacious veranda, shielded on both sides by hanging blinds, the house standing about north and south. The front veranda commands a fine view of the ocean, and some cocoanut groves along the coast.

By dint of scraping the rocks around, and the help of a cow and goat pen, some soil has been gathered in the yard, and there are growing there two *kou* trees, the mustard and castor-oil bean plants, a flourishing *cactus* (prickly pear), and some grass that is trying hard to be green. Lucy's range for play was small, and would have been any thing but attractive had she ever known the luxury of green fields, and babbling brooks, and flowers that drink the dew. And yet, I suppose, she loved her island lava home, as much as children do theirs where Nature has been more benignant and prodigal of her charms. What a pity (one can not help saying) that she should not have been kept here, as a specimen-product of the growth of Hawaii, to take root, and blossom, and shed fragrance only here. But of this more by-and-by.

Near the house of Mr. Thurston is the entrance of a cave, called Laniakea, which once formed a valuable appendage, a kind of donjon-keep to an old fort hard by, whose walls have been the inexhaustible quarry for all Mr. Thurston's building and fencing. In times of war, the wives, children, and infirm used to be put there, in case of assault or sally from the fort. Mrs. Thurston used it for a while as her dairy-house, until the shock of an earthquake one day, just after she had come out of it, made the idea of being buried alive there so appalling, or being struck by some loosened fragment from the roof, that she has since deserted it.

I have explored it to the distance of nearly a quarter of a mile, until stopped by a wide and deep pool of brackish water, which, it is said, rises and falls with the tide. The native guide who was with me left his torch on a rock and boldly plunged into the subterranean pool, whose waters splashed more at his odd capers than ever Stygian Lake at the skiff and paddle of old Charon.

The bottom of the cave is about twenty feet wide, exceedingly rough with fragments that have dropped from above, and the various shapes in which the lava cooled below. The roof is in some places thirty feet high ; in others so low, and the passage so narrow, as to oblige one to stoop in passing. The sides are in many places white with an effervescence like magnesia or nitre. The roof is stalactical black lava, and was once evidently dropping with fused earth and minerals, while the fiery fluid ran as in a sluice-way to the sea. A little way in, the walls are damp and the air close ; and there is a stillness and gloom in these bowels of the earth that may be felt by more of the senses than one.

For laughing sunshine never look'd
Into that fire-scoop'd cave.

The church at this station is one of the oldest at the islands. The first admissions were in the year 1825. The whole number admitted up to 1848 is two thousand three hundred and thirty-nine. Number admitted the past year, in which there has been an unusual interest at all the stations on Hawaii, is seven hundred and seventy-nine. Mr. Thurston's labors are more concentrated, and the care of his church requires less long touring than any of the churches on Hawaii. Natives assert that by long use he has become so skilled in the vernacular Hawaiian, that they can not tell his speaking from one of themselves, except by its being more full of thoughts. Probably for that very reason, its idiomatic exactness, his preaching is less intelligible to a *novus homo* than that of the younger missionaries.

It is a pleasure to abide a while in his orderly household. One feels to respond most fervently to his frequent family prayer, *That the Church may endure here so long as the sun and moon shall endure*, and to add to the petition that he may survive yet many years, to behold its prosperity, and to see his children after him useful and happy in the land that claims them as the place of their birth.

Although no binding rule can be established, yet we can not help thinking that, by virtue of the bond of birth-place, and the implied consecration of parents, the country where missionaries children are born, and where their parents live and labor, and, it may be, lay their bones, has the strongest claim upon them also. And we can not help wishing that it had been the rule or habit from the outset, in this mission especially, to bring up families and settle them here, in sight of the people whom they came to bless.

We are well persuaded that, with the safeguards adopted in missionary families here, it could have been safely done, and with incalculable benefit to the nation of Hawaiians. If compared with the New England Puritans, the missionaries here are far better educated, and able of themselves to educate families, than they were; and their children need no more return to America to be educated than the children of the Pilgrims to Old England, excepting those who are to be liberally educated, and they only when they had been fitted for, and were of the age to enter college.

After considerable observation, we are confident in saying that the children of missionaries here know far less of evil and more of good than the same number of well-educated children in America. By means of a purely home education, and that which is to be had at the Punahou mission school, boys and girls may be kept safer from contamination, and from imbibing evil, than they can be if educated in schools in the United States, and their characters will be more unsophisticated and natural; and they will be better fitted to perform the duties of Christian men and women in Christian society as it should be, than they would be if reared in the United States. And you will hear some of the most judicious mothers of this mission, after their experience, say that they would rather have a missionary's well-ordered home in Hawaii to rear young children in than the circumstances of most parents in America.

Why, then, might not the education of boys and girls be here completed, under the eye and affectionate regards of the natural parents, and with all the holy affections and sympathies of unestranged brothers and sisters, so as best to fit them for all the duties they would have to perform here? By the cordial intercourse and close union of different mission families, the intimacies formed in early life would ripen into happy alliances at adult age, and the posterity of missionaries might settle in and possess the land as farmers, mechanics, merchants, and teachers, and incumbents of honorable offices now filled by others.

Missionaries whose health failed them, or proved inadequate to severe missionary labors, as in several instances here, could devote themselves to rearing their families, managing model farms, teaching the children of other families the mechanic arts, agricultural pursuits, and forming them to industrious manual labor habits, and skill in the management of secular affairs; while all along showing to the natives how families can be reared, and made industrious, virtuous, and affluent.

Instead of which, as the custom is now, just as children are getting to the age when temptations are to be withstood, when they could have classes in Sabbath schools, and when their example in favor of virtue, and industry, and filial piety are most needed, they are separated from country, and home, and each other, and sent off eighteen thousand miles to America, to complete an education which, except they are intended for the learned professions, can be better completed here.

True, in this case the system of managing missionaries must be somewhat different. They should be allowed to own property themselves, precisely like ministers at home, and be put, in all respects, upon the same footing, and be made more independent of a board legislating so at arm's length and at such a disadvantageous distance. Approved farmers, builders, and artisans should be sent out, who could now be of immense service to the Hawaiians, and not less to the families of the missionaries. And there should be provision for the support of invalid missionaries and orphans out here, where it can be done much more advantageously, at less cost, and with more benefit to the Hawaiian people, and ease to the American Church, than in America.

Communities would thus have been established all over these islands; not of profligate, runaway sailors, or men bent only upon gain, having no part or lot with the people, and not caring whether they become extinct or are perpetuated, so long as they make money; but, as there is good reason to believe, communities of the intelligent and pious, loving the country as their birth-place, and the residence and sepulchre of their fathers, and loving the people as those for whom their fathers had lived and toiled, to whom God had given the Holy Spirit, and whom they had been educated to pity and pray for, and try to benefit.

The mental discipline and acquirements of Mrs. Thurston's daughters, obtained here, as evinced in the memoirs of Lucy, show conclusively that girls, at least, need not go to America in order to get an adequate intellectual education. And it will not, for a moment, be denied by any one that domestic virtues and accomplishments can be acquired as easily at a missionary mother's home as at a boarding school or missionary friends' in America. The same holds true of boys, except where they are devoted to the learned professions.

There will always be cases of some returning, in which friends in America will desire it, and take upon themselves the expense and care of education. And now and then, as missionary operations enlarge, there will be whole families to return. But we can not help thinking that such cases ought to be exceptions; that, both as a matter of economy and wisdom, and in order to secure to unevangelized nations all the benign results of the missionary enterprise, missionary families ought to be brought up and settled among them, and thus little missionary colonies be formed all over the world. And a missionary couple ought to feel, when they go to the heathen, that they go for life, they and their posterity.

The example of well-ordered Christian families, of children growing up around their parents obedient and virtuous, entering into their labors, and becoming co-workers with them, like the sons of Drs. William Cary and Scudder, in doing good, is what is eminently needed, especially at such a time as this in the progress of the Hawaiian nation. It was just as Mr. Thurston's eldest children had learned the native language, and were teachers in the Sabbath school, that they were, as the natives expressed it, taken away and put out of their sight, by being carried to America. Ought it so to be? Does the well-being of the parents or the future usefulness of the children require this sacrifice? Perhaps we are mistaken, but we honestly and earnestly think not; and we can not help wishing that the opposite experiment might be fairly tried here.

The knowledge which the world has obtained, through the touching Memoirs of Lucy G. Thurston, of the household influences under which that "daughter of the isles" was reared, makes it a thing not improper, but rather to be expected, that a visitor at her island home would speak of those influences, and of that system of home education and discipline, under which she was trained, since the same is continued, and may now be seen in operation with two other children that remain at home.

Mrs. Thurston had been a teacher in the United States, and, since the first two or three years of her missionary life out here, she has devoted herself almost exclusively to her own children—more so, perhaps, than any other mother of this mission. She felt that her first duty was the care of her own household, and with a most commendable assiduity, and a tact and ability that increased by use, she gave herself up to the mental and moral culture of her offspring, with a success of which the Memoirs of Lucy, to say nothing of her other children, the subjects of the same experiment, are a sufficient proof.

The book knowledge, discipline of mind, and solid accomplishments acquired under the maternal roof at Laniakea much exceed (if we mistake not) those generally obtained at schools in the United States. And we are of opinion that, in the case of the daughters, their education might have been completed, and a preparation secured for almost any station which woman is called to fill, in the self-same place where so good a foundation was laid.

As wives for missionaries, it is not clear but that missionaries' daughters would be all the better for completing their education here, and never seeing the land of their forefathers. But on that subject no man, or body of men, has a right to impose upon parents a rule that shall be binding. We are merely venturing an opinion as to what we deem possible and best. It will go for what it is worth, which may be nothing. But we can not help wishing to see the experiment tried, of settling and educating missionaries' children on missionary ground.

Mrs. Thurston's daily plan with her children is to devote every other half hour from early dawn to twilight to some form of mental employment. The other half hours are for amusement, exercise, and domestic avocations, the time included that is spent at meals, and at morning and evening family worship, which is directly after breakfast and supper, the children removing the cloth, and placing upon the table the hymn-books and Bibles, without their parents' rising. Some of the half hours are spent in recitation ; some by Mrs. Thurston in reading to her children ; some in study and reading by themselves. Each of them keeps a daily journal, their mother acting as their amanuensis till they are able to write. Their father instructs them in music and the languages, Mrs. Andrews in drawing, botany, and ornamental needle-work.

Thus employed, I do not see that life with them is any more monotonous, childhood any less joyous and delightful, on this black, radiating lava, within sight and sound of the glorious azure and everlasting roar of the Pacific, and with nothing else in nature that is pleasant to look upon but the morning sun as he comes up over Mauna Hualalai, and the evening canopy of stars, than it is in the sweet fields of their father-land, " beyond the swelling flood," whose " living green" there are aching eyes would be glad just now to see.

But then I can not help thinking that they sustain a loss, or, more properly, forego an advantage, and that the mind can hardly acquire that purity of taste, refinement, and delicacy of feeling, or desirable sensibility to the sublime and beautiful, which a birth and education among the more grand and lovely scenes of nature are likely to insure. Nature and the human mind are made to each other; wisely and wonderfully are they adapted; and that man is likely to be the happiest and best (other things being equal) who has the most of nature's beauties for his birthright and daily observation, from infancy to old age.

It is of great consequence, says Alison, in the education of the young, to encourage their instinctive taste for the beauty and sublimity of nature. "While it opens to the years of infancy and youth a source of pure and permanent enjoyment, it has consequences on the character and happiness of future life, which they are unable to foresee. It is to provide them, amid all the agitations and trials of society, with one gentle and unreproaching friend, whose voice is ever in alliance with goodness and virtue, and which, when once understood, is able both to smooth misfortune and reclaim from folly. It is to identify them with the happiness of that nature to which they belong; to give them an interest in every species of being which surrounds them; and, amid the hours of curiosity and delight, to awaken those latent feelings of benevolence and of sympathy, from which all the moral or intellectual greatness of man finally arises.

"It is to lay the foundation of an early and of a manly piety; amid the magnificent system of material signs in which they reside, to give them the mighty key which can interpret them; and to make them look upon the universe which they inhabit, not as the abode only of human cares or human joys, but as the temple of the living God, in which praise is due, and where service is to be performed."

There is a truth of universal experience in the first stanza of Byron's magnificent Apostrophe to the Ocean, which no teachers of youth, nor any who are striving to build for themselves characters of greatness, should ever suffer to go out of mind.

> There is a pleasure in the pathless woods,
> There is a rapture on the lonely shore,
> There is society which none intrudes
> By the deep sea, and music in its roar.
> *I love not man the less, but Nature more,*
> From these our interviews, in which I steal
> From all I may be or have been before,
> To mingle with the universe, and feel
> What I can ne'er express, yet can not all conceal.

Bryant, in his Thanatopsis, expresses it better:

> To him who, in the love of Nature, holds
> Communion with her visible forms, she speaks
> A various language; for his gayer hours
> She has a voice of gladness, and a smile,
> And eloquence of beauty, and she glides
> Into his darker musings with a mild
> And gentle sympathy, that steals away
> Their sharpness ere he is aware.

And Wordsworth, better than either:

> Nature never did betray
> The heart that loved her; 'tis her privilege,
> Through all the years of this our life, to lead
> From joy to joy; for she can so inform
> The mind that is within us, so impress
> With quietness and beauty, and so feed
> With lofty thoughts, that neither evil tongues,
> Rash judgments, nor the sneers of selfish men,
> Nor greetings where no kindness is, nor all
> The dreary intercourse of daily life,
> Shall e'er prevail against us, or disturb
> Our cheerful faith, that all which we behold
> Is full of blessings.

And again, in the Poem of The Excursion:

> Wisdom and spirit of the universe!
> Thou soul, that art the eternity of thought!
> And giv'st to forms and images a breath
> And everlasting motion! not in vain,
> By day or star-light, thus from my first dawn
> Of childhood didst thou intertwine for me
> The passions that build up our human soul;
> Not with the mean and vulgar works of man,
> But with high objects, with enduring things,
> With life and nature; purifying thus
> The elements of feeling and of thought,
> And sanctifying by such discipline
> Both pain and fear, until we recognize
> A grandeur in the beatings of the heart.

This has been too long a chapter of glimpses and echoes, some readers may say of moralizings, in which I may seem to have wandered from the beaten track of prose, and will not therefore go back, except to bid good-by to the Kailua Thurston household, and to wish them all success and joy in their honorable work. That, we are persuaded, will not be wanting, although the situation Providence has allotted them does not combine *all* the advantages of genial natural scenery that could be desired.

May the children left to this honored pair be as full of promise and hope as she was whom God took so early to himself. And may the parents live to see every bud of promise blossom and ripen with generous fruit!

CHAPTER X.

FRUITS OF FOREIGN INTERCOURSE, WORK OF THE MISSIONARY, AND DISABILITIES OF THE PEOPLE.

Like the shadows in the stream,
Like the evanescent gleam
Of the twilight's failing blaze;
Like the fleeting years and days,
Like all things that soon decay,
Pass the Indian tribes away.
Ah! the Indian's heart is ailing,
And the Indian's blood is failing:
Red men and their realms must sever;
They forsake them, and forever!

I. M'Clellan.

The celebrity which Kealakekua Bay acquired by Cook's visit and death, and its being laid down, for a long time, more accurately on the charts than any other place, has caused it to be more or less visited, from time to time, by whale ships and men-of-war. I arrived here a few days ago from Kailua, and find the anchorage good, so that vessels of the largest burden may ride safely at all times of the year, and recruit with wood, hogs, sweet potatoes, and bananas. Supplies, however, of every thing but wood are often scarce and dear, and good water is not to be had at all.

Foreigners have left the marks of their lust deep and destructive in the constitution of the people, from Cap-

View of Kealakekua Bay.

tain Cook's ships until the present time. Seamen now begin to have to smart for their lewdness, and it is considerably repressed. A case was tried a few days ago, just after my arrival from Kailua, of a man belonging to one of the ships now in port. Notwithstanding his stout denial, he was clearly convicted, and compelled to pay a fine of $15—that is, a barrel of oil. There were two trials of the offender, and every effort was made by his shipmates to evade the law; but the Hawaiian judge and justice triumphed, and the captain, unlike too many of his fraternity who have visited these seas, was too conscientious and just to set at naught the law, and refuse to pay the man's fine.

Disease here is rife, and some forms of it, consequent upon the taint from licentiousness, are truly dreadful. Cases of secondary syphilis are frequent, and horrid syphilitic ulcers, such as are seen in those wards of hospitals devoted to this class of diseases. From what one sees who has much to do with their maladies, his conclusion is, that the very national blood is so corrupted, the Hawaiian constitution so deeply, venomously diseased, and the habits of the people such, in their living, and intercourse one with another, and with lewd foreigners, that there is little hope of their preservation and perpetuity as a race. Unwilling as a benevolent man feels to admit it, yet must it be acknowledged that all facts and reasonings look that way. Unless there speedily ensue a great change in the habits of the people, unless the youth be kept from early vice and untimely marriages, and the married learn chastity, the race *will* run out and cease to be.

There are causes at work, which, if they are not

soon arrested, will insure national depopulation and decay. Whether it is not even now too late to apply a remedy; whether the national stock is not already so much impaired as to preclude recovery, as in the case of an individual who has ruined himself by his excesses, and whose repentance comes too late, remains to be seen Certain it is, they are dying off fast, rotten with disease. *Like sheep they are laid in the grave.* They seem to have little or no constitutional stamina to rally against the incursions of their maladies, which are always aggravated, too, by neglect, or the want of proper nourishment and nursing, and frequently by the villainous abuse of native doctors, who give large doses of emetic and drastic medicines, especially the seeds and juice of a certain gourd that has often been known to produce death. What is done for their salvation must be done quickly to be of any avail, or they too will be written among the nations whom the sons of Japheth have dispossessed.

It will be worth while for some one here to note the fate of those men who have infamously distinguished themselves by the injury they have done at these islands, through licentiousness and rum, and by their opposition to the Gospel; from early navigators and the English whaling captains, whose crews at different times threatened the missionaries, and fired upon the missionary establishment at Lahaina; and the American lieutenant, who disgraced himself and his nation's flag, by a licentious defiance of the law, and insults to God's ministers at Honolulu; down to loose men and slanderers of the present day, whose mouths, indeed, have been stopped, but who have not yet passed off the stage. The record might afford an instructive comment upon three passages of Scripture: *Though hand join in hand, the wicked shall not be unpunished; his mischief shall return upon his own head, and his violent dealing shall come down upon his own pate.—Whoso diggeth a pit shall fall therein; and he that rolleth a stone, it will return upon him.—A false witness shall not be unpunished; and he that speaketh lies shall not escape.*

We are of the opinion that the missionaries have been somewhat too sparing in their exposure and rebuke of infamous deeds and infamous living at these islands; while at the same time they have had to bear the brunt of all the blows struck in men's blind fury at the gradual leaking out and disclosure at home of their evil lives beyond the seas. It was not strange that there should be wrath and revenge, to find that *there is no darkness, neither shadow of death, where the workers of iniquity can hide themselves.*

Men once thought to play the libertine in these seas as they liked, to wallow a while in the sensual sty, and then, after amassing property, to return to England or America, and be accounted as faithful husbands and reputable livers, as if they had been pure as Joseph all their days. Some have been mad to find themselves mistaken; and others equally angry that the moral influence of missionaries has become so great upon chiefs and people, that they can not now try the experiment, and give full swing to passion, as men once could. This is the well-known, though under-ground cause of all the opposition and slander missionaries have here met with. The stale charges of persecuting the Catholics and meddling with government were the mere raised letters in the stereotype plate, *to take the ink and be printed*, while vexation and wrath at the restraints put upon the license they call liberty were the metal bed in which the types were fixed, and without which they could never be *steady* enough to make an impression.

As to the charge of meddling with government, we think it would have been much better for the nation had it been truer,* and had missionaries much earlier been concerned in the councils and laws of the kingdom. Nor do we see any good reason why they should wish to avoid the imputation of being implicated in government measures that are good, any more than Christians any where of being concerned

* With admirable good humor and satire, Mr. Bingham advised the Oregon Mission after this wise, having an eye to men and things at the Sandwich Islands:

In laying the foundations of learning, and religion, and civilization, be wiser and better than your brethren in the Sandwich Islands; and, unless he who contended with Michael the archangel about the body of Moses be too strong for you, do not suffer a dozen or twenty tippling-houses to follow you into the wilderness, and set up their shameless standards in sight of the humble temples you build for God, to compete with a less number of missionaries fifteen or twenty years, in the struggle between light and darkness, lest some well-bred friend of humanity should laugh at your ill success to convert the Indians to a pure and elevated Christianity, to raise them to intelligence, sobriety, and dignity, and confirm them in a steady practice of their duties to one another, to strangers, and to God.

Give the dying people now, as fast as possible, or as fast as they can receive it, if you are able, the unadulterated word of God, in some shape, and you need not shrink and tremble if some Horonite should sneer at what you build, pretending that a fox would break down your wall, or that it has already fallen by its own incumbency, because he fancied it could have no foundation.—*Hawaiian Spectator.*

in politics (in the proper sense), to be interested in which is one of the duties of a good citizen.

For ministers any where to avoid giving good advice to rulers, or proposing salutary laws, especially in an infant state like the Hawaiian, merely because some graceless Jacobins, for whose countenance or discountenance a man of rectitude (*mens sibi conscia recti*) does not care a straw—because *they* bawl out "Priestcraft—Persecution—Church and State!"—would be no less a cowardly dereliction of duty than unwise. As if a censor of Rome should forego the privileges of his censorship, lest he should be thought meddling with the duties, or aiming to unite with his, the office of consul! Or, as if a free Roman tribune should waive the rights of his tribuneship, lest, forsooth, he should seem to be grasping at the consulate!

We hold it to be as much the duty of ministers nowadays to instruct kings and governors in the law of God, to inform and rebuke them when wrong, and to advise them to what is right, as it was the duty of Jewish prophets of old. If this be meddling, the more faithfully *such meddling* is practiced, the better; and in this sense, we take it, the missionaries at the Sandwich Islands have *meddled*, though not, perhaps, as early or as much as they should have done, for fear of the consequences. If this be all the priestcraft among Protestants, the more of it the better; the sooner will the laws of men be molded by the law of God, and human governments be brought to a likeness with the divine.

It was meddling in this sense for the missionaries, at their general meeting at Honolulu in 1848, in an interview with the king, to remind him, as they did, of the wretched estate of himself and his whole kingdom in 1820, and of the marvelous and happy change which had been since effected, through the blessing of God upon their labors as missionaries. Perhaps, in the view of the United States commissioner, who so gratuitously placed himself in an attitude of hostility to the Sandwich Island mission and government, it was meddling for the missionaries to draw up and give to the world so complete an answer to all fault-finders and traducers, and so triumphant a vindication of themselves and their work, as that which is contained in the January number of the Missionary Herald for 1849.

We thank them for that admirable document, and none need be sorry for the occasion that has called forth, and put on file, in the archives of the world's history, so convincing a demonstration of the feasibility and success of the Missionary enterprise—a success which will be none the less real and true, though, in the mysterious providence of God, the whole native race expire just as it is Christianized.

The Church at Kealakekua numbers ten hundred and eighty-nine, of whom three hundred and forty were admitted in one year (1844). A substantial stone meeting-house is completed, one hundred and twenty feet long and fifty-seven wide, and things are getting into a trim, settled way, that we can not but think is full of promise, if only the Church hold its own. The house is strong, commodious, and airy. It would look more secure were it made with a hip-roof instead of high gable-ends, which, being of bare stone, without cornice or coping, and running up far, like a tall isosceles triangle, look rather toppling and precarious, and seem to say to earthquakes, *Noli me tangere.*

The audience assembled on the Sabbath varies from six to eight hundred. Many of them have procured rude settees and stools,

> Like that on which the immortal Alfred sat,
> And sway'd the sceptre of his infant realms,

where they show themselves above the popular savage posture on the ground. The Sabbath school of children before the morning service is an interesting one, numbering two hundred and forty pupils. There is another for adults between meetings, and the native services are generally through by three or half past three, in order that people from a distance may have time to return home before nightfall. When ships are in port, there is an English sermon in the afternoon at one of the mission-houses, and an English meeting always. There is a native meeting also at the church, by bell ringing at early dawn, at which one of the missionaries is generally present.

The resident ministers occupy the desk each half the day when both are here; but Mr. Ives is often absent at Kealia, a place twenty miles to the south, accessible only by canoe, where there is a large church, and a Sabbath congregation of four hundred, of which he is constituted the pastor. Mr. Ives has a select school of twelve promising boys, with whom he spends three or four hours daily. Mr. Forbes has a school of deacons, whom he has formed into a sort of theological class, and is giving them systematic instruction on

Scripture subjects, *teaching them that they may teach others.* The missionary ladies have weekly meetings when their health will permit, the one of unmarried and the other of married females. There is here also, as at all stations where there are two families, a weekly prayer-meeting, which is made a pleasant season of social intercourse, and often an occasion of much spiritual edification.

The families are separated by only a narrow lane, whose walls on each side are covered with the night-blooming Cereus, which no one that has seen it in its glory will be slow to acknowledge as the most splendid of flowers. There is much more of verdure here than at Kailua. Considerable soil has been scraped from the lava, and brought within the two inclosures; and fig-trees, acacias, pride of China, anetto, the passion flower, and other flowering shrubs and vines, freely exhale their fragrance and beauty, and more than pay for their attendance in shade, and odors, and smiles. Heaven oftener pours on them a reviving shower than at Kailua, and sun and dews here shed selectest influence, and, with the alternating gentle land and sea breezes, form a climate which, though warm and dry, is singularly salubrious.

All water for common purposes has to be brought from brackish springs at the sea-side, nearly a mile off. That for drinking is brought from pools up in the mountains, two or three miles, except when it can be caught from transient rains. The village of Kealakekua is by the sea-side, and thus at a desirable distance from the mission-houses. The meeting-house is on a rising ground, midway between them, conspicuous from the sea to ships, and to those who approach the town inland from Kailua, over a precipice six or seven hundred feet high, the perpendicular face of which, all pierced with caves that have been conduits of molten lava, and latterly depositories for the dead, forms the head of the bay. Over it, they say, is the track of some god in Hawaiian mythology, as he went up to heaven from below, whence the place has its name, *Ke ala ke akua*—the path of the god.

Mr. Forbes's own sketch of the process by which his church edifice was raised to its present standing shows the way in which missionaries have to accomplish such works in Hawaii nei. "The building is one hundred and twenty feet by fifty-seven on the outside, laid up in stone and lime, with side walls twelve feet high, and lathed and plastered overhead in the form of a hollow half hexagon. The whole cost of the building can not be easily computed. But I think we could not have erected it for less than $6000, had every thing been paid for. In the first place, every stone had to be carried by Church-members about one eighth of a mile to the building. This was gratuitous labor. Our lime had then to be obtained in the following manner: The coral was taken from the sea, and, as there are no reefs here, it was procured from the bottom, in from ten to twenty feet water, by diving down, detaching a piece, and, if large, ascending to take breath, and then descending again with a rope which they make fast, and draw up the mass.

"In this way the coral was laden, then rowed ashore, and the coral piled on the beach. Thus all the limestone was procured, about thirty-six cubic fathoms in all. It was then to be burned. For this purpose they had to procure more than forty cords of wood, every stick of which was carried from the mountain, from one to two miles, on the shoulders of Church-members. After the wood was got and the lime burned, it still had to be taken from the beach to the building, about one quarter of a mile. This was done by the women, in calabashes, each one filling her calabash with lime, and carrying it on her shoulder to the building; in all, about seven hundred barrels. In like manner, they carried full as much sand, and about an equal quantity of water, carried solely by the women in calabashes. This labor of female members was entirely gratuitous, besides many contributions in other ways.

"Then the plates, beams, sills, rafters, and posts, which support the work overhead, joists, lath, thatching grass, &c., were still to be got. This fell on the men, of course; and, as we had no cattle to drag large sticks, such things not being owned by any person who is a member of my Church, the male Church-members divided themselves off into companies, according to the size of the stick to be dragged down; and taking with them ropes, each company selected their stick, going up in the mountain by daylight. The posts and beams required from about forty to sixty men for each stick. Generally, they got down the stick by dark, after much toil, over beds of lava and ravines. The distance was from six to ten miles. In this way all our timbers were obtained. Sometimes I went with them myself to encourage them, and found that by the time we reached the place where the timbers were, we had performed quite a fatiguing morning's journey, besides being benumbed with the cold, and thoroughly wet with the dew on the fern and underwood through which we had to make our way.

"To pay the workmen who laid up the walls and did the carpenter work, the members of the Church each subscribed according to his ability, some ten dollars, some five, some two, and some one. This they paid in whatever they could that the workmen would take. Some paid in hogs, some in fish, some in potatoes, some in turkeys, fowls, and goats. Some in *tapas* and *malos*, and a few in cloth and money. The usual monthly contributions at our concerts averaged about fifteen dollars from the females alone.

"Thus we have a comfortable house of worship, the fruit of the people's own industry and voluntary effort. It has been to me a vast burden of care and anxiety, during the two years of its erection. I have had to superintend the whole process, and many times to lay out and correct the work with my own hands; and many a hard hour's labor have I spent on it in various ways."

Unless there had been this ungrudging expenditure of the missionary's time, and skill, and resources, I am sure, from the knowledge I have obtained of the people's poverty and ignorance, this Christian temple would never have been reared. It is, then, a monument at once to the missionary's zeal and the Christianized Hawaiian docility; and great is the joy of both in its completion. The poor people and the energetic pastor may alike be proud of it; let not posterity forget through what and how it has been realized

By going round, of late, into the miserable wigwams of natives, in order to visit and administer medicine to the sick, I have been deeply affected by the destitution and distress almost every where to be seen. With an observing eye it is, as it were, taking the gauge and dimensions of human misery in this part of the world. Rev. Mr. Armstrong was right in saying, six or seven years ago, that the whole nation is wretched and poor. The common people, he said, are distressingly so. "There is not one man, woman, or child in ten, throughout my Church, that would not be regarded as a fit subject for a poor-house, or an object of charity in Massachusetts. More than half of a common man's gains goes to the government, and the other half is not half sufficient to support half his family. Besides, the people lack skill, enterprise, and industry to such a degree, and lie under so many restrictions, that their temporal prosperity, and even their existence as a nation, is altogether problematical."

Mr. Forbes's testimony to the same point, his people's exceeding poverty at the time his meeting-house was built, is yet more specific. You can have but a faint idea, he wrote, after all I have said, of what this effort cost us—the building of his meeting-house. "You must keep in mind all the time, that there are not forty families in the Church whose whole wardrobe and household furniture, taking it together, would amount to more than twenty dollars. The whole property of a family, in this region, usually consists of a canoe to about one family in three, worth from ten to thirty dollars ; a hog or two, and a few fowls ; a grass house, worth from ten to forty dollars; a few mats, in value perhaps three or four dollars; a few calabashes, say worth two dollars; a shirt apiece for each male, and sometimes one pair of pantaloons; one loose-dress for each female, with a few *tapas* to sleep in. They rarely have seats in their houses, and still more rarely any dishes or pots, except one wooden dish for the whole family. Their mats form seats, tables, and often beds.

"Axes are very rare. A few of them have fish-nets, and but here and there one. A few of them own goats; perhaps twenty persons in the whole district of four thousand souls, who own twenty goats apiece. There is not one native blacksmith among the whole four thousand who can purchase bellows and tools. There is not a native carpenter who owns a set of tools, to my knowledge, on this island, the population of which is thirty thousand, or more. Here and there one owns a saw and an adze; rarely any, however, except canoe-diggers, and the tools they have usually belong to some chief, for whom they work. A few of them have doors to close the entrance to their houses. But a lock is almost as rare here as a comfortable dwelling."

Mr. Forbes adds, furthermore: "Let it not be said I have given a highly-colored picture. I believe facts will bear me out in all I have stated. Many a one pays fish, fowls, or something which he values at fifty cents, to get him a New Testament, when he has absolutely not got clothes to cover his back. Yet it will not do, in ordinary cases of poverty, to give books gratis. They would sell them for fish, and speculate, and the next day come and buy again. The people are poor, and lazy, and oppressed; yet they are greedy to get work for cloth. When they know I have a little cotton cloth on hand, they will often make application for work so often, that I am tempted to devise something for the poor wretches to do to get a shirt; but my restricted means oblige me to say to hundreds, I have got no work for you. They will sometimes hang about the door for hours, in hopes of employment, to get just cloth enough to make a shirt.

"You will say, Let them cultivate the soil. True; if some benevolent persons would only settle among them, for the purpose of teaching them how to make the most of their soil, and, when done, take the products and make a market for them, I believe much of the laziness and poverty of this people would vanish in a few years. But missionaries can not, dare not, ought not to enter on such experiments. It would require too much of their time and energies, and bring down on their enterprise a double portion of the slander already heaped heavily on them."

To this inventory of property, of correct application to the mass of people on this island, it should be added that most families have a potato or *kalo* patch, or both, and some banana-trees growing up in the country, which furnish them with the food not supplied by the sea. Their supply is by no means abundant or regular, through laziness and want of thrift. Often, after feeding a few days to the full, a Hawaiian family will go entirely without food for one or two days, or more, until compelled to bestir themselves to fish, or dig, or beg. They are generally to be found either quite full or quite empty; and a poor Hawaiian's hunger has often to be stayed upon moss and roots, and muscles or snails. The curse of the whole nation, perhaps after all the greatest reason for its wasting away so fast, is found in this indolence, indulged, probably, more now than when the nation was a nation of savages, and the people had to work more for the chiefs, and the women were more occupied than now in making *kapa*.

So much for Hawaiian poverty. As to mortality from disease, Dr. Andrews, of Kailua, made an effort, a few years ago, to ascertain what proportion of children survive the period of infancy. The result was to show that more than one half die under two years of age, and a very considerable proportion of these at a period of from six to twelve months; while the deaths among children of the mission, of all ages, do not exceed one seventh of the whole.

To those acquainted with the habits of Sandwich Islanders the cause of so many early deaths is plain. It is to be found in insufficient clothing, or, as is often the case, in an entire destitution of covering, in improper food, and want of cleanliness. It is the practice of natives to feed their children at a very early age, and often from birth, with *poi*, raw fish, sea-eggs, sea-weed, and whatever else they themselves eat. The consequence is indigestion, dropsy, diarrhea, and other complaints. Disease having supervened, no alteration is made in the diet, but a mistaken kindness indulges the sufferer in every thing his appetite craves, until death closes the scene. With such treatment the wonder is, not that so many perish, but that any survive.

As to disease among adults, with the exception of malignant fevers, I do not see but that its forms are as common and various as any where. The representations we had heard made in America would make us believe that there were no diseases out here indigenous, but only those consequent upon licentiousness, and that a prudent man need hardly die here at all, except of old age. Too much, it is true, can not be said in praise of the climate of certain localities of this favored group. But how wide representations like those referred to are from the truth, a catalogue of native names for maladies and pains would alone show. They are too numerous and specific to detail here. It is enough to say, that wherever sin is found, and especially in a rude country as Hawaii nei, where the remedy of the Gospel is not applied until long after the inoculation of the native stock with foreign vice and virus, *there* are found disease and death in all their Protean forms, more numerous than "the monstrous crew" which Michael in vision showed to Adam,

> That he might know
> What misery the inabstinence of Eve
> Should bring on men. * *
> * * * All maladies
> Of ghastly spasm, or racking torture,
> Convulsions, epilepsies, fierce catarrhs,
> Intestine stone and ulcer, colic-pangs,
> Demoniac phrensy, moping melancholy,
> And moon-struck madness, pining atrophy,
> Marasmus, and wide-wasting pestilence,
> Dropsies, and asthmas, and joint-racking rheums.

The three last of this list, together with palsies, partial madness, dysentery, and disorders of digestion, are especially common. Many die of induced phthisis, and consumption of the lungs is frequently the termination of long ailments. But hereditary or tubercular phthisis is, it is believed, never or rarely known. A missionary *kauka* (doctor), among Hawaiians, is generally a very popular man, and has it in his power to do much good. But one can have little pleasure or consolation in merely administering medicine, while their exposures are such, and their habits of living so at variance with the laws of health, and there is such an utter want of knowledge and means to nurse the sick. The missionary families do in this line, perhaps, all they can; but that, with other work pressing, is necessarily very little.

There ought to be a hospital on every island, in which natives might be supplied with the means, and taught how to take care of the sick. Any benevolent man in New York or Boston, who is amassing his thousands, could make no better investment of some of them than in founding hospitals for the native race at these islands. *The blessing of the poor, and of many ready to perish, would come upon him, and he would cause the widow's heart to sing for joy.* Such a boon is naturally to be expected from the United States, on the principle that the man who has once greatly befriended us will be most likely to do so, if need be, again.

To America, under God, the Hawaiian nation owes the Gospel. Would that they could, in like manner, be indebted to her benevolence for their temporal salvation and perpetuity as a race! Will not some generous Man of Ross that reads these pages take the hint? Let Carlos Wilcox, though dead, yet speaking at these ends of the earth—let the Cowper of New England instruct us as to the blessedness of such an investment, and urge its philanthropic realization upon some unknown reader with whom God may have intrusted the means, and whose heart shall be "finely touched," like a Howard's or Lyman's, to this "fine issue."

Rouse to this work of high and holy love,
  And thou an angel's happiness shalt know—
Shalt bless the earth while in the world above;
  The good begun by thee shall onward flow
  In many a branching stream, and wider grow:
The seed that, in these few and fleeting hours,
  Thy hands unsparing and unwearied sow,
Shall deck thy grave with amaranthine flowers,
And yield thee fruits divine in heaven's immortal bowers.

CHAPTER XI.

A BARBECUE WITH THE NATIVES, CORAL-HUNTING, AND MEMORIALS OF KAPIOLANI.

Down in the depths of the lonely sea
I work at my mystic masonry;
Ages behold my ceaseless toil,
When the sea is calm or the waters boil;
The kraken glides from my prickly home,
And there the tribes of the deep ne'er come.
I've crusted the plants of the deep with stone,
And given them coloring not their own,
And now on the ocean fields they spread
Their fan-like branches of white and red.
Oh! who can fashion a work like me,
The mason of God in the boundless sea.

Anon.

I HAVE been out recently with native divers, hunting for coral, and on an excursion with the missionary families to Kealia, the diocese of Mr. Ives. Our early departure in canoes by torch-light, hearty greetings by naked barbarians on shore, landings in the surf, exploration of a lava-dripping stalactite cave, and pitching in native tents, would have a pleasing dash of the romantic, were it not for the sundry inconveniences of getting wet and dirty, flea-bitten, and robbed of rest; all which, and other nameless items of discomfort, do considerably abate the edge of a man's relish for such excursions, after he has once had a little of a missionary's experience in that line.

However, meetings with the natives were pleasant,

especially with a large number of fine-looking, clear olive-colored boys and girls. Mr. Forbes interpreted to them my *aloha*, and a few words of congratulation and counsel. How we would like to introduce them, with their Hawaiian skin and costume, and bright eyes, to a Sabbath school in London or New York! They are merry as boys any where now; for in this mild climate nature, in spite of neglect, and dirt, and ill-feeding, *will have* children happy as long as they can live. Would that they could hold their joyousness always.

> My weary soul they seem to soothe,
> And, redolent of joy and youth,
> To breathe a second spring.

Different as childhood here is from childhood in England or America, yet I often think of passages in Gray's Ode on a Prospect of Eton College, when I see a troop of Hawaiian boys and girls rush out of school, whooping and laughing, and down to the sea to play and bathe.

> Gay hope is theirs, by fancy fed,
> Less pleasing when possess'd;
> The tear forgot as soon as shed,
> The sunshine of the breast.
> Their's buxom health, of rosy hue;
> Wild wit, invention ever new,
> And lively cheer of vigor born;
> The thoughtless day, the easy night,
> The spirits pure, the slumbers light,
> That fly the approach of morn.
>
> Alas! regardless of their doom,
> The little victims play;
> No sense have they of ills to come,
> No care beyond to-day.

Yet see how all around them wait,
The ministers of human fate,
  And black misfortune's baleful train.
Ah! show them where in ambush stand,
To seize their prey, the murderous band.
  Ah! tell them, they are men.

The natives entertained us with true Hawaiian hospitality, giving up for our own use one ample house, whose owners were not at all to blame for the fleas and cockroaches that disputed our possession, by right of pre-emption or pre-occupancy, like a squatter in the West. In the evening they went, literally, the "whole hog," burning off his bristles by fire, stuffing him with red-hot stones, and then clapping him into their oven all buried and swaddled with *ki* leaf. A while after, the porker was brought in smoking, with all his natural juices, on a large wooden tray, much, probably, like the Israelites' kneading-troughs, which they bound up in their clothes upon their shoulders when they went up out of Egypt. The head and some other parts were forthwith severed, and served up to the men that came with us. They presented a singular, gipsy-like spectacle while eating round a fire in an out-house, of which one end was exposed, and showed them in the reflected fire-light like a company of banditti feasting after a foray, or a party of the vagabond tribe described by Cowper in the skirts of a wild wood in "Merrie England:"

  A kettle, slung
Between two poles upon a stick transverse,
Receives their morsel—flesh obscene of dog,
Or vermin, or, at best, of cock purloin'd
From his accustom'd haunt. Hard-faring race!
They pick their fuel out of every hedge,
Which, kindled with dry leaves, just saves unquench'd

> The spark of life. The sportive wind blows wide
> Their fluttering rags, and shows a tawny skin,
> The vellum of the pedigree they claim.

This barbecue was followed by a Hawaiian hymn and prayer, after which we bivouacked, and composed ourselves all together for the night, so far as a constant fight with fleas, roaches, musquitoes, and musquito hawks comports with composedness.

We embarked, on our return, by friendly morning star-light, and, by dint of paddles and land breezes, reached Kealakekua by eight o'clock, hardly bested, and hungry. A native dove repeatedly for coral where the water was fifteen or twenty feet deep, and so clear and still that he could be seen below dislodging the coral, or indistinctly creeping along upon all fours on the bottom, like some great marine quadruped. He brought up a number of pieces of brain-coral, that were of a beautiful carnation tinge when first taken from the water; others of the horned and branching, and some red and yellow, and also a number of sea hedgehogs (echini), full of little spiculæ, and several anomalous creatures covered all over with red blunt horns, that used to be employed in the South Seas for slate pencils. Others were armed with a great many long, sharp, needle-like spines, each of which seemed endued with the power of motion.

Almost every body has dreamed some time or other, like Clarence, of being in the heart of the deep, and seeing

> Wedges of gold, great anchors, heaps of pearls,
> Inestimable stones, unvalued jewels,
> All scatter'd in the bottom of the sea;

Wonders of the Deep

And, as in scorn of eyes, reflecting gems,
That woo the slimy bottom of the deep.

But dreams are realities here, for when the sea is still, you can put your eye close to the water from a canoe, and look down thirty or forty feet among the knolls and copses of coral, and see, beautifully defined in robes of gold and Tyrian blue, the various fish that swim noiselessly, and have their dwelling among the submarine shrubbery.

With a skill you can not help envying, an expert fisherman will sometimes mark one of the larger fish for his prey, suddenly dive down with his spear, and capture the unsuspecting freeholder of the deep in his own secluded domain; where, if fishes have codes of laws, one of them probably is the maxim that goes so current among men, that every man's home is his castle. With Cowper,

I never ask'd Jean Jacques Rousseau,
If *fish* confabulate or *no*.

But I have no doubt, if they *do* talk, that they call the fishing *kanakas* worse pirates than the Hawaiians do English Paulet or French La Place. It is doubtful, however, whether there be a fishy tyrant in all the realms of Neptune that makes so free with his subject's wives as the former, or exacts so heavy a tribute as the latter. Notwithstanding all the enemies fish have, I think, if the balance were nicely drawn at these islands between the disabilities of those who live in the water and those who live on the land, the latter would be found to have much the heaviest list of grievances. So that the subjects of Neptune may thank their stars that they are not the subjects of men, like the poor Hawaiians, and exposed to the insults of every lewd naval pirate, whether set on by French Jesuits, and coaxed by a brandy-loving, missionary-hating party, as La Place; or hooked in the nose by men of consular rank and Protestant name, as his English lordship; or the admirals of the magnanimous Republic of 1849, Du Petit Thouars and Tromelin.

If the plebeian denizens of the deep on these coasts had the right of petition, they would, probably, protest as earnestly against the encroachments of Hawaiian fishermen, as Kamehameha III., and Kekauluohi, his premier, did against the illegal acts of Hon. Lord George Paulet, and his Lieutenant John Frere. And they would, doubtless, hail an aquatic deliverer as gladly as the whole Hawaiian nation did the advent of the excellent English Rear-Admiral Thomas, and his restoration of the AUPUNI (kingdom) to whom it rightly belonged. Very likely it was with an eye to some such events and acts elsewhere, as have been enacted within late years at the Sandwich Islands that Barry Cornwall said, satirically,

When you catch
A trout, who has the right, and who the law?
Why, *you, who are the strong*. If he could rise,
And shake his tail against your lawful right,
He'd say, All this is 'gainst our marine laws!
You rascals on dry land invade our realms
By wrong, and by no law. You send abroad
No proclamations; prove no injuries;
Quote no good reasons; no specific code;
But straight, when you desire some trout to eat,
You pounce upon us with your barbed hooks,
And treat us worse than we were Africans
We'll not endure it.

About two miles inland from the steep volcanic cliff, at the head of this bay, where we have been gathering coral and deriving a parable from trout, and fifteen hundred feet above the sea, is the notable place called Kuapehu, first chosen as the site for the missionary station on this part of Hawaii. It has its name from looking, as seen at sea, like a humpback. Mr. Ruggles, one of the first missionaries, built a house and resided there for some time; but his successor moved down nearer to the sea, for the greater salubrity of climate, and in order to be nearer to the majority of the people. The families now go there occasionally for a change of air, as the inhabitants of cities resort to the country.

The distinguished chief woman, Kapiolani, built a fine stone house near by the old meeting-house, and resided there for some time, living decently and in order to the day of her death, an ornament of religion, and a wonderful trophy of the grace of God. She entered more fully into the views and sympathies of the missionaries, and imbibed more from them, than probably any other convert ever did at these islands, whether of the chiefs or common people, excepting, perhaps, blind Bartimeus. She interested herself in the missionary's American friends, shared with them the pleasure of foreign letters, and was in all things the sympathizing mother and friend.

She had a large and generous heart. In her tours among the people, she would visit the hovels of the poor and sick, and supply them with *kapas*, and mats, and food. Her soul, too, *followed hard after God.* His word she hid in her heart, and by it confounded

Popish priests and foreigners, when they dared to confront her. They say that often in the night she used to waken her women that were by, to pray for the king, then dissolute and unpromising, that he might be turned to the *pono*, the way of righteousness.

Captain Finch, of the U. S. ship Vincennes, when here in 1829, called upon her one evening, and took tea, in company with Rev. Lorrin Andrews. He was to leave port that night, and had fixed the time when he would be on board ; but the hour came and passed, and yet another, and found him still detained at the table of this interesting woman, listening to the details of her history and experience, and admiring the propriety and truly lady-like ease and courtesy with which she entertained her guests. At length he said he must reluctantly leave, but not without saying through his interpreter, Mr. Andrews (from whom I have the story), that he had not spent an evening so agreeably since he left his own family in America. The lives of Kaahumanu, and Hoapili, and Kapiolani should, ere this, have been written, and have become the property of the Church and Hawaiian nation, which their lives so honored after they embraced Christianity.

Kapiolani died in peace on the 5th of May, 1841. Her pastor then said of her that her life was a continual evidence of the elevating and purifying effects of the Gospel. " She was confessedly the most decided Christian, the most civilized in her manners, and the most thoroughly read in her Bible, of all chiefs this nation ever had ; and it is saying no more than truth to assert, that her equal, in these respects, is not left in the nation. There may be those who had more external polish of manner, but none who combined her excellences. She has gone to her rest, and the nation has lost one of its brightest ornaments."

It is of Kapiolani that Carlyle tells this story, in the course of one of his volumes of Cromwell's Letters and Speeches: A certain queen in some South Sea Island I have read of in missionary books, had been converted to Christianity; did not any longer believe in the old gods. She assembled her people; said to them, "My faithful people, the gods do *not* dwell in that burning mountain in the centre of our isle. That is not God; no, that is a common burning mountain—mere culinary fire, burning under peculiar circumstances. See, I will walk before you to that burning mountain; will empty my wash-bowl into it, cast my slipper over it, defy it to the utmost, and stand the consequences!" She walked, accordingly, this South Sea heroine, moved to the sticking-place, her people following in pale horror and expectancy. She did her experiment, and I am told they have truer notions of the gods in that island ever since. Honor to the brave who deliver us from phantom-dynasties in South Sea islands and in North!

The facts of this truly heroic experiment are these, as detailed substantially in Bingham's Sandwich Islands, the best authority. Early in 1825, five years after the first landing of missionaries on Hawaii, this strong-minded and courageous woman, seeing the spell which held many of the people in superstitious awe of the volcano, resolved, of her own accord, to visit the great crater of Kilanea, the residence from time immemorial of the great Goddess Pele, and to set at naught her *tabus*, and dare her fires.

In order to accomplish this, she must make a journey of about a hundred miles, mostly on foot, from Kealakekua to Hilo. This bold design was, of course, opposed by almost all around her, some fearing she would bring into contempt the regard they sacredly cherished for Pele, and others dreading the danger to her own person from attempting to break the ancient *tabus* of the Hawaiian Vulcan. Even Naihe, her husband, whose powerful person and oratory might be supposed almost to set him above fear, yet not having his mind wholly freed from the shackles of superstition, was unwilling to do what she proposed, and felt an indefinable repugnance to his wife's thus exposing herself. But doing all she could to reason away their apprehensions, she perseveringly pursued her course.

In approaching the region of the volcano, she was met by a prophetess claiming authority from Pele herself, and solemnly warning her off from those sacred grounds, and predicting her death from the fury of the goddess if she should dare invade her domain with the feelings of hostility and contempt which she professed. "Who are you?" demanded Kapiolani. "One in whom *Ke Akua* dwells," she replied. "If God dwells in you, then you are wise, and can teach me," said Kapiolani: "come hither and sit down." After some urging, she complied.

Refreshments were kindly offered her, but, in the haughtiness of her assumed dignity as a supernatural being, she said, "I am a god; I will not eat." Holding in her hand a piece of bark cloth, she said, "This is a *palapala* (writing) from the Goddess Pele." "Read it to us," said Kapiolani; and, when the prophetess declined, she resolutely insisted on her proving that she had a book or writing from the god by her reading it. Then cunningly carrying out her device, and, with unexpected presence of mind, holding the cloth before her eyes, the prophetess poured forth a torrent of unintelligible words or sounds, which she would have them believe were in the dialect of the ancient Pele.

Then Kapiolani, producing her Christian books, said to the impostor, "You pretend to have received and to deliver a message from your god, which none of us can comprehend. I have a *palapala* as well as you, and will read you a message from the true God, which you can understand." She then read several passages, and called her attention to the character, works, and will of the great Jehovah, and to Jesus Christ as the Savior of the lost. The haughty prophetess quailed; her head drooped, and her garrulity ceased. She confessed that *Ke Akua* had left her, and she could not, therefore, reply. The oracle being silenced, the deluded prophetess herself joined in the repast; the conviction of Kapiolani that she ought to proceed was strengthened, and, true to her purpose, she went forward.

The missionaries at Hilo, hearing that Kapiolani had set out to visit them, were desirous to meet her at the volcano, and one of them accordingly traveled on foot twenty-five or thirty miles, till he joined her retinue on the brink of that stupendous wonder of the world. Kapiolani was much affected on meeting there a missionary coadjutor, and, accompanied by him, with a train of about eighty natives, she descended from the rim of the crater to the black ledge.

There, in full view of the terrific panorama before them, the effects of an agency always appalling, she calmly addressed the company thus: "Jehovah is my God. He kindled these fires. I fear not Pele. If I perish by the anger of Pele, then you may fear the power of Pele. But if I trust in Jehovah, and he shall save me from the wrath of Pele when I break through her *tabus*, then you must fear and serve the Lord Jehovah. All the gods of Hawaii are vain. Great is the goodness of Jehovah in sending missionaries to turn us from these vanities, to the living God and the way of righteousness."

Then, with the terrific bellowing and whizzing of the volcanic gases, they mingled their voices in a solemn hymn of praise to the true God; and at the instance of the chiefess, Alapai led them in prayer, while all bowed in adoration before Jehovah, as the Creator and Governor of all things. The great God of heaven heard their prayer. Kapiolani and her party went down courageously on that truly heroic mission, for so worthy an end, into that vast fire-eaten pit, called *Lua Pele*, and came up therefrom unharmed. The spell was broken; the dread *Pele-tabu* was violated with impunity; and the death blow was given to the tyrant superstition, which had hitherto brooded over the Hawaiian imagination like a nightmare in a long reign of terror.

"Here was heroism (says the historian) of a more

sublime and immortal character than that which rushes to the battle-field. Here was a philosophy which puts to the blush the pride of pagan Athens and Rome, whose philosophers would risk nothing in suppressing idolatry, though they admitted its pretensions were unfounded. Here was a movement which, in its character and consequences to a nation, was not unlike that of the sublime preacher on Mars Hill, whose 'spirit was stirred in him when he saw the whole city given to idolatry.' What visitor to the great Kilauea has ever gone there with a nobler object, or to better purpose, than did this noble princess, on her first becoming established in the Christian faith?"

The narrative states, that after this transaction, so important in its bearing upon the system of Hawaiian idolatry, Kapiolani and her party proceeded to the missionary station of Hilo the following day. On their arrival at night, with feet swollen, and lamed by the long and weary traveling, this Christian princess would not rest till she had secured lodging for all her company and had united with them in evening worship. She told the missionaries she had come to strengthen their hearts and help them in their work; a practical help which they at once began to reap the benefits of; for she went about, while there, doing good; and not a person, it was said, came into her presence without receiving her Christian counsel or reproof; and her salutary influence in favor of education and reform was long felt in Hilo after she had returned home to Kuapehu.

Here she resumed her energetic administration;

and to the day of her death she was a firm promoter of good morals and religion, both by her own blameless example, and her impartial enforcement of the law upon others, both natives and foreigners. It once happened that a sailor belonging to an American ship was arrested and put in prison, having been convicted of the offense for which persons were sentenced to labor on the roads of Hawaii. The captain of the ship waited upon Kapiolani, and threatened to fire the village unless the sailor should be instantly released. "Here is my law," said Kapiolani; "the sailor shall pay the fine of fifteen dollars, or he shall work four months on the roads—the same as his associate in guilt. Now, if you have the force, fire the village; but while Kapiolani lives, her law shall be executed in her country." The captain was obliged to pay the fine, in order to obtain the release of the sailor.

For these cherished memorials of Kapiolani, and others which I have learned of the truly Christian princess, I love to linger at Kuapehu. All its memories are green, and its vegetation too, unlike what is seen at the bay, is very abundant, by reason of frequent rains and lack of tendance, as in Eve's garden,

> To repress wanton growth, running to wild,
> And keep from wilderness.

The indigo and guava, first planted there by Mr. Ruggles, have made a dense dwarf forest all about. The anetto, fig, peach, mango, lime-tree, and others, have a luxurious growth within the inclosure; but interloper rats and mice get most of the fruits, and a great terrapin turtle, who will walk off with a man on his back, is the LOCUM TENENS and landlord of the place.

Near by is a luxuriant shading grape-vine, which possesses not a little interest, when one comes to know that it was the occasion of a beautiful Hawaiian *mele*, song, from the aged chief woman, Kekupuohi, one of the wives of Kalaniopuu, the reigning king of Hawaii when the island was first visited by Captain Cook. She was on a visit to Mr. Ruggles when she composed this song, the portion of which following is found translated in the Memoirs of Lucy G. Thurston. It is worth preserving, as a specimen of the old style of Hawaiian poetry Christianized, and suggested, probably, to the mind of this ancient survivor of heathenism by the New Testament figure of Christ as the true vine.

> Once only hath that appeared which is glorious;
> It is wonderful, it is altogether holy;
> It is a blooming glory; its nature is unwithering;
> Rare is its stock, most singular, unrivaled,
> *One only true vine.* It is the Lord.
> The branch that adheres to it becomes fruitful;
> The fruit comes forth *fruit;* it is good fruit,
> Whence its character is clearly made known.
> Let the branch merely making fair show be cut off,
> Lest the stock should be injuriously encumbered;
> Lest it be also, by it, wrongfully burdened.

This woman was said, in the days of heathenism, to have been the *wahine* of some forty different husbands, and of several of them at the same time. Upon hearing the Gospel, she was one of the first on Hawaii to give heed to it, and to befriend its teachers. In her eagerness to learn to read the word of God, she entered school as a pupil; but from her advanced age, her dullness, and unretentive memory, she found it difficult to get even the alphabet, so as to remember it.

Before she could read at all, the missionaries, having the supervision of thousands, advised her to give up the attempt to learn. But not satisfied with remaining unable to read the Scriptures, and choosing one of her younger female attendants for her teacher, she strenuously persevered till the mystic art was acquired, and the *palapala hemolele* (sacred writings) became thenceforth her daily companion to the end of life. Reared in the untold depravities of heathenism, and continuing therein to old age, as if to prove that nothing in the line of human regeneration is too hard for grace divine, she was then chosen to illustrate the transforming power of the Gospel, by putting on Christianity as a conscientious Christian, and dying at last with good hope in Christ.

How true now of this heavenly metamorphosis of a gray relic of idolatry are those lines in The Task, that proclaim the nature and necessity of such a change in every son and daughter of Adam!

The still small voice is wanted. He must speak,
Whose word leaps forth at once to its effect;
Who calls for things that are not, and they come.
Grace makes the slave a freeman. 'Tis a change
That turns to ridicule the turgid speech
And stately tone of moralists, who boast,
As if, like him of fabulous renown,
They had, indeed, ability to smooth
The shag of savage nature, and were each
An Orpheus, and omnipotent in song:
But transformation of apostate man

From fool to wise, from earthly to divine,
Is work for Him that made him. He alone,
And he by means, in philosophic eyes,
Trivial and worthy of disdain, achieves
The wonder; *humanizing what is brute*
In the lost kind; extracting from the lips
Of asps their venom; overpowering strength
By weakness, and hostility by love.

From Kuapehu one may ride, by a horse-path, three or four miles up into the mountain, through belts of gigantic ferns and brakes, that have formed, in their decay, a very deep and rich vegetable mold. It is matter of curious interest to the traveler to mark the progress and change of productions with the different zones, till you get into the region of koa forests, from which the natives procure their canoes, and timber for all other purposes. One admires there the tangled woods and mosses, and wild bowers made by the con volvuli and other larger vines o'ermantling both decayed and living trees, as in the woods of Florida and Louisiana. Birds, too, carol there with joy, secure from molestation by Indian's arrow or hunter's rifle.

I have visited a little school in the woods not far from that region, where the instructor was knowingly teaching geography by a globe he had made out of a calabash; covering it over with cotton cloth, then marking meridians, parallels, and names with ink and native dyes, and besmearing all with a coat of varnish (to keep it from being devoured by cockroaches) made of a native gum they call *pi-lali*, not unlike gum Arabic. His earth was considerably flattened at the poles, and rather too pursy at the equator; but for all that, it turned easier on its axis than many a fat alderman could on his heel, whom ease and good living have formed into an oblate spheroid, not unlike the honest Hawaiian teacher's earth. I have no doubt many a bright-eyed, tawny urchin, the Flibbertegibbet of his native village, will learn more from it of the round world he treads on than was ever known to Aristotle or Plato.

CHAPTER XII.

CANOEING BY SEA AND SURVEY OF VOLCANOES BY LAND.

WINGS have we, and as far as we can go
We may find pleasure; wilderness and wood,
Blank ocean and mere sky, support that mood,
Which with the lofty sanctifies the low:
Dreams, books are each a world; and books, we know,
Are a substantial world, both pure and good.
Hence have I genial seasons, hence have I
Smooth passions, smooth discourse, and joyous thought:
And thus from day to day my little boat
Rocks in its harbor or puts out to sea.

WORDSWORTH.

LIKE a bird of passage, again am I on the wing, spirits refreshed and health recruited by nestling so long in the happy missionary dove-cot at Kealakekua. Four days ago, at one o'clock in the morning, my boat and I put out again to sea from that quiet harbor, where pen, and books, and prayer, and confiding Christian converse, together with true hospitality, combined to constitute one of those genial seasons in the life of a traveler which are like a pilgrim's rest in one of the arbors erected by the Lord of the Way.

The memory of this grateful episode in my life's drama, and of the friends that made it so, will be always fresh and green. How could it, then, be otherwise than with reluctance that I resumed my wanderings, though under favorable auspices, and com mended *to God and the word of his grace* by those with whom I had been so pleasantly sojourning? A double canoe, especially when loaded with boards as this was, affords quite a comfortable conveyance for one or more passengers. The boards were piled on much as they are wont to be upon the deck of a "down-east" or Hudson River lumber sloop, away up above the vessel's rail. My place was on the top of them, where one can lie at length and sleep, if he like, and is not afraid of being rolled off into the sea.

A double canoe is composed of two single ones of the same size, placed parallel to each other, three or four feet apart, and secured in their places by four or five cross-pieces of wood, curved just in the shape of a bit-stock. These are lashed to both canoes with the strongest cinet, made of cocoa-nut fibre, so as to make the two almost as much one as some of the double ferry-boats that ply between Brooklyn and New York. A flattened arch is thus made by the bow-like cross-pieces over the space between the canoes, upon which a board, or a couple of stout poles laid lengthwise, constitute an elevated platform for passenger and freight, while those who paddle and steer sit in the bodies of the canoes at the sides. A slender mast, which may be unstepped in a minute, rises from about the centre of this platform, to give support to a very simple sail, now universally made of white cotton cloth, but formerly of mats.

It was comfortable sailing all the day along the cavernous lava-coast of Kona, sometimes within hearing and sight of great funnel-shaped blow-holes in the rocks along the shore, by which the spray of a great wave, and even stones, would sometimes be ejected with great force, and a noise much louder, but not unlike, that of a spouting whale. At night the natives would not be kept from putting into a little bay, between out-jutting masses of lava, and dropping anchor there—they alleging that the wind would be ahead, and sailing dangerous, but, in reality (I think), more to enjoy a comfortable sleep, which all Hawaiians love only next best to eating *poi*. I endured for a couple of hours, unwittingly catching a nap myself; then a few repetitions of *Ala!* and *Hoe, hoe!* broke their slumbers, and we again made sail.

Morning light found us on the borders of the county of Kau, right opposite where there rise up, a hundred and fifty or two hundred feet, several conical hills of volcanic sand and cinders, and which seem to be the basins of extinct volcanoes. The early hour, and stars fading in the light of dawn, made me call to mind those fine lines of Dana:

> The silent night has passed into the prime
> Of day—to thoughtful souls a solemn time.
> For man has waken'd from his mighty death
> And shut-up sense, to morning's life and breath.
> He sees go out in heaven the stars that kept
> Their glorious watch, while he, unconscious, slept—
> Feels God was round him, while he knew it not—
> Is awed—then meets the world—and God's forgot—
> So may I not forget Thee, holy Power!
> Be ever to me as at this calm hour.

We touched at a landing-place for the natives to eat, and to take in a new paddler before meeting with the violent trades which are felt in coming from leeward some time before reaching the southern point of Hawaii. Some wild girls there seemed very glad to show their boldness in leaping from precipices into the sea. They swam around us, as we lay off a little ways, to avoid the outrageous surf, like so many Nereids, as much at home in the realms of Neptune as ever the Peris were, or any of that fabulous train, the maids of the sea, that graced the court of Thetis.

By dint of vigorous paddling against a strong wind and current, we got to Kailikii some time before noon. It was near this that two of the missionaries in the year 1828 had well nigh lost their lives. They arrived in a double canoe like ours, and as they doubled a point of land in this vicinity, the trade-winds suddenly struck them unprepared. It was like Paul's ship falling into a place where two seas met; for between the swell from the south and the current and wind from the north, the waves dashed over their canoe and nearly swamped it, and they were rapidly swept to sea. By vigorous baling and paddling, however, the natives succeeded in making the canoe buoyant and manageable again, and bringing it in to the nearest landing-place. But there the surf was rolling ashore so roughly that the danger was imminent of dashing the canoe to pieces, and leaving their own mangled corpses on the jagged lava-rocks. The natives, therefore, determining to coast along further, and the missionaries not daring to proceed, they leaped into the water as a wave retired, and through God's goodness secured a standing on the rocks before the sea returned.

The canoe passed on, but was soon overwhelmed and wrecked by the furious billows; but the natives, buoyant as a bladder, rose to the surface and struggled for the shore. Through their unequaled power of endurance in the water, and their skill in the surf, they all escaped alive, although two of their number were drawn out by the others bruised and insensible. Their valuable canoe, belonging to Kuakini (Governor Adams), was entirely destroyed. When afterward the missionaries and captain of the canoe narrated the facts to Kuakini, and feared that he would demand indemnification for his loss, he merely asked if all on board escaped alive, and, being answered in the affirmative, he tersely replied, not surely in the temper of a Shylock, which he has sometimes been said to be, but in the true spirit of his noble sister, Kaahumanu, "I AM SATISFIED"—UA OLUOLU.

At our landing-place we descried, away over a precipice three or four hundred feet high, a man and a horse, kindly sent there for me by the missionary, Rev. Mr. Paris, who was apprised of my being at hand, and had been led to expect my arrival that day. I forthwith started alone across a stream of ancient lava, about a mile wide, that intervened between the precipice and the sea, hoping to be seen and waited for by the man with the horse. Climbing the *pali*, from which the plain had been severed and sunk in the throes of some earthquake, was a desperate work for one fasting, and by no means well. It was so very like a picture of the Hill Difficulty, which I remember in an old boyhood edition of the Pilgrim's Progress, where "Christian fell from running to going, and from going to clambering upon his hands and knees," that, if these islands had been known, one might almost think the designer had traveled through these parts. But it is doubtful whether Bunyan's imagination, or even Milton's, ever conceived of abrupt precipices, or sunken pits and plains, like those which earthquakes have rent, and volcanic fires have eaten here in Hawaii.

Reeking with perspiration, though as much divested of clothing as one well could be without becoming a *kanaka maole*, I at length reached the top, and was met by a blast of the trades as fierce as if old Boreas himself were riding them. The wall-eyed Hawaiian who had charge of the horse had not seen us, and, supposing the canoe was not to come that day, had put about for home. All that was to be seen of them was their trail in the loam and sand, which I had nothing else to do but to trudge after as best I could, with all patience and philosophy, in the teeth of the wind and a drizzling rain. It was twelve or fourteen miles to Waiohinu:

> Hills peeped o'er hills, and Alps on Alps arose,

before I got there; but a warm reception and a warm bath did much to dispel fatigue, while a wheaten loaf and a tumbler of rich goat's milk, equal to any the patriarchs ever drank in the land of Uz, exercised the digestive faculty enough to allay hunger and renew the strength.

I had the pleasure of being the first lodger, and taking the first meal with the family in the mission house, which is altogether the best contrived and most commodious we have seen in all the mission. It is a frame house, of two stories, having five rooms, and an entry through from side to side, below stairs, and four rooms above, besides a large garret for lumber and stowage room. The kitchen is of stone, directly joining the house, and of a commodious size, being the room in which the family have been living ever since the station was taken in 1842. Although the largest and best built, it will probably prove one of the most economical houses in the mission, as there will be no necessity of after additions, which have made almost every other house, built small and stintedly at first, on a meagre appropriation, a constant bill of expense, and at the sacrifice, too, of all proper plan and symmetry.

The house is situated at the head of a valley, just at the foot of very high and abrupt hills in the rear and on one side, and a more gentle declivity on the other. The trades blow in upon it strongly, and, from its relative position to the hills that attract the clouds, it receives a great deal of rain. It is five miles from the sea in a direct line, and twelve or fifteen hundred feet above it. There is all about great vegetative luxuriance. A brook, from which the place derives its name, *Waiohinu*, or sparkling water, runs directly through the inclosure, but a foot from the kitchen-door. By a location one half or quarter of a mile lower down, a better climate would have been secured, and much rain avoided, but with the loss of the water privilege, and a fine view of the sea now commanded from the front veranda.

It remains to be seen whether health will be affected by the dampness caused by almost daily showers. The sun generally shines out so clear both before and after, and water passes off so readily through the cavernous ground, that it may not be felt. But the climate is singularly different from that which is found five miles off by the sea side, or even only two miles lower down. Thus, in a ride recently through fishing villages, and over a tract along the sea where they make salt by evaporating sea-water in the natural pans of the lava, while we were melting in the sun, we saw it raining heavily before us at Waiohinu, but reached the house without a wetting by a little after six, to a well-spread supper-table, and a cheerful fireside, whose light streamed out of the windows as we approached, and made me think more of fireside scenes in dear New England than any thing yet met with in Hawaii nei. May that gracious Being, who is at the same time a *God near and afar off*, befriend that *home* in the heart of a Northern winter, which has been so vividly brought to mind!

Probably this is the first Christian fireside whose light has ever gleamed in Kau, and seldom will it be needed in such a climate, except to cheer some tired traveler, or make home more dear to the missionary husband and father, when he is waited for by the patient wife at evening, returning, wet and weary, from work in his wide sheepfold. Other fire light there is no lack of in a region like this, which used to be the play-ground of the primeval volcanic element itself. Old Kilauea's lurid glow can be seen here every night from the northern windows; and earthquake shocks are frequent enough to afford lively mementoes of the internal fires over which this part of Hawaii is but an oven-like dome, whose crust may any where slump and admit the egress of the pent-up fiery flood.

From the tops of the grassy mountains in our rear, themselves once the overflow of a crater, there may be always descried the pillar of smoke that hangs over the volcano by day, fifty miles off. Molten rock once flowed as freely behind the house as the sparkling waters do now, from which the place has its name. It would be no strange thing should it gush again in a metallic stream from the bowels of the hill near by, and it would find a sluice-way ready made to disgorge by, even a cave through which it ran of old, whose open mouth you can look into from the back door.

We visited the other day a large and deep subterranean gallery, about six miles from Waiohinu, which was once a sluice-way to the sea from some pent-stock of liquid lava further inland. The way to it was a novel one, over rough, unworn lava, and for a while through a dense growth of the *wiliwili* and *ohi* trees. The one is a wood almost as light as cork, of which the natives make the outriggers to their canoes. The latter is more like the white beech of an American forest than any thing I have seen at these islands, where you look in vain for the majestic, pillar-like growth of centuries, that forms one of the grandest features in a country where all the works of nature are in a corresponding style of magnificence.

The gallery we went to see opens at a deep pit, made by the falling in of its roof in that part. It is about fifty feet high at the entrance, and the descent is steep for several yards. We found within a woman washing *kapas*, with her child, by fresh water that drops from the vault into calabashes. Proceeding further, we found a fort, consisting of a wall thrown up across the way where it went between steep rocks. Behind it were places leveled off and built up for sleeping. It was resorted to by the natives in time of war.

We lighted a lantern, and explored for some rods, finding here and there, in the crevices, shells and sea-eggs, and pieces of bone, left, probably, by natives living there in time of siege. Rocks have from time to time been dropped from the roof in earthquakes, and the bottom is the most jagged and irregular possible. How far under ground it goes, rock-ribbed and vast, it is impossible to say—probably several miles, up to the place whence issued the last eruption. A quarter of a mile nearer to the ocean the same cave opens again, and, descending to about a level with the sea, there is found a pool of water, as at the cave in Kailua, in which one of our natives soon waded beyond his depth.

There is nothing beautiful, but much that is titanic and sublime, in the silence, and gloom, and vastness of such a place, where you stand, seemingly, in the bowels of the earth, along where liquid fire has flowed ages ago, and where earthquakes have dislodged vast fragments of rock from the ragged roof. It was, in the language of the natives, a *kupainaha*, a mighty wonder of Jehovah, where a man must be insensate and stupid indeed who does not call to mind and adore that great God *in whose hand are the deep places of the earth;* where, in view of the vestiges of Omnipotence, we can only adopt the language of men awe-struck and inspired by God himself: *Lo, these are a part of his ways, but the thunder of his power who can understand!* Dr. Watts, in his hymns for *infant* minds, expresses the idea of God's omnipresence so admirably for the *maturest*, that I never enter such a place but that I think of it:

> If I should find some *cave unknown*,
> Where human feet have never trod,
> Even there I should not be alone;
> On every side there would be God.

To live almost any where upon this part of Hawaii, and especially to go to the volcano, and observe there, as at a great safety-valve or escape-pipe, the vast force and intensity of this earth's internal fires, makes one feelingly realize how easily that dread catastrophe, foretold in the Scriptures, can be consummated, when *the heavens being on fire, shall be dissolved, and the elements shall melt with fervent heat; the earth also, and the works therein, shall be burned up.*

Volcanoes may be held as a collateral, standing evidence to the senses, to render, naturally and physically, probable that dread event which the Bible makes sure. Herein do we see the treasures of fire KEPT IN STORE and pent in the bowels of the earth, constituting there

> A capacious reservoir of means,
> Form'd for God's use, and ready at His will,

waiting only the signal word and the predestined moment to leap out and wrap in fiery ruin earth, air, and sea, which are said in Scripture to be *reserved to fire against the day of judgment and perdition of ungodly men.*

Aside from revelation, it is proved, by the researches of geology, that the physical history of our globe has included more than one chaotic convulsion. It has once, at least, already undergone a fusion by fire, as well as an universal submersion by water.* It

* What, asks Tayler Lewis, in his Phi Beta Kappa Discourse on Naturalism, what is this marred and still chaotic earth on which man dwells, that after so many geological convulsions she should be supposed to have reached a harbor where she is secure from all danger of any future wreck; or to have arrived at a state in which there is to be, henceforth, an everlasting onward movement unto all physical excellence? In other words, what is there in her present *anno eternitatis*, the present epoch of her palæontological chronology, to shield her from the apprehension of any future Plutonic fires, or outbursting floods, or continents upheaved, or oceans settling down, such as have begun and ended many a cycle in the long past periods of her interminable history?

Lecturers on astronomy sometimes attempt to prove the stability of our world and of the universe. That may be if God wills it. A belief grounded on the divine word or promise would be in the highest degree rational; but science never has shown it, and never can show it. Neither does it require any great amount of science to detect the fallacy of the pretended demonstration. It all proceeds from applying to a part of the phenomena of the universe (a very small part, too, even when we take into the account the utmost the telescope has ever reached) what can only be sound and conclusive when it embraces all actual and all possible phenomena, and then, too, only by bringing in something above nature as a regulative force. The animalcule in the snow-flake (supposing him capable of scientific reasoning) might as rationally infer the perpetuity of his own crystallized habitation. He has all the arguments that can be drawn from the most perfect beauty and regularity of structure; all that can be drawn from the laws of equilibrium; all that can be drawn from what might seem the most exquisite harmony of means and end. Its form, too, and its organization may have remained unchanged for long centuries in some polar latitude; and yet how brief a transition to another climate may reduce it, together with the *iceberg universe*, of which it forms a part, to a state of utter dissolution. From any objection arising out of the minuteness of the comparison, we appeal to one of the most rigid formulas of the pure reason. The largest differences between parts become small, beyond all commensurable ratio, when both are viewed in reference to an immeasurable whole. The snow may, then, naturally speaking, without any other evidence than this collateral line of proof furnished by the present existence and activity of volcanoes, it may include in its future history another period of fusion by fire, when, by the gradually advancing vehemence of its vast central furnace, the pent-up energy of internal combustion shall exceed its ancient bounds, and get vent as never before. Then how easily, in the space of a week or a day, might it destroy all the structures of the earth's surface, and leave nothing undissolved that is of the nature to be molten by intensity of heat.

Such, then, it is a remark of Isaac Taylor, in the Physical Theory of Another Life, being the probable fate of this planet, and perhaps of others of the system, "it is what we are to be looking for; and our position is like that of the occupiers of the vine-valleys on the trembling flanks of Ætna or Vesuvius, whom we may imagine to have been informed, or to know on some rational grounds, that by the slow but incessant enlargement of the fiery abyss beneath them, the entire crust and frame-work of the mountain must, within some calculable period, fall in, and the vast circuit of its base be converted into a sea of flame and sulphur. On just such conditions do the human family tread, from age to age, the soil of their native planet."

With what reasonableness and force, then, does Peter argue, Seeing that all these things shall be dissolved, what manner of persons ought we to be in all holy

flake has a greater ratio to the earth, that is, is a greater part of the earth than the earth is of the universe.—*A Discourse on Naturalism. By Tayler Lewis, LL.D., Schenectady.*

conversation and godliness ; looking for and hastening unto the coming of the day of God, wherein the heavens, being on fire, shall be dissolved, and the elements shall melt with fervent heat? Nevertheless we, according to his promise, look for new heavens and a new earth, wherein dwelleth righteousness, when fire shall have purged the old. That final purge will come (none know how soon), when all things are ripe for the dread consummation, though it be at such a day and hour as we think not. Then, as we are instructed in one of Milton's early dramas,

> Even that which mischief meant most harm
> Shall in the happy trial prove most glory:
> But evil on itself shall back recoil,
> And mix no more with goodness: then, at last,
> Gather'd like scum, and settled to itself,
> It shall be, in eternal restless change,
> Self-fed and self-consumed ; if this fail,
> The pillar'd firmament is rottenness,
> And earth's base built on stubble.

CHAPTER XIII.

A DIAMOND IN THE ROUGH—HOW IT WAS QUARRIED; WITH NOTES ON ITS LOCALITY AND ASSOCIATES.

No man e'er found a happy life by chance,
Or yawn'd it into being with a wish;
Or, with the snout of groveling appetite,
E'er smell'd it out, and grubb'd it from the dirt.
YOUNG.

He is the happy man, whose life e'en now
Shows somewhat of that happier life to come;
Who, by Love divine and perfect Wisdom,
Appointed to a state obscure but useful,
With it is pleased, and, were he free to choose,
Would make his lot his choice.
COWPER.

IN the great scheme of Providence there is a niche, prominent or secluded, for every man to fill; tnere is a circle of usefulness and enjoyment for every one to revolve in, without infringing on any other, if he can but find it. Happy is he who early in active life gets into it; who traces the round of labor, where Providence has cast his lot, with cheerfulness and alacrity, his time divided by a wise method, and duties running orderly into duties, but no more clashing with each other, or crowded out of place, than the hours are jostled or trodden upon by one another in their everlasting rounds.

I have found several such niches and spheres of

motion exactly filled at these islands, whose occupants, if free to choose, as free they have been under God for their guide, would make their lot their choice. They are, consequently, useful and happy, and the whole world of mankind feels their benign influence, although to a casual view it might seem not to extend at all beyond the narrow circle they steadily move round in. When Shakspeare makes Portia say to Nerissa, in the Merchant of Venice,

> How far that little candle throws his beams!
> So shines a good deed in a naughty world,

he happily utters a truth, of which I have several times been certified by exemplification, in the course of my travels through this far land. There are candles shining here, whose rays, because we would like to see them beaming to the ends of the earth, we do therefore gather up as we go, and endeavor to reflect them from the pages of this book.

Even the district of Kau, though distant and unknown to the great world, has its own lamps, both native and missionary, by which I have discerned some things in mental philosophy and theology clearer than I had seen them before, and have found practical confirmation of other truths by instances of no little value.

Thus there is a fine saying of Augustine, which I have often pondered, and which every man who has truly learned the *Gnôthi Seauton* of the ancients has found the truth of, namely, that a man must first descend into the hell of his own heart before he can ascend to the heaven of God. That is, plainly, a man must have let down the sounding lead and line into the abyss of his own heart's depravity; he must have done something toward taking the gauge and dimensions of its misery and sin; he must have seen how near he is to the roaring rocks and quicksands of ruin; yea, he must have heard the surf beating upon the lee-shore of perdition, and have seen the white caps gather and flash upon the gloom of his night, before he will put his helm hard down, wear ship, and stand about for heaven. And then, alas! how often is it too late: mast and yards go by the board; the ship misstays, and becomes a fearful wreck; and, distracted with agitation and alarm, the poor procrastinating soul is cast upon the rocks and lost in the breakers of opening eternity.

Ah! of how many a sailor especially this is only the condensed history. But it was not so in the following instance, which we have learned at Waiohinu. One day, soon after his settlement in Kau, when Mr. Paris was away from home, and his wife could as yet understand but little of the native tongue, a very wicked and strong man came into the rude grass house where they lived, without knocking, and sitting down upon the mat-floor with nothing on but his *kapa* (loose blanket, made by pounding out the inner bark of a tree to the thickness of coarse paper), he fastened his eye upon Mrs. Paris, as she was tending her young babe and overseeing her household. He stared upon her very strangely, without speaking, gloomy and sullen as a thunder-cloud.

A native servant-woman with her said, "The man wants you to speak to him." "But I know not how," said she, "or what to say;" and there the brawny barbarian still sat in gloom, gazing steadily, and following her with his lowering eye till she was frightened. At length the fixed, inquiring look of those coal-black eyes, and the despairing, gloomy face of the tawny Hawaiian, compelled her to ask him, in his own tongue, "*Heaha kona manao?*"—what was his thought. Oh! he said, with a deep groan, he was *hewa*—a sinner. "And what were his sins?" He was *hoomanakii*—an idolater; he had stolen, *aihue;* he was a murderer, had spilled blood, *pepe-hi kanaka;* he was an adulterer, *moekolohe.* "And where are you now?" asked Mrs. Paris. He answered, trembling all over, "UA LILO, UA LILO"—"I AM LOST, I AM LOST!"

Then, taking up his word as her clew, and led, she believed, by the Spirit of God, she told him, in the best broken native she could summon, the good news that *Christ came to seek and to save those that are lost*—the very persons that were *lilo* like him; and then, turning to her English Testament, she pointed him to those corresponding passages in the Hawaiian that tell of Christ as the Savior of sinners, and had the native woman with her read them there to the dark-minded, conscience-stricken barbarian, till he gathered comfort from the words and went away relieved.

He was soon hopefully converted, finding Christ, and joyfully believing the words, The Son of Man is come to seek and to save that which was lost, and himself, therefore, as one of the lost. He has held on well to the present time, and has been made a deacon in the church, and the hand of this rescued barbarian of Kau, now sitting at the feet of Jesus clothed and in his right mind, has grasped mine with a cordial *aloha*.

Thus it is that all human experience shows alike, whether Jew or Greek, barbarian or Scythian, bond or free, that fallen man must *feel* himself to be ruined before he can be saved; a captive before he can be delivered; a slave to sin and Satan before he can be set free; lost before he can be found of Jesus Christ. One must *experimentally find* himself to be blind before he can truly see; deaf, before he can truly hear; poor, before he can become rich; sick, before he can be made whole; weak, before he can be really strong; dead in trespasses and sins, before he can truly live. The thunders of God's violated law must have been heard rolling; its vivid lightning flashes must startle the soul; and the avenger of blood must be heard close at the heels, before there will be a swift flight of the awakened, immortal man to the Lamb of God that taketh away the sin of the world.

The evil of sin must have been keenly felt by him. Its plague spots and livid hue must have been noticed by the sinner upon his own soul, threatening, like the gangrene of mortification, a speedy dissolution before he will have recourse to the only Physician that can do him any good. Then how quickly, if not too late, will the burdened spirit fly to Christ, just as a tired, panting bird will to the tender hand and bosom that offers it shelter.

Even as in these tropic seas I have seen the beautiful flying-fish, when chased by the dolphin, spring suddenly from the water and skim along the waves, and light sometimes upon parts of the ship, so must the soul, pursued by its sins and the avenging law of God, leap at once, as for its life, into the outstretched arms of that Savior who is able, as he is willing, to save unto the uttermost all that come unto God through him.

How truly, though quaintly, it was that Giles Fletcher said of this all-sufficing Savior for savage and sage:

> He is a path, if any be misled;
> He is a robe, if any naked be;
> If any chance to hunger, He is bread;
> If any be a bondman, He is free;
> If any be but weak, how strong is He;
> To dead men life is He; to sick men health;
> To blind men sight, and to the needy wealth;
> A pleasure without loss, a treasure without stealth.

The county of Kau, in which this gem has been quarried from the dark caves of depraved humanity, forms the eighth and southern division of this island, and it is the most remote and secluded of all the missionary fields. Not a foreigner lives here, and travelers very seldom pass through, except missionaries. The number that will go to the volcano by this way will undoubtedly be much greater, now that there is a hospitable house where will be afforded the entertainment and help which travelers need, and missionaries know so well how to bestow. The district is thinly peopled, and the inhabitants much dispersed. Mr. Paris is sometimes absent from his family on tours eight and ten days, though never so far away but that he can be summoned, in case of sickness, by a special messenger, and get back in twenty-four or thirty hours.

At Punaluu, which is twelve miles from this by a good horse-path, there is the largest village; and a little stone house has been half built there, in contemplation of its being a missionary station, the probable residence of an associate missionary family, when one shall be granted from the next re-enforcement. It is a pleasant place on the sea-board, in view of romantic hills and recesses inland, and having several lakes of brackish and fresh water, that were dammed up some years ago from the sea by an eruption of lava. It has an atmosphere, also, of remarkable purity; and were it not for the strong trades which generally blow, the difficulty of getting supplies there, and its remoteness from all the rest of the world, it would be a most desirable place for missionary residence and service.

To some, the very objections alleged against it would be circumstances in its favor, as presenting a clearer field to do good in, unopposed by corrupting foreigners, whose influence at these islands has been hitherto so rarely of the right sort that a missionary would, on the whole, much rather be without it. Were I going to labor here for the native race, and allowed to choose my field, it would be on the Island of Molokai, or in some of the secluded districts of Hawaii, the furthest possible from places frequented by foreigners. Those missionaries may, we have thought thus far, be deemed the happiest in their missionary work who have the least to do with any others but Hawaiians.

Not far from this village there is a beach that used to be famous for having stones that propagated their kind. It also supplied the stones for native adzes, before they were acquainted with iron, those which they employed in slinging and playing at *konani*, and the very idol gods themselves that presided over the Hawaiian games. Thus, with a strange, besotted blindness, characteristic of man every where without the Gospel, like that which Isaiah so keenly satirizes in the idolaters of his day, with one stone they made a hatchet to cut down a tree, or dig out a canoe; with others they played at drafts; another they put into slings, and its mate they made into a god and worshiped it. *The residue thereof he maketh a god, even his graven image: he falleth down unto it, and worshipeth it, and prayeth unto it, and saith, Deliver me, for thou art my god.*

Or, if the plastic, god-making material be a tree, it is all the same.—Then shall it be for a man to burn, for he will take thereof and warm himself; yea, he kindleth it, and baketh bread; with part thereof he eateth flesh; he roasteth roast, and is satisfied; yea, he warmeth himself, and saith, Aha, I am warm, I have seen the fire; then he maketh a god, and worshipeth it; he maketh it a graven image, and falleth down thereto. And none considereth in his heart, neither is there knowledge nor understanding to say, I have burned part of it in the fire; yea, also, I have baked bread upon the coals thereof; I have roasted flesh and eaten it, and shall I make the residue thereof an abomination? Shall I fall down to the stock of a tree? He feedeth on ashes; a deceived heart hath turned him aside, that he can not deliver his soul, nor say, Is there not a lie in my right hand?

Ellis, on the authority of the natives, who fully believed in the procreative powers of these stones, says that some powers of discrimination were necessary to discover the stones that would answer to be deified. When selected, they were taken to the *heiau*, and there several ceremonies were performed over them. Afterward, when dressed, and taken to the place where the games were practiced, if the parties to whom they belonged were successful, their fame was established; but if unsuccessful for several times together, they were either broken to pieces or thrown contemptuously away. When any were removed for the purpose of being transformed into gods, a pair of them were wrapped very carefully together in a piece of native cloth, and duly married.

The people of this district no longer believe in these follies or practice these games, and the stone-begetting stones of Ninole are not sought after as they once were. With their idolatry, they have thrown away the most of their foolish superstitions. But the Gospel has not yet greatly bettered the external condition of the mass of them, nor has it taught them industry or thrift. They are, many of them, miserably poor, while the country back is foodful; living in leaky, narrow grass houses, hardly fit for a dog-kennel, or sometimes in caves, and dens, and holes of the earth. From numerous old walls, marking the former divisions of *kihapais* (cultivated plats), and other evidences of extensive cultivation, it has once supported a much larger population than now.

They manufacture here a good deal of the *mama-ka-kapa*, and send it to Hilo and Kona. It is the strongest and most highly prized native cloth, beaten out of the bark of the paper mulberry (*hibiscus*). The numerous specimens sent home by missionaries have made it familiar to almost every one, as well as the process of pounding it out from the inner bark of the tree. They also drive a few hogs and goats eighty miles to Hilo, live there a while, according to Hawaiian custom, upon their *maka-makas* (friends), get some of their cotton cloth in the way of presents, and then return, to have the same friends come in due time to live on them, and take off some of their *kapas* and hogs.

This system of *makana*, as it is called, is very injurious to thrift and enterprise. The missionaries, perhaps, do all they can to break it up; but immemorial usage on Hawaii, and public sentiment, make it very niggardly for a Hawaiian to refuse any thing to his friends, who are very sure to be pretty numerous if a man has considerable *waiwai* (property) on hand.

Few yet dare be so singular as to be called mean, though there is now and then one, and he is the man who is familiarly said to be looking up in the world, and getting forehanded. At sea-ports the value and uses of property are better known, and it is, consequently, somewhat less readily parted with: individuals are more avaricious and less liberal to their friends, and the ancient *regime* is almost abandoned. But here, and at other places inland, it still holds sway, to the no small detriment both of the giver and the *givee*.

I have been not a little amused to hear it adduced

by an old foreigner, in proof that the people were growing worse rather than better, that formerly, whenever a man killed a hog, he used to invite all his friends in to help eat it up; but that now it was otherwise, and, if he could, he sold some of it instead of giving it away. It is quite of a piece with an argument I once heard, to prove that missionaries had spoiled these islands as recruiting-places, because, forsooth, before they came here, a whale-ship could get a barrel of potatoes or a good-sized pig for a few feet of iron hoop: like the admirable inductive argument of the old man quoted by Latimer, to show that Tenterden steeple was the cause of the Goodwin Sands, because Goodwin Sands began to make about the time that Tenterden steeple was erected. Or say, rather, it is like the jocose, after-dinner induction of an eminent English judge, to prove that the cause of the prevalence of Jacobinism was the practice of men's bearing three names, because several leading Jacobins whom he named did actually happen thus to bear the three appellations.

It should be noticed here, that while hospitable and generous enough to their *friends*, Hawaiians are by no means so distinguished for the exercise of these virtues toward those whom they do not recognize as acquaintances. A poor and strange Hawaiian, who is so luckless as to have no *maka-makas* in a place (a thing, to be sure, which does not often happen), may whistle in vain for lodging and food, unless he carry a certificate of being a *hoa-hanau* (Church-member), which, to their credit be it spoken, will seldom fail, as in the primitive ages of the Church, of securing him entertainment from some of the Christian brotherhood

The universal Hawaiian custom is, to go to a friend and beg whatever one wants, and, on the authority of those who best know, it is said no man has a heart to refuse his friends the last *kapa* or *malo* he has in the house, if asked for it. But they begin now to see the impropriety and disadvantage of a custom like this.

When the missionaries, a few years ago, were first making efforts to get the Hilo boarding-school supported by the people, one of them said to his neighbor, "This is just right. There is some meaning in this effort. We make ourselves destitute, it is true, but, then, we are doing good by it. *Not so when we give to friends who come to beg of us.*"

One of the contributors at the same time said, "Put down three dollars to my name. I have a jacket and pantaloons not much worn; perhaps I can get three dollars for them. I will sell them to some one." Another said, "Put down two dollars for me. I have a pair of trowsers, for which, I think, I can get two dollars. If not, I will seek it some other way, and pay in what I can get, to the value of two dollars." Another said he had a pig, and would sell it for his portion; and a poor woman said, "Put down a dollar for me and my husband, and I will braid two hats to get it."

In the same manner they pay nominally for their books; but oftentimes such a dialogue as this ensues between the applicant for a book and the missionary: "I will work for it," says the poor Hawaiian. "But I have no work for you," answers the missionary; "you must pay for it something that will be valuable, or you can not have the book." "I have no money; will you take fish?" "I do not want fish." "Will you take wood?" "I do not want any more wood." "Will you take fowls?" "I have a plenty of fowls." "Will you let it go for *kapas?*" "What can I do with *kapas?*"

The poor applicant knows well enough their uselessness to a missionary; and sometimes, though I would fain hope not often, he looks down, turns about, and walks off sadly, unable to get the book he was after.

One of the missionaries tells me, "Often have I paid in books for work, and other things, merely to get the books among the people, when for cotton cloth I could have procured the same labor and articles for half the price. My custom has been to contrive some means for the people to procure books, while in multitudes of cases the avails were more trouble than profit. And I have often said to a child, go and do such a thing for your book, when I should not care whether the job was done or not, were not the book and the child's improvement by it in question."

This station of Waiohinu is separated from Kealakekua, as we have found, by a day and night's sail in a canoe, or by a rough foot-path inland, traveled only by natives; and it is forty miles from a neighbor on one side, and seventy on the other. Mr. Forbes used often to make flying tours here before 1842; and he had several Church-members in this region. But the mass of the people being far from any post, and but seldom seen by their *kumu* (religious teacher), were exceedingly heathenish and *naaupo*, as they express it, or dark-minded, when Mr. Paris and his wife came

M 2

to take up their abode with them. But their joy was none the less for that, and their simple estimate of their new teacher's love for them, in particular, as evinced in coming so far from America to make his *nohopuana* (dwelling together) with them, was very exaggerated.

The Papists made an onset in Kau about the same time with Mr. Paris, headed by an indefatigable foreign Jesuit; who seemed to think the field fairly his own, and who has steadily disputed every inch of ground with the Protestants by fair means or foul. Pointing to the Protestant missionaries, who pay natives only for work done for themselves, and who have availed themselves, whenever they could, of native aid in building churches and school houses, and their own dwellings, he accused them of oppression and taxing the people; and by gifts of cotton cloth, and, when his stock failed, by liberal promises of more, grounded on the expectation of a brig from France, he attached to himself a good many of the license-loving natives.

By loud words, and threats that the *aupuni* (kingdom) would soon be taken away from the Kaluinas (Calvinists), and that they would soon have no foothold in the land, he engaged others; so that the Catholics for a while made a formidable array, and even in one or two instances proceeded to blows with the Protestants. Whole villages went over to them; and they had the control of more than three hundred children, subjected to a discipline but little better than the old heathenism.

The confident promises of the priests, and their bold declarations, over and over again, that they were to have the kingdom, and that the Protestants should be put out, plainly shows that they were privy to a plan of the French, of taking these islands, only prevented, in the providence of God, by Paulet's taking them for the English. If, now, the re-enforcement of priests and goods do not soon appear, not a few will declare off from the Pope as a prophet of lies. And the providence of God, in averting the calamity of a French possession of these islands, will be as marked as were similar providences in the early history of New England.

There was a deep interest in religion soon after Mr. Paris's arrival here. Indeed, it had commenced some time before; and the minds of the people were greatly moved by the reports brought from Hilo, and Puna, and Kona, of the multitudes that were turning to the *pono* there. Not a few Kau men, who went there to see for themselves, were converted, and came back exciting the people with accounts of what they had seen and heard; so that Mr. Paris very soon found himself, with his slender knowledge of the language, in the midst of a powerful religious excitement, and multitudes pressing into the Church. It will not be strange if many shall prove to have been received who are unworthy members, although, so far, most of them have run well. Some of the scenes to which they were ushered very soon after arriving here in 1842, as we have heard them reviewed in conversation, must have been highly amusing, others deeply interesting.

When they landed, ten miles from the station, at least one hundred and fifty different natives took their goods, and of them all, in so many hands, after the lapse of four weeks, not the smallest article was found missing. For several weeks, at every meal-time, the all but naked natives would form a line a long ways from the door of their grass house, to see them eat, and would express the greatest wonder at seeing them laugh and talk so cheerfully while at meals.

The necessary absence of the pastor at general meeting, and the engrossment of his time for most of a year in building, have proved religiously disastrous. But few, at present, are seeking earnestly the *pono;* the love of many waxes cold, and some are falling into sin, for which they will have to be cut off. The Church numbers one thousand and twenty-four, of whom eight hundred and forty-five were received on examination in one year. The Sabbath congregation is now about eight hundred; the Sabbath school at the station, about two hundred and fifty. The population of the entire district is not far from five thousand.

It is now the time of reaction and stupidity, and the pastor begins to be greatly tried (as all on Hawaii have been, and as Paul was with his Corinthian converts) with cases of *hihia*, or persons in the Church who have got entangled, and done things worthy of censure and discipline. The people, being unstable, and addicted to falsehood and deception, as it is one universal testimony of missionaries every where that heathen are wont to be, where so many are admitted, some plainly proving unworthy; the lines of discipline also being drawn tighter than in the churches at home; habits allowed there, such, for instance, as smoking, being here generally visited with discipline; the number of Church-members under the pastoral care of one man being much greater than in the churches at home, where also the pastor's responsibility is shared by a company of deacons and elders more than here: for all these reasons, the care and discipline of a church in Hawaii nei are very heavy and trying, if faithfully attended to.

Cases are continually coming up that greatly perplex the mind and try the feelings and patience of a man that loves souls. Besides some cases, as usual, of the prevalent sin of the land, there has been one instance recently in this church, in a woman, of the old heathenish act of knocking out teeth (*kui niho*). They do it at the death of a friend. Two lovers sometimes knock out the same tooth as a pledge; and there are few persons over forty who are not disfigured by the loss of one or more.

There is also another case, which, as giving some insight into the management of missionaries, and the difficulties they have to contend with, I will detail. A hitherto blameless member of the Church, by the name of Ziba, having lost his wife by divorce, became infatuated lately with an ungodly woman, whom he said he must marry, even if it were his death. He was labored with in private and before the deacons of the Church, and would weep when talked to; but could not give up the purpose of marrying the woman. There being no legal objection (and, having seen the woman, we can not help commending his good taste for personal beauty), he procured a certificate for marriage from the *lunakanawai* (magistrate); but his pastor, it seems, could not conscientiously marry him, his former wife still living, and warned him, therefore, against getting entangled with the woman he loved.

He immediately, in consequence, became an object of suspicion to the *makai*, or native constables, among whose duties is that of looking out for offenses, with a share in the fine of those found out. Ziba, finding himself thus watched, and catching, one night, a man prying about his premises, demanded his name, held him fast, and made an alarm, till his friends brought a light, and he found it was a constable. The next day he was summoned to a *hokolokolo*, as it is called, an investigation before the *lunakanawai*, and fined for insulting an officer.

Mr. Paris had to interpose, lest the man should receive gross injustice.* Thus it comes to pass, in some

* The religion, morals, civilization, and the administration of justice among the people of Kau, have greatly improved within a few years. As late as June, 1849, the missionary writes from there concerning a Temperance Celebration of the Protestant Schools, just before a visit from the King, that the whole number present, including parents, children, and friends, amounted to nineteen hundred or two thousand persons. "It was a delightful day, and we had the stillest and most orderly feast, for so many children, that I have ever witnessed. The children were also all clothed neatly, most of them in uniform. I could not but think how differently these children appeared, with their bright and happy faces, from what they and others did eight years ago, when I first came among them. Then there was scarcely a child in Kau who had a shirt, or any other article of clothing of foreign manufacture, and many of them were more destitute of covering than the beasts of the field.

"When all had feasted and spent a little time in pleasant, social intercourse, we were marched to the house of God, where we had several short but very appropriate addresses on the subject of temperance. These were accompanied with temperance songs and instrumental music; after which we closed with prayer.

cases, if a man is censured in the Church, the officers proceed to get him before the courts, and if a man is fined or punished for any thing before the *lunakanawai*, the *hoahanau* are wont to think he must be disciplined also by the Church. The poor Hawaiian thus gets hung on both horns of a dilemma; or if he navigate clear of Charybdis, he is by no means sure of saving shipwreck on the rocks of Scylla.

"On the Sabbath following the King addressed our Sabbath school, and was followed by appropriate addresses from Dr. Judd, and Mr. Cooke, formerly a native of Tahiti, the King's chaplain. To-day the King has attended a meeting of the people of this district. The assembly was held in a beautiful grove. His Majesty made a speech of about an hour, which was listened to with the deepest interest. He alluded to the sovereign love of God in sending the blessed Gospel to his fathers; to his providential care of himself and his subjects in past years; and he referred to this Gospel, as preached by the Protestant missionaries, as the source of all their blessings and privileges, and the only foundation and safeguard of their civil and religious liberties. His appropriate and deeply interesting address was followed by others from his ministers."—***Miss.*** *Herald,* ***March,*** 1850.

CHAPTER XIV.

EXPLORATION AND REVIEW OF THE VOLCANIC CRATER KILAUEA.

AN upland isle, by molten streams embraced,
It tower'd to heaven amid a lava waste;
Below, impenetrable woods display'd
Depths of mysterious solitude and shade:
Above, with adamantine bulwarks crown'd,
Primeval rocks in hoary masses frown'd:
By noon a dusky cloud appear'd to rise,
But blazed, a beacon, through nocturnal skies.
As Ætna, view'd from ocean far away,
Slumbers in blue revolving smoke by day,
Till darkness, with terrific splendor, shows
The eternal fires that crest the eternal snows;
So high it rose, so bright the mountain shone,
It seem'd the footstool of Jehovah's throne.

World Before the Flood.

IF a man come for the first time to the eastern part of Hawaii by the way of the volcano of Kilauea, his brain, and body too, will have gotten such an impress from its tremendous fires, and his imagination will be so engrossed with the novel and stupendous displays of nature which his eyes have been beholding, that it will be some days before he can think or talk of any thing else. It will not be strange if he visit it again in dreams, and stand upon the blackened brink of that stupendous crater, and descend once more, in his sleep, into that great pit of fire,

Whose combustible and fuel'd entrails,
Sublimed with mineral fury, aid the winds,
And leave a sing'd bottom, all involved
With sulphurous stench and smoke.

I have found myself thus exercised ever since arriving at Hilo, at the close of last week, and, though suffering sorely with feverishness and general *mauvaise*, induced by exposure, fatigue, and excitement, I am anxious to record first observations before their vividness and zest shall have at all abated.

We left Waiohinu the first Tuesday of the year, Mr. Paris having anticipated his quarterly communion by one week, so bringing the sacrament and monthly concert on two successive days, in order to accompany me and make the tour of that part of his field at the same time. Through the favor of Providence, we had fine weather, although it rained early in the morning, and threatened a storm.

The horseback ride, and the more favorable climate of the sea-side and Punaluu, soon proved invigorating, and restored, in a measure, the tone of languid nature. The path from that village goes up very gradually to the volcano, distant from Waiohinu about fifty-five miles, of which we went the first day about thirty, stopping that night in a little mountain hamlet, at the house of a Church-member of the name of Jakobo.

Arriving there before our men, we went down into a valley that serves, in rains, for a tumbling water-course, and, after refreshing ourselves with a bath, we kneeled upon the rocks at even-tide in prayer to that overruling and wise Providence, who, leading us in a way that we knew not, had strangely brought together, in this volcanic heart of the Pacific, two quondam class-mates in the School of the Prophets. Returning, we found the natives of the village assembled for a meeting. Their pastor read the Scriptures, prayed and sang hymns, and addressed them at some length on their duties and the way of salvation. It was a pleasant meeting, in the open, still air of evening; Mauna Loa towering up to the northwest, the evening star pouring down its mellow radiance, the blue abyss of ocean faintly visible in the distance below us, and the illuminated cloud of the volcano just beginning to reflect its beams.

Sleep scarcely visited me for the night, but an early departure next morning, and the fresh mountain air, revived the spirits. Our ride was, for a long time, through banana-trees, *ohias*, *ko-us*, and a species of mimosa, until we came to an immense field of smooth, flat, unbroken lava, called by the Hawaiians *Pahoehoe.* It was once evidently a great upland lake of mineral fire, seeming to have been suddenly congealed into a vitreous black rock, while its billows were still rolling, as if it had suddenly heard the voice of God—

Here shall thy billows stiffen, and have rest.

Not only are the large swells and hollows distinctly marked, but in many places it is to be observed that the surface of the great waves is ruffled by a ripple like that seen on the ocean in a calm, at the first springing up of a light breeze. There are interspersed a few tracts of volcanic sand, shining with crystals of olivine, pyroxene, and obsidian.* And the furrows

* Milner, in The Gallery of Nature, says that lava is chiefly composed of the two minerals feldspar and augite, with titaniferous iron. When the feldspar predominates, light-colored lavas are the result, called feldspatnic or trachytic; but when the augite is in excess, dark varieties, augitic or basaltic lavas, are produced. Other simple minerals occur, but in very inconsiderable proportions. (Humboldt says that he found five metals among the products of existing volcanoes—iron, copper, lead, arsenic, and selenium, in the crater of one volcano.) Besides varying in chemical composition, the character of lava is greatly modified by the circumstances under which it is cooled down, compact rock resulting from cooling under pressure, but a porous, fibrous, and light material being produced when cooled with the sole weight of the atmosphere upon it. If we suppose a current of matter of the consistency of honey, we shall have a tolerably correct picture of a stream of lava, which, as it moves over a district, is not thinned, but walled at the sides, and, a crust soon forming upon the surface, tends still more to prevent it spreading out laterally. Hence it is sometimes possible, when the ground favors the attempt, to deflect one of these fiery floods from its course by attacking the sides, and removing the crust, which has succeeded in turning it away from towns that have been threatened by it. In one instance the inhabitants of Catania assailed a lava current in this way, to divert it from their city, when the people of another locality, who were placed in jeopardy, took up arms to resist the operation.

Lava rapidly cools externally, but the crust formed being a bad conductor of heat, the interior of the mass remains hot, semi-fluid, and moves on after the surface has solidified. The stream thrown out of Ætna in 1819 was in motion, at the rate of a yard per day, nine months after the eruption; and another from the same mountain is stated not to have become completely consolidated and at rest ten years after its emission. Dr. Daubeny states, speaking of temperature, that some days after ejection lava has raised the thermometer from fifty-nine to ninety-five degrees at the distance of twelve feet, while three feet off the heat greatly exceeded that of boiling water; that it has rendered a mass of lead fluid in four minutes, when the same mass, placed on red-hot iron, would have required double that time to enter into fusion; and that even stones have been melted when thrown into the lavas of Ætna and Vesuvius.

Obsidian, another volcanic product, is a black, glassy lava, containing a large proportion of silica, named, according to Pliny, after its between the swells and petrified waves are filled with the same, or with a light spumous lava, like the froth of the sea drifted by the wind.

Across this fire-frozen sea, like a vast Alpine glacier, there runs a high, ragged ridge, burst up and broken, no one can tell how, till it is jagged as a mill-saw, which you can no more get over, or get round it, than you can scale one of those high walls which are sometimes to be seen at fortified places and elsewhere, thickly planted and bristling all over with sharp pieces of junk bottle. Being ahead of our guides, we lost our way there, and wandered some time in that

> Dreary plain, forlorn and wild,
> The seat of desolation,

like that which offered rest to Satan's feet,

> From off the tossing of the fiery waves.

Once we came suddenly upon a tall, oven-like cone, so much like a sentry-box, that, with Milton's description in mind of the place

> Eternal Justice has prepared for those rebellious,

you might almost look to see some sentinel fiend come out from it, and hail you gruffly, "Who goes there?"

At length, by retracing all our steps, we got out of this dreary domain into the traveled tract, and made for the volcano, whose sulphurous smoke and stench

---

first observer, Obsidius. Scoriæ, cinders, ashes, and stones are identical, in mineral composition, with the lava currents, and are portions of them, abstracted while yet in the fiery funnel, and shot upward by the explosive energies in operation.

we now began to perceive driven along by the trade wind, and to see the vitreous threads of Pele's hair, caught in crevices and cobwebs, and shining in the sun with a metallic lustre. As you proceed, the lava is more decomposed, and the ground cracked and rent into fissures and chasms, from which there is issuing steam and vapor of smoke, and you seem to be in a region of lime-kilns or smelting-furnaces. A mile or two further on you descend two or three hundred feet, on to a vast terrace-like, sunken plain, rent here and there by earthquakes, and strewed with great boulders of lava, and sounding unsafe and hollow under the tramp of your horse, who begins to show his consciousness of a dangerous proximity to the great laboratory of nature, to which this is the vast outer court and hall of entrance.

By the time you reach the skirts of this sunken plain you begin to get an idea of the unique Hawaiian volcano; not like the pictures we have of other volcanoes, the truncated top of a mountain with a broad base and furrowed sides made by the overflow and hardening of its lava, and its summit distinguishable at a distance as the raised brim of a mighty caldron, but an immense gaping chasm, or hideous fire-eaten pit, variously estimated from nine to fifteen hundred feet deep, and from nine to fifteen miles in circumference.

The scientific Pole, Count Strezelecki, thus roughly sketched the results of his observations for a friend, in the Hawaiian Spectator: "What I remember, and long shall recollect, as showing the mighty influence of mighty objects upon me, are the difficulties I had to struggle with before my eye could be torn away from the idle, vacant, but ecstatic gazing with which I regarded the great WHOLE, down to the analytical part of the wondrous and unparalleled scene before me—I say unparalleled, because, having visited most of the European and American volcanoes, I find the greatest of them inferior to Kilauea in intensity, grandeur, and extent or area.

"The abrupt and precipitous cliff which forms the north-northeast wall of the crater, found, after my repeated observations, to be elevated four thousand one hundred and four feet above the level of the sea, overhangs an area of three million one hundred and fifty thousand square yards of half-cooled scoria, sunk to the depth of three hundred yards, and containing more than three hundred and twenty-eight thousand square yards of convulsed torrents of earths in igneous fusion, and gaseous fluids constantly effervescing, boiling, spouting, rolling in all directions like waves of a disturbed sea, violently beating the edge of the caldrons like an infuriated surf, and, like surf, spreading all around its spray in the form of capillary glass, which fills the air, and adheres in a flaky and pendulous form to the distorted and broken masses of the lava all around; five caldrons, each of about five thousand seven hundred square yards, almost at the level of the great area, and containing only the twelfth part of the red liquid.

"The sixth caldron is encircled by a wall of accumulated scoria of fifty yards high, forming the south-southwest point; the *Hale mau mau*, to which the bones of the former high chiefs were consigned, the

Walls of the Crater of Kilauea.

sacrifices to the goddess Pele offered, the abyss of abysses, the caldron of caldrons, exhibiting the most frightful area of three hundred thousand square yards of bubbling red-hot lava, changing incessantly its level, sometimes rolling the long, curled waves with broken masses of cooled crust to one side of the horrible laboratory; sometimes, as if they had made a mistake, turning them back with spouting fury, and a subterraneous, terrific noise, of a sound more infernal and earthly. Around are blocks of lava, scoria, slags of every description and combination, here elevated, by the endless number of superimposed layers, in perpendicular walls one thousand feet high; there torn asunder, cracked, or remolded; every where terror, convulsion—mighty engine of nature—nothingness of man!"

The traveler does not at once behold the living volcanic fires and boiling caldron, but the sudden view of the blackened perpendicular sides of such a vast abyss, steaming and smoking at a million pores, and glimmering all over like a bed of live coals—the playground of primeval fire and earthquakes—fills one with amazement and awe at the vast force and intensity of those inward fires, that first uplifted and then fused such a stupendous mass of rocky materials, and after spouting over, and letting off, by its great subterranean sluice-ways, floods of mineral blood, has kept supplied with fuel, from age to age, its glowing furnaces. *Great and marvelous are thy works, Lord God Almighty! Who shall not fear thee, and glorify thy name? He looketh upon the earth, and it trembleth; he toucheth the hills, and they smoke. They melt like wax at the presence of the Lord, at the presence of the Lord of the whole earth. Let all the nations say unto God, How terrible art thou in thy works!*

No susceptible mind, though but in a low degree religious, can survey such a scene without his thoughts involuntarily turning to the great Author of Nature with adoration and awe, from the new illustration of the divine attribute of Omnipotence thence derived; and if familiar with the language of Young, in view of the same dread attribute, he will be likely to think, if not to say, with him,

Oh Thou! whose balance does the mountains weigh,
Whose will the wild tumultuous seas obey;
Whose breath can turn those watery worlds to flame,
That flame to tempest, and that tempest tame;
Earth's meanest son, all trembling, prostrate falls,
And on thy boundless power and mercy calls.
Canst thou not shake the centre? THEN, CONTROL,
SUBDUE BY GRACE THE REBEL IN MY SOUL!

It was about four o'clock in the afternoon that we arrived near the brink of this mighty crater of Kilauea, at a place near the northwest end, where our screen was to be erected for the night. It being too late to explore the abyss that day, and our natives not yet having come up with food and baggage, we went to visit a sulphur bank a few hundred yards from the crater, out of which sulphureous vapor was issuing by various crevices, so hot in some places as instantly to scald the hand. It is one hundred and fifty to two hundred yards long, forty wide, and thirty or forty feet high.

The mound seems to have been originally lava, now

decomposed by the powerful action of hot sulphureous gases, and made into a material not inappropriately called by the natives *Kukaepele*, or Pele's excrements, hardened into a red crust at top, but moist underneath, and all interlaid with shining crystals of sulphur, which you will hear curiously crepitate and rustle, whenever the outside is broken and the external air let in.

This mound can be ascended and traveled over its entire length, only that it is very hot and enveloped in mineral vapors, and will shake sometimes rather alarmingly under the feet, like a patch of tenacious clay in spring from which the frost is coming out. There are apertures all along its sides, whose edges are fringed with the finest crystals of a delicate yellow color, but so fragile and soft that a touch will crush them. At a few feet from the apertures the crust has somewhat hardened and cooled, and you may dig out with a staff some of the most beautiful specimens of crystallized sulphur that can be found the world over. They are of an orange yellow, in the form of acicular prisms and tetrahedral pyramids, attached on one side as a bed to embossed cakes of joint mud and sulphur, that sparkle like any thing powdered or fretted with gold.

The grief of a traveler is, that he can so rarely carry away whole and safe any of these exquisite specimens. In packing or transporting, the crystals will almost inevitably get detached from their nidus, and after all his pains he will find some of his best specimens spoiled. Detached crystals can be collected by the peck, if one will have patience to gather them.

On one side of the mound is a ravine to which you can see no bottom, it being probably as deep as the volcanic abyss into which you look,

> Through caverns measureless to man,
> Down to a sunless sea.

The trees and shrubs that grow on its sides as far down as you can look are completely whitened, and, in some cases, even crystallized over with sulphur. The genial heat and incessant condensation of steam there constitute a natural hot-house for those species of vegetation that can bear it. The entire hill, and region of inflammable matter under it, forms undoubtedly one of the great reservoirs from which the volcano is fed,

> With ever-burning sulphur unconsumed.

It makes one think of that hill told of in Paradise Lost, in which the fallen spirits opened a spacious wound and digged out ribs of gold to make Pandemonium of.

> There stood a hill not far, whose grisly top
> Belch'd fire and rolling smoke; the rest entire
> Shone with a glossy scurf; undoubted sign
> That in his womb was hid metallic ore,
> The work of sulphur. Thither, wing'd with speed,
> A numerous brigade hasten'd; as when bands
> Of pioneers, with spade and pickax arm'd,
> Forerun the royal camp, to trench a field
> Or cast a rampart. Mammon led them on.
> * * * * Soon had his crew
> Open'd into the hill a spacious wound,
> And digg'd out ribs of gold.

Undermined as it constantly must be by the subduction of fuel for the volcano, and shaken by earthquakes, it will not be strange if this hill, and the entire sunken plain on which visitors encamp, shall some day slide off into the abyss. The rock there, in some places on the surface, shows a heat of one hundred and twenty degrees Fahrenheit, and travelers have often slept within a foot of a fissure from which steam was escaping hot enough to cook their potatoes. Such seams are numerous and wide, extending undoubtedly down to the igneous bed in which the whole tract has its slippery foundation, like a vast iceberg in the sea.

It is from steam escaping at these chasms, and immediately condensed by the cold mountain air, and falling by drops into hollows on the leeward, that the region is providentially supplied with water. The pools so formed on the compact lava are six or eight feet from the seams, surrounded with moss and rushes, and furnishing a copious supply of distilled water for man and beast. When the wind is strong, and especially mornings and evenings, this vapor is flying like scud over the brink of the crater, as a drizzling rain.

By the time of our return to the crater's brink, some of our party of natives, and other stragglers from both the Hilo and Kau side, had arrived singly and with their hogs, at the common encamping ground. The lurid fires of the caldron in the southwestern part of the crater began to be visible, looking just as any one who has seen molten ore in a foundery or smelting furnace, may imagine great liquid masses of that would look in the night, tossed to and fro on an ocean, and rising up and down in a mass, without losing its red heat or viscidity.

Night and the drizzling vapor having overtaken us before our tired natives could make any thing better, we had to nestle altogether under a screen or "*Lean-to*" of cane and brakes, thrown up against the wind, but open in front and looking toward the caldron. It was only a few feet from the precipice, so that by lifting one's self up from the reclining posture you could have in full view

The fearful tossing of those fiery waves.

Natives and hogs having, it is probable, stopped under the same screen before, we found the *ukulele* tribe so numerous and rapacious that it was impossible to sleep. They would make their biting onsets in such numbers, and with such desperate fury, that a man could hardly help screaming out with very anguish. If, while our assailants took breath, we dozed a moment, it was only to be awakened by a more fell gripe from these pitiless robbers of your rest, that were no more to be shaken off or got rid of than Hercules's poisoned robe. At length finding, as the proverb goes, what can't be cured must be endured, we fell to making merry with our torment and our tormentors, and to shaking our flea-bitten sides with woebegone bursts of laughter at each other's jokes. And we concluded, not without reason, that the remembrance of Pele's *fleas* would be quite as indelible as that of her *fires.*

After much wearisome tossing and rolling, getting up and lying down, viewing now the salient jets and coruscations, and beautiful fire-works of the volcano, and now the placid moon and stars, I managed, with aching, flea-flayed fingers, to put together grass for a fire. It was so cold that ice had formed on a calabash that lay outside our screen. Our natives being wakened from sleep, which the *ukulele* did not care to harass when they had better blood for game, we soon dispatched breakfast and other duties.

After a morning hymn, and prayer by one of Mr. Paris's deacons that accompanied us as a body-guard, we made ready to descend into the hideous pit, saying to one another as we went down,

> Facilis est descensus Averni:
> Sed revocare gradus, superasque ad auras evadere,
> Hoc opus, hic labor est.

So sang the Mantuan bard of Æneas's fabulous descent into the realms of Tartarus. The ancients never knew of the easy opening into Hades by this crater of Kilauea, or bold men would have oftener tried the passage, and Empedocles need not have leaped into Ætna.

Let a man only have a good stout pole to put before him and lean upon, and a descent may be accomplished with tolerable ease by the northeastern cliff of the crater, where the side has fallen in and slidden downward, leaving a number of huge, outjutting rocks, like giants' stepping-stones, or the courses of the pyramid of Ghizeh.

By hanging to these, and the mere aid of a pole, you may descend the first *pali* (precipice) to where the avalanche brought up and was stayed—a wild region, broken into abrupt hills and deep glens, thickly set with shrubs and old ohias, and producing in great abundance the *ohelo* (Hawaiian whortleberry, formerly sacred to the goddess of the volcano), and a beautiful lustrous-black berry that grows on a branching vine close to the ground. Thousands of birds find there a safe and warm retreat; and they will continue, I suppose, the innocent warblers, to pair and sing there, till the fires from beneath, having once more eaten through its foundations, the entire tract, with all its miniature mountains and woody glens, shall slide off suddenly into the abyss below to feed the hunger of all-devouring fire.

No one who passes over it, and looks back upon the tall, jagged cliffs at the rear and side, can doubt that it was severed and shattered by one such ruin into its present forms. And the bottomless pits and yawning caverns, in some places ejecting hot steam, with which it is traversed, prove that the raging element which once sapped its foundations is still busy beneath.

The path that winds over and down through this tract, crossing some of these unsightly seams by a natural bridge of only a foot's breadth, is safe enough by daylight, if one will keep in it. But be careful that you do not diverge far on either side, or let the shades of night overtake you there, lest a single misstep in the grass and ferns, concealing some horrible hole, or an accidental stumble, shall plunge you beyond the reach of sunlight into a covered penstock of mineral fire, or into the heart of some deep, sunken cavern.

One can hardly wander through that place alone, even in the daytime (as I was in coming up from the crater at evening), without having his fancy swarm with forms of evil. In spite of himself, there will

"Throng thick into his mind the busy shapes
Of cover'd pits, unfathomably deep,
A dire descent! of precipices huge—
Rocks, caves, lakes, fens, bogs, dens, and shades of death."

The way through this tract descends not abruptly for about half a mile, to a steep bank of partially decomposed lava, somewhat furrowed by water-courses, by which you go down some hundreds of feet more to what every body calls the Black Ledge.

This is an immense rampart or gallery of grisly black scoria and lava, about half a mile wide, running all round the pit, slightly sloping inward, and not unfrequently overflowed in eruptions. By it you learn the dimensions of the great lake to which this is now the shore. It may be compared to the wide beach of an ocean, seldom flooded all over except in very high tides; or to a great field of thick shore ice, from under which the tide has retired, leaving it cracked and rent, but not so as to break up the general evenness of its surface.

The upper crust is generally glossy, cellular, and cinder-like, brittle and crackling under the feet; but directly underneath the superficies, hard and compact, as proved by inspecting the great seams and fissures, from some of which flickering currents of hot air, and from others scalding steam and smoke are continually issuing. Pound on it, and you will hear deep, hollow reverberations, and sometimes your pole will break through a place like the rotten trap-door of some old ruin, and open upon you a hideous black hole without bottom.

Over this great volcanic mole or offset, we proceeded to make our way toward the caldron in the south-east, pounding before us with our pole, like men crossing a river to find whether the ice ahead will bear them. We stopped every now and then to examine and get up on to some great cone or oven, which had been formed after the congelation of the crust, by pent-up gas blowing out from beneath the cooling lava, raising it as in great bubbles, and letting its black, viscous vomit dribble from the top, and flow down sluggishly and congeal before it had found a level, like ice in very cold weather over a waterfall. Thus it would flow over the Black Ledge, hardening sometimes in round streams like a cable, or in serpentine forms like a great anaconda; and again it would spread out from the foot of the cone a little ways in forms like a bronze lion's foot.

The surface was frequently broken, or ready to break, with the weight of one's body, from the fiery liquid having subsided after the petrifaction of the crust. Generally, too, the hardened lava seemed to have been flowed over, like ice near the shore when the tide rises and goes down, with a thin scum of lava that became shelly and crepitated under the foot like shelly ice.

Then, as we went further into the bed of the crater, gradually going down, we would come to places where, like as in frozen mill-ponds, whence the water has been drawn off, the congealed lava had broken in to the depth sometimes of fifty and one hundred feet. Every where, too, there were great fissures and cracks, as in fields of river ice, now and then a large air-hole, and here and there great bulges and breaks, and places from which a thin flame would be curling, or over which you would see a glimmer like that which trembles over a body of fresh coals or a recently-burned lime-kiln. Touch your stick there, and it would immediately kindle.

There were also deep, wide ditches, through which a stream of liquid lava had flowed since the petrifaction of the main body through which it passed. Cascades of fire are said to be often seen in the course of these canals or rivers as they leap some precipice, presenting in the night a scene of unequaled splendor and sublimity. In some places the banks or dikes of these rivers are excavated and fallen in with hideous crash and ruin; and often you may go up, if you dare, to the edge on one side and look over into the gulf, and away under the opposite overhanging bank, where the igneous fluid has worn away and scooped it out till the cliff hangs on air, and seems to topple and lean like the tower of Pisa, just ready to fall.

It would be no very comfortable reflection, if a man were not too curiously eager and bold, and intent upon the novelties he is drinking in by the senses, to have much reflection or fear at such a time, to think how easily an earthquake might tumble down the bank on which he is standing, undermined in like manner with that which you are looking at right opposite.

On our left, as we passed on to the Great Caldron, we explored, as far as was possible between the heat and vapor, the great bank, or, more properly, mountain-side of sulphur and sulphate of lime (plaster of Paris), and obtained some specimens of no little beauty. There are cliffs of sulphur through which scalding hot vapor is escaping as high up above you as eight hundred feet; and lower down there are seams from which lambent and flickering flames are darting, and jets of hot air will sometimes whirl by you, involving no little danger by their inhalation. Around these fissures are yellow and green incrustations of sulphur, which afford a new variety of specimens.

When we had got to the leeward of the caldron, we found large quantities of the finest threads of metallic vitrified lava, like the spears and filaments of sealing-wax, called Pele's hair. The wind has caught them from the jets and bubbling springs of gory lava, and carried them away on its wings till they have lodged in nests and crevices, where they may be collected like shed wool about the time of sheep-shearing. Sometimes this is found twenty miles to the leeward of the volcano.

The heat and sulphur gas, irritating the throat and lungs, are so great on that side, that we had to sheer away off from the brim of the caldron, and could not observe close at hand the part where there was the most gushing and bubbling of the ignifluous mineral fluid. But we passed round to the windward, and were thus enabled to get up to the brim so as to look over for a minute into the molten lake, burning incessantly with brimstone and fire—

> "A furnace formidable, deep, and wide,
> O'erboiling with a mad, sulphureous tide."

But the lava which forms your precarious foothold, melted, perhaps, a hundred times, can not be handled or trusted, and the heat even there is so great as to burn the skin of one's face, although the heated air, as it rises, is instantly swept off to the leeward by the wind. It is always hazardous, not to say fool-hardy, to stand there for a moment, lest your uncertain foot-hold, crumbling and crispy by the action of fire, shall suddenly give way and throw you instantly into the fiery embrace of death.

At times, too, the caldron is so furiously boiling, and splashing, and spitting its fires, and casting up its salient, angry jets of melted lava and spume, that all approach to it is forbidden. We slumped several times near it, as a man will in the spring who is walking over a river of which the ice is beginning to thaw, and the upper stratum, made of frozen snow, is dissolved and rotten. A wary native who accompanied us wondered at our daring, and would not be kept once from pulling me back, as with the eager and bold curiosity of a discoverer, all absorbed in the view of such exciting wonders, I was getting too near.

At the time we viewed it, the brim all round was covered with splashes and spray to the width of ten or twelve feet. The surface of the lake was about a mile in its longest diameter, at a depth of thirty or forty feet from its brim, and agitated more or less all over, in some places throwing up great jets and spouts of fiery red lava, in other places spitting it out like steam from an escape-pipe when the valves are half lifted, and again squirting the molten rock as from a pop-gun.

The surface was like a river or lake when the ice is *going out* and broken up into cakes, over which you will sometimes see the water running, and sometimes it will be quite hidden. In the same manner in this lake of fire, while its surface was generally covered with a crust of half-congealed, dusky lava, and raised into elevations, or sunk into depressions, you would now and then see the live coal-red stream running along. Two cakes of lava, also, would meet like cakes of ice, and their edges crushing, would pile up and fall over precisely like the phenomena of moving fields of ice; there was, too, the same rustling, grinding noise.

Sometimes, I am told, the roar of the fiery surges is like the heavy beating of surf. Once, when Mr. Coan visited it, this caldron was heaped up in the middle, higher above its brim than his head, so that he ran up and thrust in a pyrometer, while streams were running off on different sides. At another time when he saw it, it had sunk four or five hundred feet below its brim, and he had to look down a dreadful gulf to see its fires.

Again, when Mr. Bingham was there, it was full, and concentric waves were flowing out and around from its centre. Having carefully observed its movements a while, he threw a stick of wood upon the thin crust of a moving wave where he thought it would bear him, even if it should bend a little, and then stood upon it a few moments. In that position, thrusting his cane down through the cooling tough crust, about half an inch thick, and immediately withdrawing it, forthwith there gushed up, like ooze in a marsh or melted tar under a plank, enough of the viscid lava to form a globular mass, which afterward, as it cooled, he broke off and bore away.

It is not easy for one that has not himself been in

a similar position, to sympathize with and pardon the traveler at such a point, for he is unwilling to forbear and leave it till fairly surfeited and seared with heat and admiration, or driven off by some sudden spout and roar, or splash of the caldron. You gaze, and gaze, and gaze in amazement, without conscious thought, like a man in a trance, reluctant to go away, and you want to spend at least a day and night, viewing close at hand its ever-varying phenomena.

Had we only brought with us wrappers, I believe we should have been the first to have slept on the Black Ledge. Now that the edge of curiosity is a little blunted and the judgment cool, we can see that there would be a degree of hazard and temerity in it which is not felt under the excitement of novelty and in the full tide of discovery. Forced by startling admonitions of instant danger, I had to quit suddenly the precarious footing I had gained on the caldron's edge, like a hungry man hurried from his repast ere he has snatched a mouthful. But the look I caught there, and the impression of horror, awfulness, and sublimity thence obtained, live and will live in my conscious being forever and ever; and it is this shall help me utter what many have experienced, and have wished to say before the poet said it for them:

> One compact hour of crowded life
> Is worth an age without a name.

A moment of being under such circumstances is an epoch in the history of one's mind; and he, perhaps, may be deemed the most highly favored of mortals who has the most of such epochs in remembrance, provided only that the incommunicable thoughts and emotions which, in the moment of that experience, seemed to permeate the very substance of the mind, have given it a moral tone and impulse running through all its subsequent life. It is thus that thoughts are waked "to perish never," being instamped ineffaceably upon the spiritual frame-work and foundation stones of the soul, dignifying and consecrating them to noble uses.

It was not, I trust, without some valuable additions to our stock of impressions in this line, that we reluctantly left that spot. Departing thence, we passed over a tract between the level of the brim of the caldron and the Black Ledge, in order to gain again the latter, most strangely rugged and wild, as if convulsion after convulsion had upheaved, and sunk, and rent, and piled the vast mineral and rocky masses; forming here great hills like the ruins of a hundred towers, and there deep indentations, while every block lay upon its fellow, ready to be dislodged, edgewise, crosswise, endwise, sidewise, angle-wise, and every wise, in the wildest confusion and variety possible, as if Typhœan giants had been hurling them at each other in war; or as when the warring angels

> From their foundations loosening to and fro,
> Uptore the seated hills, with all their load,
> And sent them thundering upon their adversaries.
> Then hills amid the air encounter'd hills,
> Hurled to and fro with jaculation dire :
> Horrid confusion heap'd upon confusion rose.

Rocks, too, in earthquake commotions, have been started from the perpendicular sides of the crater in this part, and have rolled down eight hundred or a thousand feet with a force, one might think, that would almost shake the world.

When we had thus encompassed the crater, and had returned to the point where we first came down upon the Black Ledge, it was getting toward night, and I found myself so excessively heated and feverish, and throbbing with the headache, which most persons there suffer from, as to be unable to go for the castellated and Gothic specimens into some ovens that are found in the sides near by.

Leaving, therefore, my companion and the natives to hunt for them, I proceeded slowly back, and toiled up, with difficulty, the steep side of this stupendous crater, which may be set down at a moderate calculation as not less than twelve miles in circumference, and one thousand feet deep. In the centre of this vast sunken amphitheatre of volcanic fire,

> "A dungeon horrible on all sides round,
> As one great furnace flaming,"

a man looks up to heaven, and to the seared walls of this great prison, and feels like a pigmy, or the veriest insect, in contrast with so mighty and terrible a work of the Lord God Almighty.

The person who can go down into it, and come up safe from it, with a light mind, unthankful and unawed, is as wanting in some of the best attributes of mental manhood as of piety; and, let me say with Cowper,

> I would not enter on my list of friends,
> Though graced with polish'd manners and fine sense,

the man who should prove himself so brutishly insensible to the sublime vestiges of Divine power, and to the providential care of Divine goodness.

Our second night by the volcano was one of rather more ease and comfort than the first, a screen having been erected for us in a new spot, beyond the domain of imported fleas. I slept a little at intervals, just raising myself at every awakening to look at Pele's fires, which spouted and played like fountains, and leaped suddenly with a flash from place to place, like electricity on wire in the experiments of the lecture-room.

Once when I arose at midnight and went out a little beyond the range of our screen, to enjoy in silence the august and grand spectacle, the violence of the wind was such as to take off my unguarded hat, and carry it clear over the brink of the crater, where it lodged for the night, but was recovered with little injury in the morning by one of our courageous natives.

One of the early visitors there said that, on coming near the rim, he fell upon his hands and knees awe-struck, and crept cautiously to the rocky brink, unwilling at once to walk up to the giddy verge and look down as from a mast-head upon the fiery gulf at his feet. In a little time, however, like a landsman after a while at sea, he was able to stand very near and gaze unalarmed upon this wonder of the world.

I have myself known seamen that had faced unfearingly all the perils of the deep, and had rushed boldly into battle with its mammoth monsters, to stand appalled on the brink of Kilauea, and depart without daring

Kilauea by Moonlight.

to try its abyss. Gazing upon it, then, at midnight, so near its brink as we were, was rather venturing upon the edge of safety, as I found to my cost. But woe to the man that should have a fit of somnambulism on the spot where our tent was pitched that last night. Baron Munchausen's seven-leagued boots could hardly save him from a warm bath in flowing lava cherry-red.

Morning broke again upon our open encampment, clear and bracing as upon the Green Mountains of Vermont. With fingers burned and bleeding from the climbing and crystal-digging of yesterday, we made all the dispatch possible in collecting and packing specimens, but it was one o'clock before we were ready to leave. Having at length got off the natives with their burdens, two for Hilo and two for Kau, we kneeled for the last time by that wonderful old furnace, where the hand of God works the bellows and keeps up his vast laboratory of elemental fire. Then we mounted our horses and bade a final good-by, the one for Hilo, and the other for his happy Hawaiian home.

It was with regret that I left half explored a region so replete with wonder and novelties, where a man might spend a week in the rarest sight-seeing without satiety. One wants to encompass the crater above as well as below; *to go round about her, to mark well her bulwarks, to tell the towers thereof*, and to spy out all the wonderful country round about; to apply the plummet and line, and take the gauge and dimensions of the vast openings into earth's fiery womb here to be met with; and to trace out some of those subterranean galleries and awful caves by which her redundant fires have from time to time flowed off seaward, and to explore all the region where, sixty years ago, Keoua and his band of warriors were fatally arrested by an eruption.*

* The army of Keoua set out on their way in three different companies. The company in advance had not proceeded far, before the ground began to shake and rock beneath their feet, and it became quite impossible to stand. Soon a dense cloud of darkness was seen to rise out of the crater, and almost at the same instant the electrical effect upon the air was so great that the thunder began to roar in the heavens and the lightning to flash. It continued to ascend and spread abroad till the whole region was enveloped, and the light of day was entirely excluded. The darkness was the more terrific, being made visible by an awful glare from streams of red and blue light variously combined, that issued from the pit below, and being lit up at intervals by the intense flashes of lightning from above. Soon followed an immense volume of sand and cinders, which were thrown in high heaven, and came down in a destructive shower for many miles around. Some persons of the forward company were burned to death by the sand and cinders, and others were seriously injured. All experienced a suffocating sensation upon the lungs, and hastened on with all possible speed.

The rear body, which was nearest the volcano at the time of the eruption, seemed to suffer the least injury, and, after the earthquake and shower of sand had passed over, hastened forward to escape the dangers which threatened them, and rejoicing in mutual congratulations that they had been preserved in the midst of such imminent peril. But what was their surprise and consternation when, on coming up with their friends of the centre party, they discovered them all to have become corpses. Some were lying down, and others were sitting upright, clasping with dying grasp their wives and children, and joining noses (their form of expressing affection) as in the act of taking a final leave. So much like life they looked, that they at first supposed them merely at rest, and it was not until they had come up to them and handled them that they could detect their mistake. The whole party, including women and children, not one of them survived to relate the catastrophe that had befallen their comrades. The only living being they found was a solitary hog, in company with one of the families which had been so suddenly bereft of life. In those perilous circumstances, the surviving party did not even stay to bewail

When some enterprising Yankee, or Yankeefied Hawaiian, shall have built there a house of entertainment, the thing will be possible, and Kilauea will be resorted to from far and near as one of the wonders of the world. Invalids and travelers from America may yet cross the Isthmus of Darien or the Rocky Mountains by rail-road, be ferried to Hawaii nei by iron steamers from San Francisco or Panama, and have their youth renewed by a sulphur bath from one of the steaming orifices of old Pele. Nor is it an impossibility, in this age of gold, that volcanic fire may yet retire from the bed of this crater, and, in the changes of mineral chemistry, leave all its veins and fissures so injected with shining metal from the central Pyrophlegethon, that Hawaii shall yet become the El Dorado of the Pacific, the Colchis of modern Argonauts, and the very *Ultima Thule* of gold hunters from all nations.

It was not till late in the evening that I reached Ola, a district in Puna, where Mr. Coan had deposited a letter for me in the time of his last tour, and had charged his good people there to pay suitable attentions to a stranger that was shortly coming through. Warned of our approach by the whoop and whistle of the natives, the hospitable inmates of a house there, with kindest intent, had kindled a large fire in the middle, and called together a goodly deputation from other houses. As the place had no outlet but by one

their fate, but, leaving their deceased companions as they found them, hurried on and overtook the company in advance at the place of their encampment.—*Dibble's History of the Sandwich Islands*, p. 65, 66. *Lahainaluna Mission Press*, 1843.

little *puka* (door) in the side, it was so dense with smoke, and oppressive with heat and twice-breathed air, as to induce a violent headache, that was by no means an equivalent for the wet feet and pure air by whose loss it was gained.

What with this and the feverishness incurred already by exposure and weariness, and the incessant fire of a flying detachment of *ukulele* that came in my skirts from the volcano, there was no sleep for the night, and I was in poor plight for travel the next day. Heavy showers, too, prevented an early departure. But by nine in the morning of Saturday I was mounted for Hilo. The route lay through the tangled forests and ferns of Puna, fallen trees lying frequently across the way, and the road for a good part of the distance being made of the large stumps of ferns, *a la mode corduroy*, or what they call "down east" a gridiron road, over which my horse traveled with more shrinking and difficulty than St. Anthony (I believe it was) used to walk barefoot, for penance, over a bridge paved with sharp flints.

To a wearied traveler, the way through that long wood seemed almost interminable. But there was something singular in the composition of the forest, and of the ground, or rather crumbled lava whereon it grew. The huge vine, called by the natives *Iie*, coiling up like a great reptile, and overhanging all the trees with its deep-red blossoms, was very conspicuous; and large trees of the ohia and kukui (candle nut) would be frequently girdled with a chaplet of moss, on which were growing ferns, and a plant with long leaves like the dandelion.

Frequently there were to be seen three or four of these garlands on the stock of the same tree, one above another, at intervals of three or four feet. Birds, too, made the wood vocal, when the rain was not pattering upon the leaves; and they never warbled finer their sweet philosophy,

> Flee from doubt and faithless sorrow:
> God provideth for the morrow.

First impressions of Hilo are always pleasant. The gentle rise of the land up to the domes of Mauna Kea and Loa; the numerous and large oak-green bread-fruit trees, and spiral pandanus, with the dense undergrowth of shrubs and grass springing from a deep and always moistened soil, interspersed with lagoons and fish-ponds of fresh water, strike the eye of the stranger very agreeably.

There are also several native houses of uncommon neatness and beauty, the posts being morticed into sills, furnished with verandas on two sides, and surrounded with neat green hedges of the *ki* plant. The three mission-houses have verdant and ample yards adjoining, in which are the Oriental lilac, mimosa, tamarind, mango, guava, coffee, lime, and fig-trees, and other shrubs and flowers, inclosed by stone walls.

A cordial greeting at Mr. Coan's, warm bathing, and change of apparel dispelled half my weariness, while the luxury of a bed and sleep, scarcely known for four nights, proved greatly restorative to over-worn and excited nature. I was at the sanctuary in the morning on the following Sabbath, where Mr. Coan preached, a neat frame structure, one hundred and twenty feet long and sixty wide, thatched with grass on the roof and sides, unceiled, and without glass windows. It has a wide veranda all round, made by the overhanging eaves, and is altogether a very handsome specimen of a native grass meeting-house. But the labor of preaching in such a structure can be little less than that of speaking in the open air, under the disadvantage, too, of an atmosphere fetid with the exhalations of palm-oiled *kanaka* bodies and *poi*-made lungs.

Mr. Coan's Sabbath labors are the care of his Sunday school at nine in the morning, preaching immediately after, then a meeting for persons under censure and seeking admission to the Church. After a short intermission, the afternoon sermon, and then, when ships are in port, an English sermon to seamen and such of the foreign residents as choose to attend. After supper, a religious exercise with the girls of Mrs. Coan's household school.

These exercises are far too much for the well-being and endurance of the pastor, who can not sustain such excessive labors many years more. Were it not for his frequent absences on tours, which, laborious as they are, and sometimes fraught with peril, yet prove invigorating, it would be impossible to hold out as he does. Sabbaths, when the pastor is away, Rev. Mr. Lyman, of the boys' boarding school, supplies the desk.

In the afternoon, it being the first Sabbath of the year, the sacrament was administered to about eight hundred communicants; but a small part of this huge Church of six thousand now coming to communion at the station, the elements being administered, in Mr. Coan's quarterly tours, at several other places The usual Sabbath audience present one would judge to be about eight or nine hundred. The girls of Mrs. Coan's school, to the number of twenty-five, sit on benches directly opposite the desk. The boys of Mr. Lyman's school, about eighty, in raised seats within a box on the right.

The singing is done by the two schools conjointly, a youth of about fourteen leading the choir and playing a viol, on which he has instructed himself, with help from Mrs. Lyman. The singing is altogether the best I have heard at the Islands; the voices of the girls, together with their bright, happy faces, are truly pleasing. They sing a verse before each meal, as well as at their morning and evening prayers, and at the opening and close of school; and a visitor will be hearing some of their merry voices all the time,

> "From morn to noon, from noon to dewy eve,
> A summer's day."

Their dormitory, dining-hall, and school-room is all one grass building, situated a few yards from the house, about thirty-five feet long and twenty wide. The school-room is at one end, furnished with desks and benches, having a single window on each side, and raised up about two feet above the ground floor of the dining-hall and dormitory. The sleeping nests are little recesses on the two sides of the dining-hall, and are made by mere partitions of mats, just large enough each for two; there they bestow themselves and live happier than so many queens.

The school has no appropriation from the mission treasury; but friends in America have been kind, and their donations are yearly needed, and could hardly be better bestowed. This interesting school, from its establishment in 1839, as well as that for boys under Mr. and Mrs. Lyman, has had the signal blessing of God. Its pupils have been preserved from sickness and death, and, as it is believed, from Hawaiian immoralities. I suppose they are the *elite* of Puna and Hilo, some among them being truly beautiful; and surely no Christian visitor can help becoming deeply interested in the welfare of these warbling Hawaiian girls, and offering in their behalf many earnest prayers. Would that their virtue, and youthful spirits, and buoyant, singing hearts might be kept always!

> O! MAY THEY KEEP IN TUNE WITH HEAVEN TILL GOD,
> ERE LONG, TO HIS CELESTIAL CONCERT THEM INVITE,
> TO LIVE WITH HIM, AND SING IN EVERLASTING
> Morn of light!—MILTON.

CHAPTER XV.

COMPARISON OF NOTES ON THE VOLCANO.

Such a boiling and broiling,
Such a whacking and thwacking,
Such a sissing and hissing,
Such a clattering and splattering,
Such a muttering and fluttering,
Such a crackling and rattling,
Such a lattering and battering,
Such a blending and rending,
Such a wearing and tearing,
Such a blowing and glowing,
Such a snapping and flapping,
Such a sizzling and frizzling,
That which end we stood on was doubtful,
For we all were demented by fear.

E. O HALL.

IT will be perceived, in what has gone before, that I have put down first impressions of the great Hawaiian volcano, taken at sight, its present phenomena being, as it were, arrested and Daguerreotyped as they passed before my eyes. But these phenomena are ever-varying, so that no two visitors at different times ever found them alike, or the aspect of the crater unchanged at two several visits.

At this time of my seeing it, its fires were uncommonly low and quiescent, and the crater almost supernaturally still. Thus my companion, who had been there twice before within two years, had never observed so little activity as now. And the changes he found and pointed out as we passed along in the bed of the crater are very great. Many huge cones, that a year ago were laboring with unearthly throes and groanings, and now and then projecting from their top smoke, and steam, and liquid lava, with terrific detonations, have entirely vanished, and the places where they stood are hardened and smooth.

The hissing of steam, the roaring as of mighty fires, and the sound of the lake, like the noise of many waters, were then distinctly heard from the top of the cliffs, and streams of bright lava were seen falling and flowing between the laboring cones. Now there was an entire absence of those appalling noises, and suppressed struggles, and inward mutterings of agony and wrath, as of immense power writhing under chains and darkness, which almost all visitors will tell of. Neither did we hear any of those underground explosions which are said sometimes to reverberate from end to end of the crater, and shake even its massive walls.

Such an explosion occurred in the night while Mr. Stewart and the English naval commander, Byron, were on a visit to the volcano in 1825. An account of it is given in the volume entitled "Journal of a Residence in the Sandwich Islands, by C. S. Stewart." The tumult and tremor awakened them, and, springing from their sleeping-places, they saw a dense column of heavy black smoke rising from the crater directly in front.

"The subterranean struggle ceased, and immediately after flames burst from a large cone near where we had been in the morning, and which then appeared to have been long inactive. Red-hot stones, cinders, and ashes were also propelled to a great height with immense violence, and shortly after the molten lava came boiling up, and flowed down the sides of the cone, and over the surrounding scoria, in two beautiful, curved streams, glittering with indescribable brilliance. At the same time a whole lake of fire opened in a more distant part, which could not have been less than two miles in circumference. Its surface had all the agitation of an ocean—billow after billow tossed its monstrous bosom in the air, and crested and broke in sheets and spray of fire, like heavy rollers sweeping over a reef to the shore, and occasionally burst with such violence as in the concussion to dash the fiery spray forty and fifty feet high."

One of those prodigious engines, which they call cones (more properly funnels or fire-pumps), he examined near at hand, and judged it to be one hundred and fifty feet high. A huge, irregularly-shapen, inverted funnel of lava, covered with clefts, orifices, and tunnels, from which bodies of steam escaped with deafening explosion, while pale flames, ashes, stones, and lava were propelled with great force and noise from its ragged and yawning mouth.

Ellis, in his "Missionary Tour through Hawaii," is believed to have been the first who described this unique and grand crater. At the time of his visit he said that the southwest and northern parts of it were one vast flood of burning matter, in a state of terrific ebullition, rolling to and fro its fiery surge and flaming billows. "Fifty-one conical islands, of varied form and size, containing as many craters, rose either round the edge or from the surface of the burning lake. Twenty-two constantly emitted columns of gray smoke, or pyramids of brilliant flame; and several of them at the same time vomited from their ignited mouths streams of lava, which rolled in blazing torrents down their black, indented sides into the boiling mass below. Streams of lava, from smaller craters in vigorous action higher up the sides of the great gulf, rolled down into the lake and mingled with the melted mass there, which, though thrown up by different apertures, had, perhaps, been originally fused in one vast furnace.

"At night, the agitated mass of liquid lava, like a flood of melted metal, raged with tumultuous whirl, and, darting its fierce light athwart the midnight gloom, unfolded a scene terrible and sublime beyond all we had yet seen. The lively flame that danced over its undulating surface, tinged with sulphureous blue, or glowing with mineral red, cast a broad glare of dazzling light on the indented sides of the insulated craters, from whose roaring mouths, amid rising flames and eddying streams of fire, shot up at frequent intervals, with loudest detonations, spherical masses of fusing lava, or bright, ignited stones. The dark, bold outline of the perpendicular and jutting rocks around formed a striking contrast with the luminous lake below, whose vivid rays, thrown on the rugged promontories, and, reflected by the overhanging clouds, combined to complete the awful grandeur of the imposing scene.

"The natives sat most of the night talking of the

achievements of Pele, and regarding with a superstitious fear, at which we were not surprised, the brilliant exhibition. They considered it the primeval abode of their volcanic deities. The conical craters, they said, were their houses, where they frequently amused themselves by playing at *konane*, a game of drafts. The roaring of the furnaces and the crackling of the flames were the *kani* of their *hula*, the music of their dances, and the red, flaming surge was the surf where they played, sportively swimming on the rolling wave.

"From their accounts we learned that it had been burning *mai ka po mai*, from chaos till now, and had overflowed some part of the country during the reign of every king that had governed Hawaii; that in earlier ages it used to boil up and overflow its banks, and inundate the adjacent country; but that for many kings' reigns it had kept below the level of the surrounding plain, continually extending its surface and increasing its depth, and occasionally throwing up, with violent explosion, huge rocks or red-hot stones.

"These eruptions were always accompanied with dreadful earthquakes, loud claps of thunder, with vivid and quick-succeeding lightning. No great explosion had taken place since the days of Keoua, a part of whose forces, while going to war, met here with a sudden and awful destruction. But many places near the sea had since been overflowed, on which occasions they supposed Pele went by a road under ground from her house in the crater to the shore."

All readers of the Missionary Herald, and a large circle besides, are familiar with Mr. Coan's graphic account of the eruption lower down in Puna, in 1840, when night was converted into day on all eastern Hawaii, and the brilliancy of the light was like a blazing firmament. Just before that eruption, it is said, the entire pit of the crater of Kilauea, about three miles long, and two or more broad, was one sea of fire. On the breaking out of the lava in Puna it immediately subsided, and even the caldron sunk several hundred feet below its present surface, revealing vast caves and galleries by which the fused material had been drawn off.

I am informed by Mr. Coan, that in Puna there is an extinct crater, ten or twelve miles from Kilauea, nearly as deep, and that there are to be met with all along in that region both sunken pits and conical mounds. They are all lateral craters to the great volcanic dome of Mauna Loa, which has been raised by successive eruptions fourteen thousand feet above the level of the sea.

It had been thought by the Scientific Corps of the Exploring Squadron, and by most other observers, that while its fires should continue to burn, no eruption could take place from a point higher than Kilauea, which is estimated at about four thousand feet above the level of the sea. But the sudden lighting of a taper one night in 1843, upon the bare top of the monarch mountain itself, revealed the fallacy of such an opinion. A fiery river took its rise there, several miles wide, which Messrs. Coan and Paris explored a couple of months after, till they found it disembogued and lost under ground in some ancient caves and galleries.

Several eruptions have taken place since from the

same point, that is, nearly fourteen thousand feet above the level of the sea, or eight thousand higher than Kilauea; and in 1849 another prodigious flood of boiling rock issued from the same quarter.

I find that Commander Wilkes, of the United States Exploring Squadron, whose annals, so far as appertains to facts and phenomena at the Sandwich Islands, are remarkably accurate and unexaggerated, was not less amazed than all others have been at the view of this mighty crater. One of the Scientific Corps wrote to a friend that "Vesuvius was a babe to it. The surface at one moment black as ink, the next exhibiting rivers, and pools, and jets of a hideous blood-red fluid, that was sometimes thrown up to the height of fifty or sixty feet, and fell back with a sullen splashing that was indescribably awful. By night it was grand beyond description. The frequent lightings up, the hissings, the deep muttering explosions, reminded me of some great city in flames, where there were magazines of gunpowder or mines continually exploding."

I will eliminate and condense from the extended volumes of Mr. Wilkes's minute narrative a few paragraphs here and there, that touch circumstances, and present points of view not, perhaps, exhibited so clearly in the narrative of the previous chapter. He described the rushing of the wind past them as they approached the abyss, just as if it were drawn inward to support the combustion of some mighty conflagration. When the edge was reached, the extent of the cavity became apparent, and its depth sensible by comparison with the figures of some of the party who had descended. The vastness thus made sensible transfixed the mind with astonishment, and every instant the impression of grandeur and magnificence increased.

To give an idea of its capacity, he estimates that the city of New York might be placed within it, and when at its bottom would hardly be noticed, for it is three and a half miles long, two and a half wide, and one thousand feet deep. A black ledge surrounds it at the depth of six hundred and sixty feet, thence to the bottom is three hundred and eighty-four feet. The bottom looks in the daytime like a heap of smouldering ruins. What is wonderful in the day, becomes ten times more so at night. The immense pool of cherry-red lava, in a state of violent ebullition, illuminates the whole expanse, and flows in all directions like water, while the illuminated cloud hangs over it like a vast canopy.

All usual ideas of volcanic craters are dissipated upon seeing this. There is no elevated cone, no igneous matter, or rocks ejected beyond the rim. The banks appear as if built of massive black blocks, which in places are clothed with ferns near the top, nourished by the issuing vapors. The pool is one thousand five hundred feet long by one thousand wide, of an oval figure. The ebullition in it was (as is the case when the heat is applied to one side of a vessel) most violent near the northern side.

They occasionally perceived stones, or masses of red-hot matter, ejected to the height of seventy feet, and falling back into the lake again. Reflecting upon the position they were in, its insecurity, and the deep and vast fires beneath, with the high basaltic walls encompassing them upon all sides, the sulphureous flames and broad glare, throwing such enormous masses of stone in strong relief by their own fusion, it was difficult to comprehend how such a reservoir could thus be pent up, and be viewed in such close proximity without accident or danger.

The whole party was perfectly silent, and the countenance of each individual expressed the feeling of awe and wonder which the writer felt in so great a degree himself, and which the scene was so well calculated to excite. No one can see all this, and yet doubt the theory of the igneous fluidity of the earth. All combustible causes that we are acquainted with are totally inadequate to produce such an effect. The whole seemed boiling up like a fountain, differing only in density and color.

The immense space occupied by the crater is gradually filled with the fluid mass of lava to a certain point, above which the walls, or the surrounding soil, are no longer able to bear the pressure. It then finds vent by an eruption, previous to which, however, a large part next to the walls of the crater has become partially cooled, and remains fixed at the level it had attained.

After the eruption, the central mass, therefore, alone subsides three or four hundred feet, and leaves the portion that has become solid, forming a kind of terrace or shelf. This is what constitutes the Black Ledge, and it is one of the most striking features of the crater. Its surface is comparatively level, though somewhat uneven, and it is generally coated with a vitreous, and, in some places, scoriaceous lava, from half an inch to one inch thick, very iridescent and brittle.

The crackling noise made in walking over this crisp surface, like a coating of blue and yellow glass, resembles that made by treading on frozen snow in very cold weather. Every here and there are seen dark pits and vaulted caverns, with heated air rushing from them. Large cracks are passed, the air issuing from which, at one hundred and eighty degrees Fahrenheit, is almost stifling.

Masses are surmounted that it would seem as if the accumulated weight of a few persons would cause to topple over, and plunge the whole into the fiery pool beneath. There were many cracks where their sticks were set on fire, and some places in the vaulted chambers where the rock might be seen red hot. The Black Ledge is of various widths, from six hundred to two hundred feet. One trip to the floor generally satisfies the most daring; and as long as a person remains, he must feel in a state of great insecurity, and in danger of undergoing the most terrible of deaths, in being cut off from escape by a sudden outbreak of the red molten fluid. Yet a hardihood is acquired, brought about by the excitement, that gives courage to encounter serious peril in so rare a situation.

To stand on the Black Ledge, and look around on the desolation which appears on every side, produces a feeling similar to that with which the scene of some dreadful conflagration would be viewed. The same description of sadness is felt that such a prospect would create, while there is in addition a feeling of insecurity, arising from the fires that are raging around, and are known to exist underneath. Rocks on the sides of the caldron are left as if spattered with pitch

To give an idea of the vastness of this volcano's capacity,* it may be stated that the discharge from the lake, during one night Wilkes was at the crater, he estimates to have been fifteen millions of cubic feet.

* The power exerted by volcanic agency may be estimated by the amount of matter protruded, by the distance to which masses of rock have been projected, and by calculating the force requisite to raise lava to the tops of existing craters from their base. Vesuvius hurled stones eight pounds in weight to Pompeii, a distance of six miles, and has cast similar masses two thousand feet above its own summit; while Cotopaxi has projected a block of one hundred and nine cubic yards in volume to the distance of nine miles. The annexed table gives the height of the respective volcanoes named above the sea, with the force requisite to cause lava to flow over their tops, and the initial velocity which such a force would produce:

Volcanoes.	Height in feet.	Force exerted upon the lava.	Velocity per second.
		Atmospheres.	*Feet.*
Stromboli . . .	2,168	176	371
Vesuvius . . .	3,874	314	496
Jorullo	2,942	319	502
Hecla	5,106	413	570
Ætna	10,892	882	832
Teneriffe . . .	12,464	1009	896
Kea S. Islands. .	14,700	1191	966
Popocatapetl . .	17,712	1435	1062
Mount Elias . .	18,079	1465	1072
Cotopaxi . . .	18,869	1492	1104

Milnor's Gallery of Nature, p. 781. London, 1846.

"The foci of active volcanoes are situated at enormous depths, and, judging from the remarkable fragments which I have found in various parts of the earth incrusted in lava currents, I should deem it more than probable that a primordial granite rock forms the substratum of the whole stratified edifice of fossil remains."—*Humboldt's Cosmos,* vol. i., p. 285.

"The mineral composition of lava differs according to the nature of the crystalline rock of which the volcano is formed, the height of the point where the eruption occurs, whether at the foot of the mountain or in the neighborhood of the crater, and the condition of temperature of the interior. Vitreous volcanic foundations, obsidian, pearl-stone, and pumice, are entirely wanting in some volcanoes, while in the case of others they only proceed from the crater, or, at any rate, from very inconsiderable heights."—*Cosmos,* vol. i., p. 234.

A small crater within the pit, measured by Dr. Judd, and found to be two hundred feet in diameter, was filled in twelve minutes, at which rate, in one day, it would have discharged two hundred million cubic feet of lava.

It was by the sudden filling up of a small crater like this that Dr. Judd came within a hair's-breadth of losing his life, while attempting to dip a ladleful of the molten rock. The lava suddenly broke out behind him, and but for the fidelity of a native, stopping when all others fled with terror, reaching out to him his hand, and drawing him up, not without burning to a blister his own face and arms, he would inevitably have perished in another minute by the most horrible of all deaths.

One of the missionaries at these islands, soon after visiting this volcano, portrayed very naturally its phenomena, and the impressions they made upon his own mind, in a familiar letter to a friend, which has been laid before me. And, inasmuch as it paints some features not presented in the foregoing, we will quote therefrom, for the sake of finishing in one chapter the *tout ensemble* of wonders appertaining to this most remarkable of all the hitherto observed exhibitions of Nature in the line of volcanoes. There might be taken a series of panoramic and particular views of this unique volcano, and exhibited through the diorama, that would doubtless be greatly admired, and bring an independent fortune to the first successful artist. Something of the kind, I have no doubt, will be tried and accomplished ere long; and then we shall have the whole world gazing at Kilauea, and tracks of travel will tend there, and tourists will be filling their books with its wonders, and rail-road, steam-ship, and Daguerreotype will be bringing them so near, and making them so familiar, that Pele will have more idolaters than ever she had in the days of old. Whether Hawaiians will gain by it remains to be proved.

The account above referred to says, that after two or three miles' walk in the crater, over steaming fissures, and around deep gorges, in the beds of which lava had recently flowed, forming so many canals of liquid fire, they came upon a vast lake of melted and boiling rock! "This lake is nearly circular, and from one half to three quarters of a mile in diameter. You attempt to approach it, but heat and sulphureous gasses compel you to a hasty retreat. At length you succeed. For a while you are permitted to stand upon its fearful brink. The whole surface below is moving with a heavy but varied motion. The dark gray mass presently cracks, and a streak of gory fire rolls heavily up into the crevice. A score of similarly irregular lines of fire, crossing and recrossing each other, and connecting the periphery of the whole like so many links of lightning, reveal on every hand the raging element. Soon these cool from exposure to the atmosphere, to be succeeded in endless rotation by new and similar phenomena.

"Suddenly every eye is turned to the left, or perhaps the attention is divided toward several spots of absorbing interest. An accumulation of heat had produced a corresponding intensity of action. In quick succession one gory jet follows another, each cooling as it falls, its crimson hue darkening and deepening from its first issue till it has reached again its element. These jets cross each other in every direction, the portions of liquid thus thrown up congealing in all shapes and sizes as they ascend and fall. Nature seems at play with the most fearful of her elements. From these boiling fountains the melted rock flows out on all sides, and, congealing upon its surface, gives to the whole mass a diverging motion.

"Different currents meeting, the congealing and plastic crust is crowded into every imaginable twist and form, till at length cracked at the line of greatest pressure, its fragments are piled up on either side of the fissure or forced under, again to be fused, and again, ere long, to supply some fresh but distant fountain. These centres of intensity at length abate their fury. The jets are less and less rapid, and soon a dark gray crust has closed over and bound them.

"While all this has transpired, heat and gas have repeatedly obliged you to escape their contagion. You look at your watch, and hours have unconsciously passed. The day is waning, and your lungs already feel the effects of the heated and noxious vapors. Still, the ever-varying phenomena bind you to the spot. Some new bursting fountain rivets your gaze. The crust pressed from beneath, and from the meeting of counter currents, assumes an irregularity and a singularity of form, and in its numerous and gaping seams draws out the sight in the course of its fiery channels; and withal so constantly is every feature modified and lost, and formed anew and again lost, that one finds himself in the midst of a volcanic panorama, the scene, however, perpetually shifting.

"Up to this time you have, perhaps, indulged but a passing thought upon the fearfulness of your position. You could not have been insensible of your proximity to so awful a place, nor yet to the rolling fire just beneath your feet. Your attention has often been fixed upon the brilliant and varying line of fire that marks the entire circumference; but you have again traced its circle, and you realize for the first time its treacherous foothold. Whither tends the sluggish yet destructive tide? Directly beneath you! A few layers of congealed scoria, already hot from the fire beneath, and that may at any time break or melt under you, this alone is your foothold! You look again at the mad element, and more of fear than of sublimity mingles with your emotions. At length your trembling feet bear you from the spot, new feelings having been kindled in the soul, and impressions received that time can never efface. You have seen 'unquenchable fire,' and felt for the first time the fearful aptness of that emblem of the world of woe. You can now realize the conflagration of the world. God has only to touch each hill and mountain top, and the whole earth would melt and flow down at His presence."

Another letter is before me of a still more recent date, written by a missionary lady who was passing a day with her children by that burning mountain's side. It will show the power of the volcano in awing and elevating alike all minds susceptible of emotion, and proves, also, that changes are in progress which may soon result in an eruption both magnificent and desolating beyond any thing yet known. "We arrived," says the writer, "at three o'clock in the after noon, enveloped in fog, while the thunder was rolling over our heads. There was soon a smart shower; then it cleared up, and was remarkably pleasant during our stay. But what shall I say of that *awful* night—the most fearful one I ever spent? I can not describe what I saw, heard, and felt. When we had been there about an hour, Henry came in and asked me to go out on the bank and *hear* the volcano. He said it made a noise like an animal with its head cut off. After listening a moment, I heard the heavy breathing; but soon there was an explosion, the noise of which equaled the thunder which we had just been hearing. We saw distinctly that the gas was escaping from the largest cone. Report followed report in quick succession, attended with a rumbling noise as though the lava was escaping, and yet we could see but a small flow. The children were greatly frightened; but the natives rushed out of the house, crying, 'Man of war! man of war!' These explosions, louder at some times than at others, occurred at intervals of about an hour during our stay. In the stillness of the night, the echo around the walls of the crater was grand and awful beyond description.

"At early dawn I started to walk till the animals overtook us. When opposite the immense mound which now covers the lake, we could feel the heat from it very sensibly (they being, it will be borne in mind, some fifteen hundred feet perpendicularly above it). The top of it is nearly on a level with the lowest side of the crater, having been thrown up, apparently, by the gases beneath, and, in being thrown up, large seams opened on every side, through which we could see Pele's fires, and out of which the lava flowed whenever gas escaped from the cones."

Another observer of a similar explosive phenomenon with that here referred to said, that while gazing intently into the crater below, his ears were suddenly saluted by five or six regular discharges from a small crater in the bottom, from which had previously issued only a light column of smoke. They were so regular and abrupt as to remind him of a consular salute from a man-of-war, and so loud as to cause the whole cavern to tremble.

> "List! to the booming sound
> From yonder crater, unobserved till now.
> Again, and yet again, it bellows forth
> Its bursting thunder with distracting noise;
> The echoing cliffs prolong the wild dismay,
> And distant mountains bear the echo on.
> Once more 'tis still. Naught but the dashing roar
> Of the huge waves in constant action toss'd,
> Salutes the ear. Again! the cavern'd sides
> Tremble beneath the pent-up energies
> Of the fierce power! while, with reverberant sound,
> Mountains and vales re-echo all around."

These waves, speaking literally, are masses of fused, viscid rock thrown out in succession from a central opening, and flowing sluggishly down the inclined plain around it, a crust being gradually formed on the surface while the molten matter is still running beneath, forcing itself and pressed along by the new matter of successive waves behind. This motion of a flowing mass, whether larger or smaller, seen from the rim of the crater by night, gives the appearance of a fiery surf, or a rolling wave of fire, or the dancing along of an extended semicircular flame on the surface of the lake.

When one wave has expended itself, or found its level, or otherwise become stationary, another succeeds and passes over it in like manner, and then another, sent out, as it were, by the pulsations of the earth's open artery at the top of the mound. This shows how a mound, cone, pyramid, or mountain can be gradually built of lava, and wide plains covered at its base with the same material.

It was in view of phenomena like these that we find it written after the following cyclopean way, indeed, but without exaggeration, in the valuable volume entitled, Bingham's Sandwich Islands: "Had Vulcan employed ten thousand giant cyclopses, each with a steam-engine of one thousand horse power, blowing anthracite coal for smelting mountain minerals, or heaving up and hammering to pieces rocks and hills, their united efforts would but begin to compare with the work of Pele. There was enough of mystery connected with the experiments going on before our eyes to give ample employment to fancy and philosophy, and materially to enhance the sublimity of the fearful scene. For it might be asked, How can such an immense mass of rocks and earth be kept incessantly in a state of fusion, without fuel or combustion? or by what process could such solid masses be fused at all in accordance with any mode of generating heat with which we are acquainted?

"If there be combustion in the crater adequate to the melting of such vast masses of substances so hard, rocky, and earthy, why is there an accumulation of the general mass, so that millions of cubic fathoms are from time to time added to the solid contents of the mountain? Or if the bowels of the mountain are supposed to be melted by intense heat somehow generated, could they be heaved up by the expansion of steam or gas, while an orifice equal to three or four square miles, like that of Kilauea, or the terminal crater on the same mountain, is kept open? for steam and gas might be supposed to pass through the fluid masses and escape, instead of raising them from a depth, just as steam rises from the bottom of a boiling caldron without materially elevating the surface of its contents.

"But if, with one class of geologists, we suppose the interior of the earth to be in a molten or fluid state, as perhaps originally created, and that Kilauea and other volcanoes are but openings to that subterranean, fiery central ocean of red or white hot matter, then we have no faint illustration of the bold imagery used by the sacred writers, and of that phraseology which seems hyperbolical or even paradoxical, 'the bottomless pit,' 'the fire that is not quenched,' 'the lake that burneth with fire and brimstone,' 'the smoke of their torment ascendeth up forever and ever.' If such a fluid mass constitutes the main portion of the interior of the earth, it is literally '*bottomless*,' and the opened surface, like that of Kilauea, may be strictly called a LAKE, a lake of fire; and, as sulphur and particles of the sulphuret of iron are present, it may be called *a lake that burns with fire and brimstone*."*

* When the questions are asked, What is it that burns in the volcano? What excites the heat, fuses together earths and metals, and imparts to lava-currents of thick layers a degree of heat that lasts for many years? it is necessarily implied that volcanoes must be connected with the existence of substances capable of maintaining combustion, like the beds of coal in subterranean fires. According to

Respecting the uses of such an open lake of fire little can be said, since so little is known. The suppo-

the different phases of chemical science, bitumen, pyrites, the moist admixture of finely-pulverized sulphur and iron, hydrophoric substances, and the metals of the alkalies and earths, have in turn been designated as the cause of intensely active volcanic phenomena. The great chemist, Sir Humphrey Davy, to whom we are indebted for the knowledge of the most combustible metallic substances, has himself renounced his bold chemical hypothesis in his last work (Consolations in Travel and Last Days of a Philosopher).

So general, deep-seated, and far-propagated an activity as that of volcanoes can not assuredly have its source in chemical affinity, or in the mere contact of individual or merely locally-distributed substances. Modern geognosy rather seeks the cause of this activity in the increased temperature with the increase of depth at all degrees of latitude, in that powerful internal heat which our planet owes to its first solidification, its formation in the regions of space, and to the spherical contraction of matter revolving elliptically in a gaseous condition. A philosophical study of nature strives ever to elevate itself above the narrow requirements of mere natural description, and does not consist, as we have already remarked, in the mere accumulation of isolated facts. The inquiring and active spirit of man must be suffered to pass from the present to the past, to conjecture all that can not yet be known with certainty, and still to dwell with pleasure on the ancient myths of geognosy which are presented to us under so many various forms. If we consider volcanoes as irregular, intermittent springs, emitting a fluid mixture of oxydized metals, alkalies, and earths, flowing gently and calmly wherever they find a passage, or being upheaved by the powerful expansive force of vapors, we are involuntarily led to remember the geognostic visions of Plato, according to which hot springs, as well as all volcanic igneous streams, were eruptions that might be traced back to one generally-distributed subterranean cause, *Pyrophlegethon*. This Pyrophlegethon of Plato plays much the same part in relation to the activity of volcanoes which we now ascribe to the augmentation of heat as we descend from the earth's surface, and to the fused condition of its internal strata. Volcanic scoriæ and lava-streams are portions of Pyrophlegethon itself, portions of the subterranean, molten, and ever-undulating mass.—*Humboldt's Cosmos*, vol. i., p. 237. *Harper & Brothers, New York* 1850.

sition that it is one of the earth's great safety-valves, in the economy of Providence, to preclude fatal explosions, would seem, at least, to have no more of fancy in it than of fact. Why may not the awful phenomena of burning mountains be considered also like *pustules* on the human skin, as symptoms and indications of disease within, and as meant to inform us, from age to age, that even as all diseases in the constitution of man must have their *crises*, in order to be thoroughly cured, so, in the nature of things, must the malady of the natural and the moral world be at length cured and thrown off at once, in the fullness of time, by a universal eruption that shall thoroughly purge with fire all its distempers?

Earthquakes and volcanoes are now only held in abeyance by the arm of Omnipotence, from their destined work of the world's renovation by destruction. They are not to be dictated to by man, nor to have their laws clearly ascertained, or the places and times at which they shall or shall not break forth declared beforehand, any more than the times and seasons of events to come in the moral world, which belong only to the Lord Almighty. This is a province of knowledge, both in the world of matter and the world of mind, which God keeps very much to himself. THE DEEPS OF FUTURITY, *as well as the deep places of the Earth, are the Lord's.* In the maturity of time they will both be uncovered, and, PURIFIED BY THE FIRES OF JUDGMENT, THE BURNING EARTH SHALL OWN AND OBEY HER LORD.

> She quakes at his approach. Her hollow womb,
> Conceiving thunders through a thousand deeps

And fiery caverns, roars beneath his feet.
The hills move lightly, and the mountains smoke,
For he has touch'd them. From the extremest point
Of elevation down into the abyss,
His wrath is busy, and his frown is felt,
The rocks fall headlong, and the valleys rise.
What solid was, by transformation strange,
Grows fluid; and the fix'd and rooted earth,
Tormented into billows, heaves and swells,
Or, with vortiginous and hideous whirl,
Sucks down its prey insatiate.—Cowper.

CHAPTER XVI.

EARTHQUAKES, NATURE, ART, AND RELIGION AT HILO.

If in the field I meet a smiling flow'r,
  Methinks it whispers, "God created me;
And I to Him devote my little hour
  In lonely sweetness and humility."
If, where the forest's darkest shadows lower,
  A serpent quick and venomous I see,
It seems to say, "I, too, extol the power
  Of Him who caused me, at his will, to be."
The fountain purling, and the river strong,
The rocks, the trees, the mountains raise one song;
  "Glory to God!" re-echoes in mine hear:
Faithless were I, in willful error blind,
  Did I not Him in all his creatures find;
His voice through heaven, and earth, and ocean hear.
MONTGOMERY'S *Imitation from the Italian.*

ALMOST every one that has visited Hilo once would like to go there again. Its salubrious climate, perpetual verdure, quiet walks and rural scenery, pleasant society, and its vicinity to the volcano of Kilauea, form a combination of attractions not found at any other place on the Islands. You may walk up to the ancient craters and cascade, or go over the other side of the river, where of old they used to hold fairs, or stroll along under the palm-trees by the beautiful mile-beach, or take a canoe and paddle over to Cocoa-nut Island for shell-hunting and bathing; or you may make your way through the bread-fruit and *hala* trees to the borders of the lakes, and take a sail there, if you like, in a boat of bulrushes, such, very likely, as Moses was laid in by the Nile.

Or a ride of thirty-five miles will carry you closer to the phenomena of an active and changeful volcano than in all the world besides. If it be winter, while you are perspiring freely under a tropical sun at the beach or from any where in the bay, you may look up to the pure snow-capped summit of Mauna Kea, and let the enchanting sight do what it can to cool and invigorate you. A few evenings since the mountain presented a spectacle of great beauty—its base encircled with a rim of thin white mist, its sides sprinkled with light patches and delicate shadings of vapor, its peak flashing with sun-lit clouds and snow-banks, that gloriously reflected the declining sunbeans, like a dome of the purest alabaster.

If you are fond of earthquakes and desirous to take a shock, your curiosity will be likely to be gratified in the course of four or five weeks; but the shock will be so sudden and short, and take you so much by surprise, whether by night or day, that you will have no chance to examine the phenomenon, and can hardly help wishing it might be continued a little longer, if it were only to scrutinize it more closely and mark your own sensations.

The first time I felt a shock at these islands, it was in the house about noon, at Kohala; and I could not help going to the door, after such a commotion, to see if there were no signs of sympathy with the laboring earth in the other elements. But it was all sunny and still; the sky looked cheerful and serene; the fair face

Mission Premises at Hilo, and Mauna Kea.

of Nature was not pale; and the throe had passed like an evil thought which will sometimes dart across the mind, and you are glad to have it go as quick as it came.

One of the two shocks experienced at Hilo was in the night, when I was awakened by its jar, but the mind took no cognizance of it till it was past. Its suddenness was like that of lightning, of which the quickest of all observers of Nature expressively takes notice in his drama,

> Brief as the lightning in the collied night,
> That, in a spleen, unfolds both earth and heav'n;
> But, ere you can have time to say, behold!
> The jaws of darkness do devour it up.
> So quick bright things come to confusion.

Another shock was more prolonged while we were at the supper-table. First, there was a premonitory jarring of the house, like as I had felt three times before; then a violent jerk, as if the house were heavily knocked in one corner, and the blow transmitted to the other until there was a recoil. Native houses were seen through the window to pitch and reel. Mr. Coan, who was absent on a tour, and sitting at the time under some trees, said that they moved to and fro, and the leaves rustled as from the blow of a woodman's ax. His little son insisted upon it, at first, that he felt something warm strike through him, but became convinced at length that it was only the natural glow of excitement and alarm, which not boys only, but boys' parents too, and almost every one else is subject to when they hear the hoarse rumble, and feel the fearful vibration of an earthquake.

This preternatural trembling of the earth gives evidence of unseen danger, that one knows not how to avoid or grapple with, and of tremendous powers at work, subject only to the control of the Mightier than the mightiest, that may in a moment rend the solid rocks, prostrate lofty trees, and tumble into ruin all the dwellings and all the works of man, and open hideous abysses that have swallowed, and may again, whole cities at once.

We have seen it somewhere remarked, that of all sensations in nature, those produced by earthquakes or volcanic agencies are the most alarming; the strongest nerves are unstrung, and the most courageous mind feels weakened and unhinged when exposed to either.*

* Before we leave the important phenomena which we have considered, not so much in their individual characteristics as in their general physical and geognostical relations, I would advert to the deep and peculiar impression left on the mind by the first earthquake which we experience, even where it is not attended by any subterranean noise. This impression is not, in my opinion, the result of a recollection of those fearful pictures of devastation presented to our imaginations by the historical narratives of the past, but is rather due to the sudden revelation of the delusive nature of the inherent faith by which we had clung to a belief in the immobility of the solid parts of the earth. We are accustomed from early childhood to draw a contrast between the mobility of water and the immobility of the soil on which we tread; and this feeling is confirmed by the evidence of our senses. When, therefore, we suddenly feel the ground move beneath us, a mysterious and natural force, with which we are previously unacquainted, is revealed to us as an active disturbance of stability. A moment destroys the illusion of a whole life; our deceptive faith in the repose of nature vanishes, and we feel transported, as it were, into a realm of unknown destructive forces. Every sound—the faintest motion in the air—arrests our attention, and we no longer trust the ground on which we stand. Animals, especially dogs and swine, participate in the same anxious disquietude; and even the crocodiles of the Orinoco, which are at other times as dumb as our little lizards, leave the trembling

You think of the devastation they have done heretofore, often, with one and the same chain of shocks, opening the ruinous chasm between lands separated by an ocean; of the awful judgments they have executed for God, of the probable agency they will yet have, as indicated by prophecy, in accomplishing the judgments written; and the thoughts naturally go forward to the consummation of all things, when

> "Final ruin fiercely drives
> His plowshare o'er creation,
> When wrapp'd in fire the realms of Ether glow,
> And heaven's *last thunder shakes* the world below."

True, the Christian knows they will only work the will of his heavenly Father; that earthquakes and storms are His ministers, unchained only to do His bidding, and bound by the decree Thus far and no further. Come what may, the believer in Jesus knows he is safe, and he shall rise

> Unhurt amid the war of elements,
> The wreck of nature and the crush of worlds.

But it is seldom that faith, taken by surprise, does at once steady the soul, and lift a man clear above hostile infirmities and fears. 'Tis not in human nature to feel, unmoved, the solid earth quaking, or to hear

---

bed of the river and run, with loud cries, into the adjacent forests. To man the earthquake conveys an idea of some universal and unlimited danger. We may flee from the crater of a volcano in active eruption, or from the dwelling whose destruction is threatened by the approach of the lava-stream; but in an earthquake, direct our flight whithersoever we will, we still feel as if we trod upon the very focus of destruction.—*Humboldt's Cosmos*, vol. i., p. 215, 216. *Harper & Brothers, New York*, 1850.

without dismay beneath one the mutterings of a power that can in a moment bury continents or upheave mountains and cast them into the sea. 'Tis not in a moment, at such emergencies, that every Christian can repress the flutter and agitation of nature, collect his energies, and repose calmly on God.

Probably it was with an eye to this, and a consciousness of natural weakness and liability to dismay under sudden terrors, that the Psalmist said to God, *In the shadow of thy wings will I make my refuge until these calamities be overpast.* And the Lord himself also, in tender compassion to human infirmity, when awakening to judgment and about to come out of his place to punish the inhabitants of the earth, addresses his children, *Come, my people, enter into thy chambers, and shut the doors about thee: hide thyself as it were for a little moment, until the indignation be overpast.* It is a precious charge and promise to the righteous, *Be not afraid of sudden fear, neither of the desolation of the wicked, when it cometh. For the Lord shall be thy confidence, and shall keep thy foot from being taken.*

Earthquakes at Hilo have not been frequent or severe for several years; but in 1838, it is said there were forty or fifty shocks in eight days, and twelve in one night.* Some persons were sure they could perceive a tremulousness or quivering of the ground all the time, and were even made sick by it. Some of

* From memoranda furnished by Rev. Mr. Lyman that there were fifty separate shocks, according to his observation, in eight years; the usual motion or jar being like that produced by the firing of distant artillery, or the falling of a heavy body on the ground; to this is added a tremulous motion when the earthquake is slight.

View of Volcanic Hills and Lava Streams in Puna.

the early missionaries here found their nerves and health not a little affected by the frequent recurrence of shocks, and were glad to be stationed at other islands of the group, where they occur but seldom. Those now resident here are no more affected by them than the majority of persons in America by an ordinary thunder-storm, from which, in fact, there is much more danger, as earthquakes here have never yet proved disastrous, whereas the lightning there, flung from the over-charged clouds, burns houses, and blasts its hundreds every year.

There is a triad of old grassy craters at this place, some ways in the rear of Rev. Mr. Lyman's house, up to which the visitor from ships in port, whose heart has long been athirst

> To gaze at Nature in her green array,

may take a pleasant stroll through fields of the schoolboys' upland *kalo*, and see the smooth basins which volcanic fire, that mighty old potter, has molded so nicely, tipping a little toward the sea. One of them is trenched around at the base for a cow pasture. The rich bottom of the bowl of another some industrious boys have made into a *kalo* patch. By getting up on to the rim of the highest, you can see the hills that were made in the sea twenty miles off in Puna, at the time of the last eruption.

Go on a mile and a half further to the right, through a dense undergrowth of *oi* (a pernicious shrub interpolated here from abroad, and gaining injuriously upon the cultivated lands, very much as foreigners are upon the natives), and you will come suddenly to the beautiful cascade of The Rainbow—*Ka Wai anue nue.*

> Lo! like a glorious hill of diamonds bright,
> Built on the steadfast cliffs, the waterfall
> Pours forth its gems of pearl and silver light;
> They sink, they rise, and sparkling, cover all
> With beautiful refulgence; while its song,
> Sublime as thunder, rolls the woods along.

This is formed by the sudden descent of the romantic river Wailuku (water of destruction) over a hollowed cliff, into a deep basin that was once probably a crater. Let yourself half way down on to a ledge from which the aquatic natives are wont to take their leaps, and the broad arch of the cascade is directly before you, its basin spanned with rainbows, and behind the descending sheet a deep, misty cave, into which venturesome swimmers sometimes penetrate, and look out through the thundering waterfall. Beneath is the deep basin, its bosom seemingly but little moved by the impetuous suit of the cataract that is making such an ado to get into her gentle lap, reminding one of Collins's Ode to Chastity,

> Cold is her breast, like flowers that drink the dew.

Piled up all around, and hung with mosses and ferns, are the solid lava walls, rent only in one place, which your position does not command, to afford a narrow outlet for the flow of the maiden river that ripples joyously over its rocky bed, and fearlessly opens its breast to the sunbeams, seeming to say in triumph to the too eager waterfall above, Now I'm free, and away to the sea.

To the right is a singular pyramidal peak of basalt,

one hundred and fifty feet high, Nature's intrusted silent keeper of this romantic spot. When the river is swollen and furious, bearing on its rapid current drift-wood and trees, and filling up that deep abyss fifty or sixty feet with its rush of waters, the scene must be truly sublime. A man should visit it alone, and stay there long, and go there often, as every visitor at Hilo, who is at all alive to the beauties of Nature, certainly will do, in order to see and enjoy what may be enjoyed there by a mind which the Spirit has touched,

> " To see the present God in nature's wild
> And savage features; in the untrodden height,
> The beetling precipice, the deep, cold glen,
> The roar of waters, and the gloom of groves."

Alison finely remarks, that Nature, in all its aspects around us, ought only to be felt as signs of his Providence, and as conducting us, by the universal language of those signs, to the throne of God. " When the eye of man opens upon any sublime, or any beautiful scene of nature, the first impression is to consider it as *designed*—as the *effect* or workmanship of the Author of nature, and as significant of his power, his wisdom, or his goodness; and, perhaps, it is chiefly for *this fine issue* that the heart of man is thus *finely touched*, that devotion may spring from delight; that imagination, in the midst of its highest enjoyments, may be led to terminate in the only object in which it can finally repose; and that all the noblest convictions and confidences of religion may be acquired in the simple school of nature, and amid the scenes which perpetually surround us."

Further down the stream are other cascades, of less height and beauty. But there is a fall just above the ships' watering-place, of forty or fifty feet, where boys and girls, and often swimmers of a larger growth, are wont to let themselves be carried down headlong into the fluid gulf, with what exposure of life and naked limbs they little care.

The facilities afforded for watering at this port are superior to what are to be found at any other place in these islands, or, perhaps, through the whole Pacific Seas. The largest line-of-battle-ship may ride safely in the bay, and her water-casks may be filled by just rafting them up to the waterfall, and either directing the water by a spout or holding them under the natural stream. Other fresh recruits of live stock and vegetables might be furnished with almost as much ease and abundance as at Lahaina or Honolulu, were it not for the lack of enterprise and industry on the part of the inhabitants. But these virtues, there can be little doubt, will come into play as a market shall be opened for their products.

The number of ships touching here is increasing every year, and such is the entertainment they get, without the usual danger in sea-port towns from strong drink, that, stopping here once, they seldom fail to come again. A number of American and English men-of-war have been here during the last four years. The Exploring Squadron also tarried several weeks. The visits of Commodore Jones, in the frigate United States, and that of the Ohio, Captain Stribbling, in 1849, were highly satisfactory and agreeable to the missionaries, beneficial to the people, and creditable

Cascade of the Rainbow, Wailuku, Hilo.

to the commodore as a naval commander, an honorable and upright man, and an independent and warm friend to the missionaries, and to the Hawaiian nation, which he has ever proved himself, from the time of his first visit to the islands, in 1826, and honest arbitration then between the missionaries and their shamed traducers.

It were happy if a like report could be given of the noted Carysfort, and other English ships of war, and of all the American whale ships that have touched at this port for a few years past. While the influence of some has been salutary, infamous facts might be stated pertaining to others of them, whose visits have been sadly demoralizing and baleful. But we forbear to give them notoriety.* *Let the memory of the just be blessed, but the name of the wicked rot.*

The so-called reflex influence of missions has been very happily exemplified at this station. The missionary pastor's faithfulness with sea-captains and others who have touched here, and with all foreigners who have come in his way, and whenever and wherever he has had the privilege of preaching the Gospel, and the hospitable, friendly acts of all the families, have not been in vain. Seed cast upon the waters

* Under date of October 16th, 1849, Rev. Mr. Coan thus writes to the American Seamen's Friend Society: "Whale ships are now in, and our streets are all alive with sailors. Hundreds are having liberty on shore, and our town is like a bee-hive. Still all are quiet. No man staggers, no man fights, none are noisy and boisterous. We have nothing here to inflame the blood, nothing to madden the brain. Our verdant landscape, our peaceful streets, our pure cold water, and the absence of those inebriating vials of wrath which consume all good, induce wise commanders to visit this port, in order to refresh and give liberty to their crews."

has been gathered again with rejoicing. I have become acquainted, while at the islands, with three cases of hopeful conversion at Hilo: a whaling-captain, a traveler, and a seaman. Other cases I have heard detailed. Three captains, to our knowledge, labored with on the subject, have pledged themselves not to whale any longer upon the Sabbath.

How many lasting impressions may have been made upon seamen and others by the pungent lessons they have heard, and the tracts and kind words they have received there, and by what they have observed of the power of the Gospel upon natives, we can never tell in time; but in eternity, I doubt not, there will be found a goodly company of foreign souls saved through the instrumentality of truth brought in their way at Hilo. They who have thus sown the seed shall reap the fruit with joy, and sing the harvest-home in another world.

On one occasion, some years ago, when Mr. Coan was absent from his station at the general meeting of missionaries in Honolulu, a whale ship entered the port of Hilo, and the captain, being in want of men, was disposed to enlist some native Hawaiians. It so happened that one man engaged himself who was a member of Mr. Coan's church, one of the rules of which obliges its members to keep the Sabbath day holy, KA LA TABU. He did not think to ask if it was a Sabbath-keeping ship until he had engaged to go the voyage to the Northwest Coast, and just before the evening had come for the vessel to sail.

Then, learning that the ship whaled on the Sabbath, and that he should have to work on the Lord's day as on other days, he came in his *pilikia*, perplexity, to Mrs. Coan, to know what he should do.

Mrs. Coan, well knowing her husband's mind and determination in like cases, and that the man, if he went the voyage in such a Sabbath-breaking ship, would be likely to become an abandoned and wretched apostate, nobly took on herself the responsibility of saying that he must by no means go, and that she would be answerable to the captain for the man's breaking his engagement under the circumstances of the case : a thing the honest Hawaiian was wishing, but afraid to do.

Telling him to put himself at rest on that score, she promised him herself to write a *palapala*, letter, to the whaling captain, respectfully explaining why the man could not go the voyage, and exculpating him from blame.

Just as he was setting sail that evening, and reckoning fully upon his man, the captain received Mrs Coan's note. The pilot was now on board, the anchor tripped, and it was too late to make up his loss. But in great wrath at what he deemed the impertinent interference of a missionary's wife, he resolved to touch off the reef at Honolulu, on his way, and expose the whole affair in the Sandwich Island Gazette, a local newspaper of the baser sort, very much given at that time to opposing and vilifying the missionaries.

General meeting was then in session, and the first news Mr. Coan had of his domestic household and flock at Hilo was in the publication of his wife's letter to the sea-captain, and the outpouring of whole vials of editorial wrath and abuse upon her and himself, and the whole *meddling* mission, in them represented. With his wonted promptitude, and a soul overflowing with thankfulness and joy at the noble conduct of his wife, the honored missionary at once took his pen and wrote simply as follows, in the language of Scripture, for which he is never at a loss, inclosing also the slip from the Sandwich Island News:

"MANY DAUGHTERS HAVE DONE VIRTUOUSLY, BUT THOU EXCELLEST THEM ALL."

We leave it to wives and sisters to imagine the delight given by such an epistle to the heart of a DAUGHTER, whom we well knew every way worthy this spontaneous commendation; and we leave it to husbands and brothers to conceive, if they can, the genuine satisfaction and pride of the missionary at this new proof of the treasure he had in A PRUDENT WIFE.

Light is sown for the righteous, and gladness for the upright in heart.—Cast thy bread upon the waters, for thou shalt find it after many days.—In the morning sow thy seed, and in the evening withhold not thy hand, for thou knowest not whether shall prosper either this or that, or whether they both shall be alike good.—He that goeth forth and weepeth, bearing precious seed, shall doubtless come again with rejoicing, bringing his sheaves with him.

In the seed that has already sprung up at Hilo, there is delightful evidence of what missionaries and the Gospel are doing for Hawaiians. No one can learn the system of faithful pastoral visitation and Church oversight adopted here, or contemplate the two boarding schools in successful operation, preparing Hawaiian youth for eminence and usefulness, without having his mind elated with joy and hope of the complete Christianization and saving of the Hawaiian race.

Mr. Lyman's school is a model for one of the kind, admirably conducted, taught, and disciplined. It was established by Mr. Lyman in 1836. Up to the year 1848, nearly three hundred youth have passed through it, of whom seventy-five have entered the mission seminary at Lahainaluna, and more than fifty have gone out directly as teachers. The number of pupils at the present time is seventy, from the ages of thirteen and fourteen to seventeen and eighteen.

The discipline and regimen of the school are rigid and thorough, but kind. The hours of study, labor, meals, relaxation, sleep, and all exercises are exactly marked, so that no boy has a moment to be idle in. They make their own clothes, cultivate the most of their food, bake, pound, and mix it for the table, and do all that is to be done for themselves, and a great part of the work required in the family of their instructors. Thus they acquire habits of diligence, order, and the improvement of their time, in all which Hawaiians, like uncivilized people every where, are lamentably deficient.

The studies pursued are reading, writing, arithmetic, geography, history, composition, and music. Most of the daily drilling, as in the girls' school, is done by assistant native teachers. Mrs. Lyman has formerly devoted a good deal of time to teaching them to sing, but native lads, whom she had taught, are now able to relieve her of much of the burden. The two schools occasionally meet of an afternoon for exercise in singing. Thirty-seven of the boys and twenty-one of the girls are members of the Church. It is intended to effect alliances between them, which will give promise of more mutual fitness and conjugal enjoyment than falls to the lot of Hawaiians generally.

Not a few of the lads are good-looking, sprightly youth, that have made very commendable proficiency in their studies, and in the practical knowledge suitable for Hawaiians. The girls have attained considerable skill in needle-work and braiding straw, which they turn to profitable account in making garments and bonnets for themselves, and doing all the work that is furnished them by foreigners. During seven months of one year they made thirty shirts, several pairs of pantaloons, a number of jackets, and fifty garments for themselves, besides attending to their regular studies, and miscellaneous housework.

A native man and his wife teach and live with the girls, always accompanying them when they go out daily to bathe, and in all their excursions, and assist in the preparation of their food. This is furnished by the Church in *kalo*, potatoes, fish, and *pia* (the native arrow-root). The country lying immediately around the station is divided into five sections, which supply the school with food for one week each in regular rotation.

On the monthly concert days some of the Church-members plant and till food for the benefit of the school, which, when it is ripe, the girls now and then go for in a body with their teacher, pull and bring it home. But this way of contributing having lost its novelty, and food, too, being scarce, and bringing a high price, supplies do not pour in as they once did, so that some food has to be bought. The boys' boarding school receives an appropriation of eight hundred dollars yearly, which is spent in the repairing and erection of buildings, paying native teachers, and furnishing cloth and food when necessary.

Missionaries have to do an immense amount of what they call *paipai ana*, that is, stimulating, stirring up, in order to get the natives to do any thing steadily and systematically. They will work well for a little while, on the spur of something new. Improve the favorable tide, and it will bear them on to considerable achievements. But when the novelty of the thing is over, and the tide is out, they are as immovable as a stranded ship from which the waves have retreated. You must invent some new stimulus to locomotion, suggest some novel expedient, and pour a fresh tide of voltaic energy through torpid minds and muscles before they will start again.

This is one of the sore trials of missionaries, the inconstancy of the people in doing good, and the necessity it lays upon their teachers of incessant repetition, *line upon line, precept upon precept, here a little and there a little*, and always urging forward. Along with their poverty, it may keep them yet a long time from supporting their ministers entirely, except at Lahaina, Honolulu, and Wailuku, and perhaps, under skillful management, here also, where the proportion of Church-members is so great that two shillings only a year from each would give their laborious and happy pastor an ample support. For the year 1848 they contributed at Hilo five hundred and forty-one dollars in cash, besides doing much for meeting-houses, schools, &c.

Probably they will give more for this object than for any or all others. And yet while schools are pinched, meeting-houses to be built, and their own dwellings so poor and miserably furnished, it would seem almost like cruelty for the missionary to be compelled to appropriate their contributions to himself.

There is no benevolent patron of missions but would have his heart made glad and his donation doubled by personal inspection of the good it is doing here; and some who have never known the luxury of contributing generously to foreign missions would be made, I think, into liberal donors. A visit here, too, by those who have argued in stately platform speeches, Preach the Gospel, convert the world by preaching the Gospel, and let schools go, would be likely to correct some theoretical crooks and distortions, and substitute a deep conviction of the absolute indispensableness of high schools and seminaries, lest the word of God, however faithfully preached, be rendered of little or no lasting effect.

Besides the schools above mentioned, Mr. Wilcox instructs a company of seventy teachers in an old stone building that was the precarious habitation of the first missionaries. They are off and on throughout the year, never all present at once, but coming up from time to time by turns to refit and polish their pedagogical armor and get themselves supplied with intellectual furniture, books, stationery, &c. So, to compare great things with small, and not meaning any slur upon the honest teachers,

So certain Cleri from the land of Romilly,
Wanting a barrel of the stuff call'd homily,
And being quite without the brains to brew it,
And never fearing they will have to rue it,
Buy it at London, lithograph'd and wrought,
And stitch'd in Sabbath leaves with careful thought.
There all things venal are, *si sint emptores,*
(Such is your vice, *O tempora, O mores!*)
From two-hour speeches made in Parliament,
To fifteen-minute sermons preach'd in Lent.

Government is under obligation to pay the teachers; but they are so miserably compensated that many are just ready to give up, and some of them would betake themselves to other ways of getting a livelihood, were it not for the degree of honor attached to the office of a *kumu-kula* (school teacher). If the missionaries should withhold their influence, and help, and oversight of the teachers, the schools would be laid flat and powerless, if not quite extinct.

Mr. Wilcox makes occasional tours through Hilo and Puna, to examine the schools, stir up parents and teachers, and set things awry to rights. But it is rather a sorry, thankless work, because he can carry to the teachers no pay. He thinks, very likely, if some of the money spent on foreigners and anniversary feasts were distributed among the poor teachers, that both the nation, the king, and the pedagogues would be much better off.

The whole number of Church-members now in regular standing in Hilo and Puna, under the pastoral care of Mr. Coan, is six thousand one hundred and nine, in a population of ten thousand. The whole number admitted since the station was taken, up to 1848, is nine thousand three hundred and eighty-two.

Whole number deceased, three thousand five hundred. Children baptized by the present pastor, three thousand and eighty-three. The yearly mortality in the Church is great, many of the members being old and infirm. More than fifteen hundred have died during the years 1848 and 1849, and it is not at all probable that this great Church will hold its own. For an account of the manner in which pastoral supervision and discipline are exercised, and the ordinances administered to this great body of professing believers, the world is indebted to the Missionary Herald.

There was an old man of the Hilo Church whom they called Joshua, whose prayers I used to listen to with deep interest when stopping at that station, for their peculiar unction and engagedness. Many things were told me of him by his pastor, illustrating his fervent piety and power in prayer. During the great sickness of 1848 and 1849, he passed away, to be, we doubt not, with the spirits of the blessed, among whom his remarkable spirituality, for a converted heathen, will exalt him to a precedence above many that had attained in their earthly career to far more head-knowledge of God and divine things than he.

The account given of him by his pastor is so characteristic and instructive, that we venture to transcribe a part of it here. He had been a member of the Church for several years prior to the Great Revival of 1838 and 1839, without evincing any special marks of uncommon spirituality; but during that work, says Mr. Coan, he became deeply and thoroughly aroused, and at the same time wonderfully transformed.

"The study of the Bible, secret and social prayer

attendance at the house of God, religious conversation, visiting from house to house, laboring for souls, &c., were his meat and his drink. With no extraordinary native powers of mind, he became one of the most active and efficient helpers, merely through the strength of his piety, or, in Scripture language, 'through the power of the Holy Ghost' resting upon him.

"He was already an old man, but his strength and his youth were renewed like the eagle's. He became my almost constant companion in travel, patiently toiling by my side over the burning lava fields of Puna, and through the rivers and ravines of Hilo. His love for Christ, his compassion for souls, seemed deep, fervent, and constant, not always, of course, equally intense, but never doubtful. His prayers were highly fervent, deeply humble, believing, and importunate. I have never met with a mightier wrestler at the throne of grace Good old Jacob, when gazing up the celestial ladder, did not see more clearly into heaven than good old Joshua, when kneeling before God. I never tired in traveling with him, and his conversation and prayers never wearied. When my spirits were sad, my resort, next to the throne of grace, was the hut of good old Joshua. He was truly spiritual, and there was an unction about him which readily attracted spiritual minds. The wicked venerated and feared him; the good loved him.

"As age and infirmity crept over him, he began to feel it more and more difficult to go with me on my tours. Several times, when invited to do so, he has excused himself, saying, 'I am too old and too feeble.

My heart goes with you; but this poor old body can not drag itself over the hills and the rivers any more. It is done.' Then, after a little reflection, all his old recollections would revive, and his desire to go again would become so strong, that he would say, 'Well, I will try once more. Perhaps God will give me strength to go through; if not, let him leave me by the way; all will be well.' Gathering up his strength and taking his staff, the pilgrim and the patriarch would set off 'faint yet pursuing.' Usually, at the close of the first day, and when bowing before the family altar, the old man would express his joy and gratitude to God that he had been persuaded to attempt the tour. Listening to the Word, and seeing the works of God, would so fill his soul with joy that he would spontaneously exclaim, 'I am glad that I came. I feel stronger than when I set out. The Word does me good. Oh how much I should have lost had I remained at home!' Such scenes were repeated several times before he finally yielded to the increasing infirmities of age.

"At length the strong man bowed beneath the pressure of years, and his active labors were confined to the circle immediately around the station. His wife, younger and more vigorous, was smitten by a paralysis, and hastened to the grave. This left his house and his heart desolate; for his conjugal relations were happy. He had no children. The measles and hooping-cough, with their attendants, prostrated his little remaining strength, and he was never again able to leave his house. He lingered, however, on the banks of Jordan, but with many longings to pass over.

"Often have I found him, while strength allowed it, lying prostrate with his old spectacles on, his Bible open on the mat (his bed), and his face downward, eagerly digging gold from that precious and exhaustless mine. While thus absorbed, and with dimmed natural vision, he would not at first notice that any one had entered; but at length, raising his eyes a little, and descrying me, he would reach out both hands, clasp one of mine, press it, hold it fast, and look up to heaven, while the tears flowed down his aged cheeks, and remain silent for some time. At length his struggling feelings would find vent in such words as follow: 'Bless the Lord! I rejoice to meet you. My heart is full. O! the word of God. Deep, high, broad, rich, wonderful! I relish it; I eat it; it is delicious food; it is sweeter than honey to my taste. I want to see Him. I long to be with Him. I long to go. But I will wait. He is good. He knows best. He will come by and by. But to be with Him! This only will satisfy my soul. This only will fill my heart.'

"Expressions of a similar character fell from his lips during almost every one of our later interviews. At length we were summoned to the general meeting; and on our return it was announced that the Master had come and called for Joshua. My soul followed him in his celestial chariot, and I involuntarily exclaimed, 'My father! my father! the chariot of Israel and the horsemen thereof.' He was a good man, and no one denies it. Both friends and foes say of Joshua, 'He was a good man.' Give me his simple faith and his sure hope, and I ask no other inheritance. Oh that my title to eternal life might appear as clear, as authentic as his!"*

Since becoming somewhat acquainted, by observation and intercourse with the missionaries, with the peculiarities of native character, having learned their liability to, and eagerness for, excitement upon the subject of religion, and their child-like inability, as of undisciplined, weak minds generally, to restrain powerful emotions, we are of opinion that a somewhat exaggerated impression of the spirituality and power of the great revival may have gone abroad. We would not abate a jot of heart or hope from those laborious, praying men who had, under God, the management of that great work on North and East Hawaii, or damp at all the joy and thanks rendered to God on their behalf by many who have read what things God hath wrought by them. Neither do we pronounce upon any of the measures and means used, that they were unauthorized or unwise, or such as should not be used in like circumstances again.

The field was new, the work was new, teachers and people were new to each other; the powerful influences of the Holy Spirit were flowing, as on the day of Pentecost, in a new channel, by which they had never run so strongly before. The Hawaiian mind was unused, like the Pagan world in the time of the Apostles, to the warm evangelic element that was now pouring through its circulation.

What wonder that its stimulating effects should be, as then, remarkable and strange, inducing the judgment, These men are beside themselves, and full of

* Missionary Herald, April, 1850.

new wine? What wonder that this new stimulus should prove too strong for undisciplined and ignorant minds, and produce novel developments, and uncontrollable bursts of feeling, that have always and every where more or less characterized its presence, even in enlightened communities, at times when it has powerfully permeated the human mind?

What matter of surprise is it that, mingling with the agitated current of human and animal feeling, it should sometimes swell and burst the vessels that contained it, or overflow its natural embankments, and bear off, somewhat confusedly, on its bosom many to whom such an element was altogether new? Or who can deem it at all strange that the constituted tillers of the Lord's vineyard should find themselves altogether inadequate or unwilling to stay the swelling torrent, or always turn it into its proper fertilizing courses, and keep it from running off?

How natural that they should err, sometimes in opening, sometimes in closing the sluice-way of excited feeling, and managing the waste-gate of the mental emotions. How unheard of, if, on the top of the tide which was rolling into the Church, many should not be carried in before their time, and some get fast moored in that much-desired haven who should afterward show colors of the hypocrite and pirate.

While never for a moment doubting the genuineness and extraordinary power of that work (which who that knows can do?), it would yet be too much, and would prove an anomalous exemption from ordinary human weakness and fallibility to say that every measure adopted in the conduct of that astonishing work was perfect, or that no mistakes were committed, nor ever undue haste or lack of wisdom evinced in admitting to the Church.

But it is much easier for a looker-on to say so, and for the actors themselves to acknowledge it—the excitement and toil of battle being done—than to avoid those errors or make use always of that Heaven-inspired wisdom that precludes alike mistake and regret. *Experience*, it is a striking remark of Coleridge, *is like lamps in the stern of a ship; they illuminate only the path that has been gone over.* Many ships have met on the high seas with fatal collision, because their lights were only in the binnacle or astern. And many a mistake might have been avoided in the management of affairs, and in the conduct of revivals of religion, many a rock and shoal passed clear, could the lamp of experience have been hung up before instead of behind.

One thing is certain, that those men ordinarily who are themselves at the head of affairs, or, to take the particular instance, those whom God has intrusted and blessed with a revival of religion, who are themselves heartily engaged in it, baptized in the revival influence, and spiritually minded, they are the most competent to its management. They can better interpret the mind of the Spirit than others, and judge more correctly than some cool looker-on, or than any distant though not indifferent co-workers, what to do and what not to do, what to allow and what to disallow, what to encourage and what to discourage, what to urge and what to oppose, what to use and what to disuse.

They can best tell, under the guidance of the Spirit, what expedients and measures to adopt and what to reject, what means will be likely to prove favorable and what unfavorable to the work, what will be for its success and what to its prejudice. If a review of things prove them to have erred, it does by no means prove that following other counsels would have been a less error.

And especially is it true that those who are engaged as ministers in a revival of religion, who preach to and talk with the people, who observe and examine the anxious, who know the most about the persons who are offered as candidates for the Church, it is those certainly who can best decide who are worthy and who are not worthy, who *shall* be admitted and who shall not. Nor does the admission of very many, or of very few, of itself prove an unbecoming haste and carelessness, or a wise caution. This man may be very wise, and right, and conscientious in admitting many, and another very unwise and wrong in excluding many, or *vice versa.* Men always, and missionaries of necessity and right, too, will be governed in this matter very much by temperament and feeling. A man in one sphere of labor or over one Church, can not dictate to and make rules for another man in another sphere of labor or over another Church.

Missionary pastors, we think, ought to be independent one of another, except so far as they voluntarily come under the rules of an association, and independent of any extra Board or other body of men in all Church affairs. Their own good sense, with the advice of their deacons, or other reliable men who know the cases in hand, and the guidance of the Spirit constantly sought in prayer, must be their only reliance. . And no man ought to complain of another for conscientiously acting on this rule. To God only he is responsible. *To his own Master he standeth or falleth. Who art thou that judgest another?* He is to be commended who acts conscientiously from love to souls, to be reasoned with calmly when deemed in error, to be found fault with slowly, and always in good temper.

There are scattered about almost every where some of the fault-finding, day-after-the-fair, *I-could-have-told-you-it-would-be-so* class of men, who do little good themselves, and those who would do good they hinder. How much better is the way of him who, by patient continuance in well-doing,

As ever in his great Task-master's eye,

with no rash judgments of other men, but privately remonstrating with his brother, if he deem him wrong, and exercising himself to keep a conscience void of offense, both toward God and man, thus holds on his even tenor, calmly putting forth all his powers for God and humanity, head, heart, and hand,

Active and firm to fight the bloodless fight
Of science, freedom, and the truth in Christ.

It is of him we can say, in the words of Horace,

Integer vitæ scelerisque purus,
Non eget Mauri jaculis neque arcu.

The man that lives upright and clear,
Nor Moorish arrows, bow, or spear,
Has ever need to use or fear.

Open opposition and fault-finding he can openly meet; secret defamation and undermining he can live down or counter-work; and, in the end, his real character comes out untarnished like a mirror, though it may be momentarily blackened by the smoke of slander or covered with the dust thrown by envious jealousy.

HEREIN DO I EXERCISE MYSELF, TO HAVE ALWAYS A CONSCIENCE VOID OF OFFENSE TOWARD GOD AND TOWARD MEN. There is a noble sonnet by Professor Upham, on those words of Paul, with which I can not deny myself the pleasure of closing this chapter, having in eye a friend and missionary brother whom I greatly admire and love:

What constitutes the true nobility?
  Not wealth, nor name, nor outward pomp, nor power.
Fools have them all; and vicious men may be
  The idols and the pageants of an hour.
But 'tis to have a good and honest heart,
  Above all meanness, and above all crime;
To act the right and honorable part
  In every circumstance of place and time.
HE WHO IS THUS, FROM GOD HIS PATENT TAKES,
  HIS MAKER FORMED HIM THE TRUE NOBLEMAN;
WHATE'ER IS LOW AND VICIOUS HE FORSAKES,
AND ACTS ON RECTITUDE'S UNCHANGING PLAN.
THINGS CHANGE AROUND HIM; CHANGES TOUCH NOT HIM;
THE STAR THAT GUIDES HIS PATH FAILS NOT, NOR WAXES DIM.

With this adopted sonnet the author takes his leave of Hilo and of the friends that may have traveled with him thus far, he hopes not without profit, through THE ISLAND WORLD OF THE PACIFIC. He promises to resume his travels through other parts of the Island-kingdom of Hawaii, should Providence allow and the reception of the present volume warrant it.

Meantime, he commends his readers to the careful perusal of the statistics and facts collected in the following pages, as containing the reliable data from which to forecast the horoscope of the future destinies of the Sandwich Islands.

APPENDIX.

APPENDIX.

STATISTICAL VIEW OF THE RESOURCES, TRADE, COMMERCE, POPULATION, PIETY, POSITION, AND PROSPECTS OF THE HAWAIIAN ISLANDS.

> Mother of Wealth, and Enterprise, and Arts,
> Her golden empire marries distant parts;
> She knits the league; she sheathes the blade of war,
> Of Earth, and Sea, and Man the conqueror:
> Dread agent, or for boundless good or ill,
> God speaks the word, and Commerce works his will.
>
> *Anon.*

We throw into the form of an appendix, for ease of reference and for the use of commercial readers and travelers, the following condensed statements and tables of statistics, gathered mainly from latest documents in the Government Journal published at Honolulu, and carefully compared and corrected for this work.

In the chain of events which have served to attract attention to this portion of the globe, the first was the seizure of these Islands by Lord George Paulet, and the subsequent restoration by Admiral Thomas. Up to that time, 1843, the trade of the Islands was limited to one or two ships which sailed from Boston, and the trade with the whaling fleet. The imports in 1843 amounted to $223,385 38, upon which a revenue of $8,468 38 was collected. So rapidly did the trade increase, that in 1847 the imports amounted to $710,133 52, and the revenue to $48,801 25, while for the current year the amount of both imports and revenue therefrom will doubtless far exceed that amount. But it should be borne in mind that this great increase of importation is not the consequence of increased consumption, for many of the goods which have been imported and paid duties here, eventually found their way out of the country.

The second event which occurred to draw public attention to the Pacific was the establishment of the French Protectorate at Tahiti. Although this event has not directly exerted any great influence upon commerce, it has, in a political sense, attracted public attention to the Pacific, and will in the end, if the right measures be pursued by the government there, exert a wholesome influence upon commerce. The consumption will be increased by the influx of foreigners, while the products will also be increased.

The settlement of the Oregon boundary question, and the influx of settlers, may be classed as the third event, which has already exerted, and is destined to exert a still greater influence upon the growth of commerce in the Pacific. The exports of Oregon, a few years since, consisted mainly of furs, and her trade was limited to one or two vessels annually. We have no statistics by which to judge of the increase of trade, but it must be apparent that it has been great. Lumber, timber, flour, and salmon are now exported from Oregon in large quantities. The occasional trader is but one of quite a fleet of vessels which now annually visit Columbia River. The natives of the forest are fast sinking away before the mighty tide of civilization which is pressing onward, and their wigwams are being displaced by the hut of the hardy pioneer. Oregon is rich in agricultural resources, and the time is not far distant when her "dark shores" will be crowned with stately warehouses, her waters be whitened with the sails of commerce, her rivers plowed by stately steamers, and her borders resound with the songs of an independent and happy people.

The occupation of California by the American forces may be called the fourth link in the chain of events to which we have alluded. The trade of California, previous to this event, was limited to an occasional hide-drogher or smuggler, her exports to hides and tallow, with now and then a sprinkling of specie. During the occupation of the country by the forces of the United States trade was better, the consumption was increased, but, on account of no export existing, the prosperity of the country was likely to suffer a serious check. In June, 1848, however, the gold placer on the American Fork was discovered, and the ease with which gold was procured soon afforded an export more than sufficient for all their wants. Subsequently, the treaty of peace between Mexico and the United States was ratified, and Upper California, gold and all, became a part and parcel of the great American Republic. California has presented an instance of commercial growth unequaled in the annals of the world, and the discovery of gold in such abundance is an event which will exert a mighty influence upon the prosperity of commerce in this ocean. A dense population will soon be in California, and if agriculture be neglected a large fleet of vessels will be required to supply their wants.

The line of steamers via Panama make California and Oregon near neighbors to the great commercial cities of the Atlantic coast. A railroad has long been talked of, and will doubtless soon be commenced.

Boston and St. Louis are already connected by a magnetic line, an extension of which is contemplated to the Pacific coast. The expense of completing a line from St. Louis to the Pacific has been estimated at $300,000.

It is impossible to foretell the mighty influence which this chain of events will exert upon the future prosperity of commerce in this ocean. The Pacific, about which so much has been written and so little known, will soon be crowded with traders—every bay and island, every nook and corner, will be explored. The mighty wave of immigration, which is now rolling toward the western shores of the American Continent, will sooner or later reach the coast of Hawaii. The geographical position of these Islands plainly point to them as the West Indies of the Pacific.

The nature of their resources and the channels of their commerce will appear from tables hereafter, which we preface with the following Compendium of Commercial Regulations, for the information of merchants, travelers, ship-captains, and sea-faring men generally who may peruse this book.

Condensed Abstract of Laws respecting Commerce, published for the information of Ship-masters and others frequenting the Ports of the Hawaiian Islands.

Vessels arriving off the ports of entry to make the usual marine signal, if they want a pilot.

The pilot will approach vessels to the windward, and present the health certificate, to be signed by the captain. If the vessel is free from any contagion, the captain will hoist the white flag, otherwise he will hoist the yellow flag, and obey the direction of the pilot and health officer.

Passports must be exhibited to the governor or collector by passengers before landing.

Masters of vessels allowing baggage to be landed before compliance with the laws are subject to a fine of $500.

Masters of vessels, on arriving at any of the ports of entry, are required to deliver all letters to the collector of customs. The law regarding the delivery of letters by shipmasters to the collector, will only take effect on promulgation by his Hawaiian Majesty in privy council.

The commanding officer of any merchant vessel, immediately after her arrival at either of the legalized ports of entry, shall make known to the collector of customs the business upon which said vessel has come to this port, furnish him with a list of her passengers, and deliver to him, under oath, a full, true, and perfect manifest of the cargo with which said vessel is laden; which manifest shall contain an account of the packages, with their marks, numbers, contents, quantities, and also the names of the importers or consignees. When any such officer shall fail to perform any or all of the acts above mentioned within forty-eight hours after his arrival, he shall be subject to a fine not exceeding $1000.

All manifests, entries, and other documents presented at any custom-house shall be either in the Hawaiian or English language.

The collector, at his discretion, and at the expense of any vessel, may provide an officer to be present on board such vessel during her discharge, to superintend the disembarkation, and see that no other or greater amount of merchandise be landed than is set forth in the permit.

All goods landed at any of the ports of these Islands are subject to a duty of five per cent. *ad valorem*, except spirituous or fermented liquors.

The following are the only ports of entry at these Islands, viz.: for merchantmen, Honolulu, Oahu, and Lahaina, Maui; and for whalers, in addition thereto, Hilo, Hanalei, Kauai, and Kealakekua, Hawaii. The port charges on merchant vessels are as follows: At Honolulu, 20 cents per ton; buoys, $2; clearance, $1; pilotage in and out, $1 per foot each way. At Lahaina, anchorage dues, $10; pilotage, $1; health certificate, $1; lights, $1; canal (if used), $2, and clearance, $1.

Merchant vessels touching at the port of Honolulu for refreshments only, and neither lading nor unlading any cargo, taking or leaving any passengers, shall pay but six cents per ton harbor dues, instead of 20 cents; but if they discharge or take cargo, leave or take passengers, they shall pay 20 cents per ton harbor dues.

By a law promulgated in the Polynesian newspaper of June 19, 1847, whale ships are, from and after that date, exempted from all charges for pilotage, tonnage dues, or anchorage fees, at all the various ports of entry for whalers of this group.

Hereafter the charges on whalers will be, clearance, $1; permits (when required), $1 each; and in addition thereto, at Honolulu, buoys, $2. At Lahaina, health certificate, $1; canal (when used), $2; and at Kealakekua, health certificate, $1.

Whale ships are allowed to land goods to the value of $200, free of duty; but if they exceed that amount, they are then liable to pay five per cent. on the whole amount landed, as well as the charges for pilotage and tonnage dues, or anchorage fees required of whalers by law previous to June 19, 1847; and if the goods landed shall exceed

$1200 (which is only permitted by law at Honolulu and Lahaina), they will then be considered as merchantmen, and subject to the like charges and legal liabilities.

The permits granted to whalers do not include the trade, sale, or landing of spirituous liquors. Any such traffic by them (which is prohibited, except at Lahaina and Honolulu) will subject them to the charges upon merchantmen, including the payment of 20 cents per ton, as well at the anchorage of Lahaina and at the roadstead of Honolulu, as within the port of Honolulu.

Any master of a whale ship who shall fail to produce his permit when called for, shall be liable to a fine not less than $10, nor more than $50, to be imposed by the collector.

Before obtaining a clearance, each shipmaster is required to produce to the collector of customs, a certificate under the seal of his consul, that all legal charges or demands in his office against said vessel have been paid, and that he knows of no reason why said vessel should not immediately depart.

Spirituous or fermented liquors landed at any of the ports of these Islands are subject to the following duties, viz.: rum, gin, brandy, whisky, &c., of more than 27, and less than 55 per cent. alcohol, $5 per gallon; if more than 55 per cent. alcohol, $10 per gallon. Wines, liqueurs, cordials, &c. (except claret, Bordeaux, Champagne, and sinclar wines, of not over 18 per cent. alcohol), $1 per gallon; claret, &c., of less than 18 per cent. alcohol, malt liquors and cider, five per cent. *ad valorem*.

Products of the whale fishery may be transhipped free from any charge of transit duty.

Vessels landing goods upon which the duties have not been paid, are liable to seizure and confiscation.

If any person commit an offense on shore, and the offender escape on board of any vessel, it shall be the duty of the commanding officer of said vessel to surrender the suspected or culprit person to any officer of the police who demands his surrender, on production of a legal warrant.

It shall not be lawful for any person on board of a vessel at anchor in the harbor of Honolulu to throw stones or other rubbish overboard, under a penalty of $100.

All sailors found ashore at Lahaina after the beating of the drum, or at Honolulu after the ringing of the bell, are subject to apprehension and a fine of $2.

Shipmasters must give notice to the harbor-master of the desertion of any of their sailors within forty-eight hours, under a penalty of $100

Seamen are not allowed to be discharged at any of the ports of these Islands, excepting those of Lahaina and Honolulu.

It shall not be lawful to discharge seamen at any of the ports of these Islands without the written consent of the Governor.

Honolulu and Lahaina are the only ports at which native seamen are allowed to be shipped, and at those places with the Governor's consent only.

Any vessel taking away a prisoner from these Islands shall be subject to a fine of $500.

To entitle any vessel to a clearance, it shall be incumbent on her commanding officer first to furnish the collector of customs with a manifest of cargo intended to be exported in such vessel.

It shall not be lawful for the commanding officer of any Hawaiian or foreign vessel to carry out of this kingdom as a passenger any domiciled alien, naturalized foreigner, or native without previous exhibition to him of a passport from his Majesty's Minister of Foreign Relations.

Retailers of spirituous liquors are not allowed to keep their houses open later than nine o'clock in the evening, and they are to be closed from Saturday evening until Monday morning.

Rapid riding in the streets is prohibited under a penalty of $5.

Office hours at the Custom-house and other public offices, every day (except Sundays and national holydays), from nine o'clock A.M. until 3 o'clock P.M.

COMMERCIAL STATISTICS.

STATEMENT OF IMPORTS, EXPORT DUTIES, &c., AT THE PORT OF HONOLULU, OAHU, HAWAIIAN ISLANDS, FOR THE YEAR ENDING DECEMBER 31, 1849.

Description of Goods.	Gross invoice value.	Gross duties.	Value re-exported.	Return duties.	Net consumption.	Net duties.
Goods paying five per cent. duty	$603,403.64	$30,174.06	$70,222.60	$2,818.68	$533,181.04	$27,355.38
Spirits, Wines, &c.	43,328.03	191,944.93	18,879.47	109,279.48	24,448.56	82,665.45
Imported by Consuls, Missions, &c., free of duty	74,890.20	——	——	——	74,890.20	——
By whale ships, under the $200 provision, free	8,117.57	——	——	——	8,117.57	——
	729,739.44	222,118.99	89,102.07	112,098.16	640,637.37	110,020.83
Deduct spirits, wines, and goods, &c., now in bond, and which will probably be exported, estimated at	——	——	18,000.00	44,000.00	18,000.00	44,000.00
Total	$729,739.44	$222,118.99	$107,102.07	$156,098.16	$622,637.37	$66,020.83

IMPORTS FOR THE YEAR 1849, AMOUNTING, AS PER TABLE, TO $729,739.44, WERE IMPORTED FROM THE FOLLOWING COUNTRIES, VIZ.:

Country	Amount	Country	Amount
United States of America	$239,246.42	Tahiti	$19,340.27
California	131,505.89	Columbia River	12,672.38
Great Britain	44,578.11	Hamburg	9,723.58
British Colonies	52,821.59	Petropaulovskoi	6,622.83
China	95,787.27	Mazatlan, Manilla, Panama, Bremen Sea, &c., &c.	6,629.27
Chili	87,356.05		
France	23,455.78	Total	$729,739.44

DOMESTIC EXPORTS FROM HONOLULU FOR THE YEAR 1849.

Article	Amount	Article	Amount
Sugar, 653,820 pounds, at 5 cents	$32,691.00	Coal, 464 baskets, at 25 cents	$116.00
Molasses, 41,235 gallons, at 25 cents	10,308.75	Wood, 30 cords, at $10	300.00
Coffee, 28,231 pounds, at 10 cents	2,823.10	Wool, 1000 pounds, at 12½ cents	125.00
Salt, 2,866 barrels, at $1	2,866.00	Coral stone	440.00
Lime, 906½ barrels, at $2	1,813.00	Furniture	1,520.56
Beef, 158 barrels, at $12	1,896.00	Mules, 12, at $30 each	360.00
Hides, 2,512 pounds, at $2 each	5.024.00	Horses, 4, at $100 each	400.00
Tallow, 17,403 pounds, at 6 cents	1,044.18	Sheep, 50, at $3 each	150.00
Goat skins, 31,488, at 20 cents each	6,297.60	Turkeys, 500, at 75 cents each	375.00
Irish potatoes, 858 barrels, at $3	2,574.00	Clothing*	1,290.25
Sweet potatoes, 306 barrels, at $1.50	459.00	Koa shingles, Timber and Boards, and eight House Frames	10,809.99
Onions $1,246.25, Pumpkins $200.50, Limes $115.75, Lime juice $152, Pickles $260, Oranges $704,50	2,680.00	Eggs, Melons, Beans, Arrow-root, Brooms, Poi, Corn, Mustard Seed, Bacon, Dried Beef, Sausages, Yams, &c., &c.	1,257.65
Butter, 994 pounds, at 37½ cents	372.75		
Hay, 35 tons, at $50	1,750.00	Total	$89,743.74

* The cloth from which the clothing was made, and most of the timber of the house frames, is foreign produce.

STATEMENT OF IMPORTS, EXPORTS, RECEIPTS, &c., AT THE CUSTOM HOUSE, PORT OF HONOLULU, OAHU, HAWAIIAN ISLANDS, FOR THE YEARS 1843–9.

Years.	Gross value of imports.	Gross duties.	Re-exported.	Return duties.	Net amounts.	Net duties.	Transit duties.	Harbor dues.	Total net receipts.
1843	$222,383.38	$6,701.84	$66,618.17	$1,670.41	$156,565.21	$5,270.74	$239.31	$2,958.33	$8,468.38
1844	350,357.12	10,326.13	60,054.06	1,501.34	289,969.77	8,970.13	411.60	4,881.33	14,263.56
1845	546,941.72	21,563.94	67,010.93	2,098.82	471,319.78	19,465.12	734.01	4,890.83	25,189.96
1846	598,382.24	53,447.78	62,325.74	21,667.02	536,056.50	31,780.76	20.56	4,705.32	36,506.64
1847	710,138.52	101,512.25	55,208.07	52,991.17	653,930.45	44,521.08	184.93	4,094.24	48,801.25
1848	605,618.73	142,357.73	33,551.55	90,148.27	572,067.18	52,209.46	264.52	3,095.96	55,568.94
1849	729,739.44	222,118.99	198,102.07	156,098.16	622,637.37	66,020.83	235.13	5,687.53	71,943.49

R

Gross Receipts at the Custom Houses of Oahu, Maui, and Kauai for the Year ending December 31, 1849.

Honolulu, Oahu.		Lahaina, Maui.	
Import duties	$66,020.83	Import duties	$1,101.22
Transit duties	235.13	Transit duties	30.16
Harbor dues	5,687.53	Stamps	724.50
Stamps	2,726.88	Anchorage dues	500.00
Fines and Forfeitures	40.70	Light	76.32
Interest	528.24	Canal	62.00
Storage	2,124.44	Shipping and discharging Seamen	836.50
	$77,363.75		$3,330.70
Harbor Master, Honolulu:		Hilo, Hanalei, and Kealakeakua:	
Shipping and discharging Seamen	1,153.00	Stamps, &c.	97.87
Stamps	1,286.00	Amount at Honolulu (brought over)	79,802.75
Total	$79,802.75	Total	$83,231.32

Whale Ships entered at the Ports of Honolulu and Lahaina during the Year 1849.

	Lahaina.	Honolulu.
American	153	108
French	—	7
Bremen	1	4
British	—	1
	154	120
		154
Total		274

Amount of Domestic Produce furnished as Supplies to Shipping.

Honolulu.		Lahaina.	
Ships of war and government vessels, estimated	$4,000	Domestic produce exported (mostly potatoes) about	$14,000
134 merchant vessels, say $80 each	10,720	154 whalers, say $250 each	38,500
108 whalers (inside), say $250 each	27,000	14 merchant vessels, $80 each	1,120
Total	$41,720	Total	$53,620

Total value of domestic produce exported to foreign markets, and furnished to foreign vessels from the Hawaiian Islands for the year 1849, estimated $190,000

Arrivals and Departures of Merchant Vessels at and from the Port of Honolulu for the Year 1849.

Whole number in 1849	162
Whole number in 1848	90
Increase in 1849	72

Arrivals and Departures of Merchant Vessels at and from the Port of Lahaina for six Months ending December 31, 1849.

Whole number arrived from San Francisco and cleared for that and other ports	18
Amount of tonnage	3398

ARRIVALS AND DEPARTURES OF GOVERNMENT VESSELS AND SHIPS OF WAR AT AND FROM THE PORT OF HONOLULU DURING THE YEAR 1849.

Date.	Nation.	Class.	Name.	Commander.	Guns.	From	Sailed.	For
January 4	United States	Sloop	Dale	Rudd	18	Mazatlan	January 18	San Francisco
April 9	United States	Propeller	Massachusetts	Wood		New York	April 18	Columbia River
April 12	Russian	Brigantine	Baikal	Nevelsky	8	Valparaiso	April 25	Sitka
May 8	Great Britain	Sloop	Herald	Kellett	22	Panama	May 19	Petropaulovskoi
May 16	Great Britain	Brigantine	Pandora	Wood		Panama	May 29	Valparaiso
May 23	Great Britain	Sloop	Amphitrite	Eden	24	Callao	July 17	Valparaiso
July 4	United States	Ship	Ohio	Stribling	90	San Francisco	July 21	San Francisco
August 12	French	Frigate	Poursuivante	Tromelin	60	Callao	September 5	San Francisco
August 14	French	Steamer	Gassendi	Faucon	10	Tahiti		San Francisco
August 21	United States	Sloop	Preble	Glynn	16	Hong Kong		San Francisco
September 6	United States	Brig	Lawrence	Fraser	10	Valparaiso	September 28	San Francisco
November 26	United States	Propeller	Massachusetts	Knox		San Francisco		In port
December 5	United States	Sloop	St. Mary	Voorhies	22	San Francisco	December 24	Hong Kong

TABLE BY C. R. BISHOP, ESQ., THE COLLECTOR GENERAL OF CUSTOMS, SHOWING THE IMPORTS AND EXPORTS OF SPIRITS, WINES, AND CORDIALS FOR THE YEAR 1849, DISTINGUISHING THE FLAG UNDER WHICH THE IMPORTATIONS AND EXPORTATIONS WERE MADE.

IMPORTED, 1849.

Under the flag of	Rum.	Gin.	Brandy.	Whisky.	Alcohol.	Cordials.	Wines $1 per gallon duty.	Absinthe.	Aquadiente.	Pisco.	Arrack.	Aniseseed.	Spirits, duty $5 per gallon and upward.	Wines and Cordials $1 per gallon and upward.
United States	$837.00	$561	$365.00	$120	$58	—	$1,567.60	—	—	$45	—	—	$1,986.00	$1,567.60
Great Britain	5,960.00	3240	7,989.00	239	—	—	2,198.00	115.00	15	115	—	—	17,673.00	2,198.00
Chili	2,229.00	160	1,460.00	—	—	24.00	846.00	—	—	—	—	—	3,849.00	870.00
Peru	76.00	—	48.00	—	—	—	—	—	155	—	—	14½	293.50	—
France	—	—	584.00	—	—	—	—	—	—	—	—	—	584.00	—
Hawaii	291.00	365	8,573.40	—	1207	225.00	2,061.00	120.00	—	—	—	—	10,556.40	2,286.00
Denmark	—	—	271.40	—	—	—	151.00	—	—	—	1200	—	1,471.00	151.00
Total	$9,393.00	$4326	$19,290.40	$359	$1265	$249.00	$6,823.60	$235.00	$170	$160	$1200	$14½	$36,412.90	$7,072.60

EXPORTED, 1849.

Under the flag of	Rum.	Gin.	Brandy.	Whisky.	Alcohol.	Cordials.	Wines $1 per gallon duty.	Absinthe.	Aquadiente.	Pisco.	Arrack.	Aniseseed.	Spirits, duty $5 per gallon and upward.	Wines and Cordials $1 per gallon and upward.
United States	$847.90	$83	$3,557.00	—	—	$14.00	$192.80	—	—	$12½	—	—	$4,500.40	$206.80
Great Britain	1,334.00	281	212.00	124	—	—	288.00	—	—	—	—	—	1,951.00	288.00
Chili	319.00	—	1,180.00	—	—	—	522.00	2.40	15	147½	—	—	1,663.00	522.00
Peru	—	—	—	—	—	—	—	—	94½	—	—	—	94.50	—
France	—	—	422.00	—	—	4.80	—	21.60	—	—	—	—	443.60	4.80
French Provinces	—	—	66.00	—	—	—	18.00	—	30¼	—	—	14½	110.75	18.00
Hawaii	144.00	235½	10,131.00	—	1173	67.50	2,332.00	321.60	—	—	—	—	12,005.10	2,399.50
Denmark	—	—	385.00	—	—	28.80	317.00	—	—	—	1120	—	1,505.00	345.80
Russia	75.00	—	—	—	—	—	—	—	—	—	80	—	155.00	—
Total	$2,719.90	$599½	$15,953.00	$124	$1173	$115.10	$3,669.80	$345.60	$139¾	$160	$1200	$14½	$22,429.25	$3,784.90

QUANTITY OF LIQUORS PAYING $5 PER GALLON AND UPWARD DUTY, TAKEN FROM THE CUSTOM HOUSE IN HONOLULU FOR CONSUMPTION IN THE HAWAIIAN ISLANDS.

1847.	1848.	1849.
From Jan. 1 to June 30, inclusive..1287 gallons.	From Jan. 1 to June 30, inclusive.. 892 gallons.	From Jan. 1 to June 30, inclusive..2262 gallons.
From July 1 to Dec. 31 inclusive..1984—3271.	From July 1 to Dec. 31, inclusive..2551—3443.	From July 1 to Dec. 31, inclusive..3456—5718.

Table of Government Schools in 1849

Islands.	Districts.	No. of Protestant schools.	No. of Catholic schools.	No. of Protestant scholars.	No. of Catholic scholars.	Whole number of schools.	Whole number of scholars.	Number of days —school.	Am't of teachers' wages for 1848.	Old debts paid during the year 1848.	Rema'ing debt.	Am't expended on school-houses, 1848.	Wages of Inspector and sundries.	Readers.	Writers.	Mental & written arithmetic.	Geography.	Moral Philosophy.	Singing.
	District 1	48	6	291	139	54	2,230	6,063	$1,082.12	$1271.11	$492.62	—	—	1274	901	1096	813	24	91
	2	13	7	355	215	20	570	1,004	154.80	—	—	—	—	144	77	258	81	10	31
	3	26	4	925	95	30	1,020	4,048	460.33	508.38	173.25	25	—	417	207	276	156	—	144
	4	21	6	972	219	27	1,191	2,818	417.11	634.86	28.72	—	35.50	441	117	457	252	—	26
	5	21	3	1,116	82	24	1,198	4,174	521.84	835.31	—	—	23.50	649	287	814	280	—	60
	6	21	2	841	37	23	878	4,337	982.53	432.58	—	6.50	26.50	415	296	376	166	—	19
Hawaii....		150	28	6,300	787	178	7,087	22,441	$3,618.83	$3682.24	$694.59	$6.75	$85.50	3340	1885	3277	1748	34	371
	District 1	25	4	1,232	96	29	1,328	5,766	1,230.90	—	47.50	239.25	20.00	721	494	644	637	—	33
	2	24	3	837	72	27	909	4,128	815.45	—	—	442.25	40.00	465	380	195	329	20	64
	3	18	9	633	223	27	856	3,486	631.87	74.00	31.37	18.00		497	234	353	229	—	—
	4	27	15	1,149	382	42	1,531	8,349	1,251.41	111.43	—	122.67	25.00	790	449	602	534	7	34
Maui......		94	31	3,851	773	125	4,624	21,729	$3,929.63	$185.43	$78.87	$822.17	$85.00	2473	1557	1794	1729	27	131
Molokai ...	5	20	2	982	34	22	1,016	—	407.79	—	—	—	—	610	273	685	300	68	422
Lanai	6	7	—	184	—	7	184	1,120	180.00	—	—	—	—	162	104	127	103	—	10
	District 1	23	7	1,068	256	30	1,324	4,088	864.05	—	—	216.81	—	516	312	463	315	110	145
	2	12	2	445	60	14	505	2,592	820.58	—	—	318.59	—	228	114	250	103	—	14
	3	27	10	820	190	37	1,010	5,430	1,196.78	—	—	84.25	20.00	540	328	464	575	5	28
	4	11	4	306	76	15	382	2,287	369.92	—	—	1.12	20.00	213	124	257	145	41	69
	5	15	4	429	81	19	510	2,661	502 97	13.50	—	20.62	15.00	243	180	212	175	—	122
	6	11	8	529	273	19	802	2,839	539.08	115.23	—	126.59	20.00	591	411	508	517	6	113
Oahu......		99	35	3,597	936	134	4,533	19,897	$4,293.38	$128.73	—	$787.99	$75.00	2331	1469	2154	1830	162	491
	District 1	15	1	400	20	16	420	2,979	386.04	388.19	53.81	—	—	230	72	176	93	—	—
	2	15	1	437	22	16	459	3,372	622.37	362.93	277.83	9.00	15.00	280	143	231	186	—	—
	3	20	1	515	22	21	537	3,762	483.14	320.20	—	38.87	15.00	339	178	262	183	21	21
Kauai.....		50	3	1,352	64	53	1,406	10,113	$1,491.55	$1061.32	$331.64	$47.87	$30.00	849	393	669	462	21	21
Niihau	4	6	2	141	37	8	178	1,360	152.80	91.35	22.00	38.50	—	90	47	41	14	—	—
	Total..	426	101	16,407	2631	527	19,028	76,663	$14,073.98	$5149.07	$1147.10	$1599.79	$275.50	9855	5728	8747	6186	312	1446

Census of the Hawaiian Islands, from Official Documents, taken January, 1849.

Islands.	Population.	Deaths.	Births.
Hawaii	27,204	2,726	586
Oahu	23,145	2,409	396
Mauai	18,671	1,619	267
Kauai	6,941	686	154
Molokai	3,429	412	52
Niihau	723	44	18
Lanai	528	47	5
Total aggregate	80,641	7,943	1,478

Aggregate amount of each description of persons included opposite.

Males.		Females.	
Under 17 years of age	10,773	Under 17 years of age	9,593
Of 17 and under 30	6,327	Of 17 and under 30	5,719
Of 30 and under 50	10,819	Of 30 and under 50	9,696
Of 50 and upward	8,353	Of 50 and upward	8,121
Total males	36,272	Total females	33,128

Excess of males, 3143.

	36,272
Blind	337
Deaf	144
Hilo (not included)	8,972
Native population	78,854

FOREIGNERS.	
Unmarried	409
Living with foreign wives	133=266
Children	239
Living with native wives	343
Half castes	471
Foreigners in Hilo	59
Total foreigners	1,787
Natives	78,854
Grand total	80,641

SCHOOLS, ETC.	
Number of English schools	9
Number of English scholars	131
Number of high schools	6
Number of high scholars	256
Number of primary and common schools	505
Number of primary and common scholars	18,022

From this census it appears that out of a total population of 80,641 souls in the year 1849, there was an excess of deaths over births of 6,465 souls, which gives a rate of mortality exceeding 8 per cent. per annum. At this rate of annual decrease the whole Hawaiian population, in 1860, would dwindle down to 32,224; in the year 1870, it would be reduced to 14,073; in 1880, to 6,134; in 1890, to 2,667; in 1900, to 1,162; in 1910, to 494; in 1920, to 207; in 1930, to 92; in 1940, to 37; and in the year 1950, to 20.

By the same census the relative mortality of the seven inhabited islands was shown to be as follows:

Hawaii . . .	$7\frac{23572}{27204}$	per cent.	yearly.
Oahu	$8\frac{16140}{23145}$	"	"
Maui	$7\frac{4503}{18671}$	"	"
Kauai . . .	$7\frac{2613}{6941}$	"	"
Molokai . . .	$10\frac{1717}{3429}$	"	"
Niihau . . .	$3\frac{431}{723}$	"	"
Lanai	$7\frac{504}{528}$	"	"

If any reliance is to be placed on the accuracy of the census, the above results satisfactorily disprove the opinion that has often been expressed, that the decrease in the native population was mainly owing to a nameless disease introduced by foreign sailors, and to their other contaminating influences. Had that been the case, the greatest relative mortality should have been found among the natives of Oahu and Maui, which are the two islands where foreign ships chiefly refresh. But the greatest mortality has been on Molokai, where foreign ships scarcely ever touch. It seems, therefore, demonstrated that, whatever may be the cause of the depopulation of the islands, intercourse with foreigners is not the cause alone.

The comparative salubrity of Niihau, the annual mortality of which is about 3½ per cent., is a very striking feature of the late census. Whether that great healthfulness is to be attributed to the great industry of the natives, occasioned by the want of taro, or that the potatoe, on which they chiefly feed, is more favorable to life, is not as yet ascertained. The census of that island was taken by an intelligent native, there being no foreigners living on it. The manufacture of mats by the natives of that place may prevent them from the same slothful indulgence that is general on the other islands, or the census may have been less correctly taken, or the late epidemic may not have been so fatal there as elsewhere.

Perhaps the census for the present year, 1850, for the taking of which Mr. Armstrong, the Minister of Public Instruction, has already issued his instructions, may enable us to solve that and other useful problems. If any means could be devised to distinguish between the mortality and the births of the industrious natives, and the mortality and births of the slothful—between the natives who live in ports frequented by ships and those who live in the country, and between natives, half-breeds, and foreigners in all situations—the results would be of great importance in leading to a correct appreciation of the true causes of that extraordinary decrease of the natives that appears to have acquired a fresh momentum with every relaxation from the severe compulsory labor of the old times of paganism.

If it be true, as has been alleged, that natives employed on board foreign ships, and subjected to the same rules of feeding and working as the foreign sailors, are free from any greater mortality than the latter; and if it be true that those natives who are regularly employed on the few plantations existing on the islands, are nearly exempt from the great mortality that prevails among those who idle their time away in their old lazy manner, then we may assume as a fact that *general indolence* is the true cause of the rapid depopulation of these healthful islands.

It is a fact well known to physicians and surgeons, that in cases of long confinement to bed from fracture or any other accident requiring a horizontal position, but not otherwise affecting the general health, the most muscular men become weak and relaxed in a few weeks. The same effects follow from imprisonment; and we believe were a regiment of healthy grenadiers landed on these islands and obliged to pass their time as listlessly and inactively as the natives generally do, many of them would die before the end of the year, and scarcely any would then possess their original strength.

It is found that those natives who are classified as laborers devote a very few hours of the day to actual exertion, unless they are hired by the day or month; and there is reason to believe that the class of natives who do not work at all, but live upon the earnings of their friends and acquaintances, is very numerous. Thus we find wherever a native servant is employed, there are sure to be five or six hangers on, who always make their appearance at meal-time, but at all other hours of the day and night are to be found stretched at full length, huddled together on one or more mats.

Hawaiian females, as well as Hawaiian men, are interested in the immediate abolition of this deplorable idleness. The Rev. A. Bishop says, "Indolence is attended with enervating effects on the constitution. This is evinced in the females, who have little to do, and yet they are more subject to sickness than the men. Perhaps there are other causes productive of sickness in many females, in consequence of *vicious* idleness."

The idleness and moral laxity of Hawaiian women are the reproach of the nation. In days of heathenism, Hawaiian mothers used to kill their own children, rather than have the trouble of bringing them up; and even now, while professing to be Christians, they sometimes see their children die of want and neglect, rather than labor to provide for and take care of them; and there is too much reason to believe that, in many cases, they resort to measures to prevent children altogether.

There are many kinds of garden and field labor in which women could engage, as well as the men; and, besides, they can card, spin, weave, sew, knit, plait, embroider, wash, and employ themselves in keeping the houses and clothes of their fathers, husbands, or brothers clean and comfortable. It is so that all civilized women employ themselves. Are the Hawaiian women forever to remain mere objects of gross desire, as if they had been created for no nobler end than venal prostitution?

Hawaiian legislators should do what they can to hold out to the common people the inducements to industry recommended by Rev. Mr. Coan, namely:

"*First.* Moral and intellectual instruction.

"*Second.* Examples of industry and thrift living and moving before their eyes.

" *Third.* Entire security of the avails of their own industry, energy, and skill.

"*Fourth.* Efforts to increase their desire for the rational comforts of life, by showing the blessings of competency, and the shame and numerous other evils attendant on that poverty which is the offspring of indolence and vice.

Fifth. Perhaps premiums, or special encouragements from government, to those who may excel in agriculture, gardening, manufacturing, art, science, and moral virtue."

In regard to the "FIRST," viz., "moral and intellectual instruction," that has been very liberally and constantly given, by the American Missionaries, since 1820, and in a degree by the Catholic Missionaries, since 1827. The natives are no longer an ignorant and uneducated multitude. They have had the benefit of good precepts in the doctrines which the missionaries have taught, and of excellent examples in the virtuous lives which they and their families have led, and they are now able, in their own language, to read the Holy Scriptures and numerous other good books, giving them greater facilities to instruct themselves than what were enjoyed by any other nation, previous to the comparatively recent date of the art of printing. In bringing the Hawaiians on this par, the missionaries have done their duty. The means of carrying them on further are beyond their proper institute. It is for the Hawaiians themselves, by exerting the capabilities of doing well, which they have acquired from the missionaries, and for the Hawaiian government, by encouraging those efforts at well-doing, to complete the good work of civilization.

But as a means of ultimately improving the Hawaiian race, of making them industrious and happy, says one of the missionaries, other agencies than civil penalties must be employed. "They must become a 'law to themselves,' or laws enacted by the chiefs will do little to cure the evils of indolence and improvidence. Still, something may be done by the rulers, and of this I will speak. Instructions from their teachers have been frequent and full. Motives drawn from the word of God have long been urged upon the people. These, we believe, are the only ones of much weight in laying the foundation for elevating and saving a degraded heathen people. Nor have these motives been urged in vain. I have found uniformly that those individuals who give the clearest evidence of piety, the humble and prayerful, are the most industrious."

To the same effect Rev. Mr. Clark remarks, that "Instruction in letters and religion is the appropriate work of missionaries, especially instruction in religion. It was for this object they were sent to these islands, and for this they are sustained in their work; and to this object they have devoted their main strength. But they have not failed to impart instruction in mechanical arts, and by example and precept to stimulate, in various ways, the people to industry. The most thriving and industrious mechanics and farmers in this place are those who have been most closely connected with missionaries, and have received the greatest amount of instruction from them. There are three or four mechanics in this place, and some others who have gone from here and are pursuing their trade in other places, who acquired their knowledge under the direction of missionaries. There are now fourteen carts, besides several trucks, in this district, owned by natives; and more than thirty yoke of oxen, kept in constant use. The owners of these were first instructed in the use of carts and oxen by missionaries. There are about thirty horned cattle owned by natives, besides donkeys, horses, &c., used as beasts of burden. Besides the four individuals from the mission seminary, before mentioned as mak ing butter for market, there are now two or three more engaged in the same business, prompted by their example. All these persons acquired their knowledge of making butter from missionaries, and were induced, by their example and precept, to engage in the business, and they are all common natives. Foreigners who own herds of cattle of their own buy butter of these natives; in fact, nearly all the enterprise and thrift in this place are among those who have come most under the stimulating influence of missionary instruction and example."

Such results, however small, are encouraging, as proving to the government the susceptibility of improvement of the natives. But the government must not look to the missionaries to do what clergymen are not expected to do to any people. The province of the missionary is the spiritual interests of the people. In that province they have done wonders. It is the province of the government to further the temporal interests of the people, and here the missionaries have set the example with greater earnestness and system than any other body of men. Further they can not go, without encroaching upon the duties of the government, and raising an outcry against themselves of wishing to arrogate the *whole* government of the country, which, however unjust, would injure the authority of the king, and impair their usefulness as missionaries.

There is one concurring cause of the diminution of the native popu lation at the Hawaiian Islands not noticed above, which is thus noted in the Sandwich Island History, by Jaroes:

"Great numbers of healthy Hawaiian youth have left in whale ships and other vessels, and never returned. The number annually afloat is computed at four thousand. At one time four hundred were counted at Tahiti, five hundred in Oregon, fifty-one at Paita, Peru, besides unknown numbers in Europe and the United States. Their wives and families, left to provide for themselves, fall into vicious habits. and both evils combined tend to diminish the native population."

This depopulation will appear at a glance the more appalling, by the following comparison of the results of census in different years. They are by no means accurate, but are relatively reliable enough for authorizing the general conclusion as to the rapid passing away of the native race.

Estimate of population for	1823	142,050.
Census of	1832	130,313.
Census of	1836	108,579.
Census of	1846	95,400.
Census of	1849	80,641.

The year 1849 will be marked in the Hawaiian calendar as THE YEAR OF DEATH, when measles, hooping-cough, and influenza swept off, at a low estimate, ten thousand of the aborigines. The same diseases, at the same time, terminated fatally with but few of the foreigners. Both their fruitfulness and their exemption from disease, over and above the native race, are matter of frequent observation and remark. Some years ago a careful comparison was instituted by an intelligent observer, to show the remarkable discrepancy of numbers between the children of missionaries and those of the chiefs, who were then the most civilized of the Hawaiian population. The following was the result:

Nine of the mission families numbered fifty-nine children—an average of six and five ninths to a family. Twenty Hawaiian chiefs had but nineteen children among them all. The mission families within less than one generation had increased one hundred and seventy-five per cent. At the same ratio of increase, in one hundred years their descendants would number fifty-nine thousand five hundred and thirty-five.

Saying nothing now of the enfeebling of the Hawaiian constitution, which has been often referred to and proven in the course of this work, the striking difference shown by this investigation in the productiveness and mortality of persons of native and of foreign origin, so far as proximate causes are concerned, must be mainly owing to the better observance of the natural laws of health and life in the one case than in the other. Native Hawaiians, having little forethought, and holding life in low esteem, pay no regard to cautions for preserving health; live in filth and among vermin; wear clothes in dry weather, but take them off when it is wet and cold; sleep abroad in the night air; freely indulge in unwholesome and excessive diet, and have nothing as suitable food in sickness. When suffering with a raging fever, their lungs laboring under a severe influenza, they will plunge into cold water to allay their internal heat. Indeed, cold water is their main specific for every kind of sickness; and a truly skillful, scientific Hydropathist might probably turn the Hawaiian fondness for a water-cure to useful account, for their benefit and his own pecuniary emolument, by establishing a Hydropathic Hospital in the vicinity of Honolulu, somewhere in the watered valleys of Nuuanu or Manoa.

With an increase of the means of comfortable living, now rapidly taking place at the Hawaiian Islands, and a proper inculcation of the rules of life and principles of physiology, there is good reason to believe that the health of the native race will improve, and its rate of mortality fall off. One of the missionaries lately writes that, since the discovery of gold in California, the price of labor and of all native produce has doubled, and articles of foreign fabric, at the same time, have fallen in value. "Every man who is industrious can and does accumulate property. It is not uncommon to find men with one or two hund red dollars in their possession. But the native who gets money, instead of improving his habitation and increasing his domestic comforts, usually spends it in buying expensive clothing and gay trappings for his horse. To see him on horseback, decked out in his expensive equipments, one might suppose him in easy circumstances; but what you see on him and about him is nearly all he is worth. His house is a mere thatched hovel, with one room, containing a few mats and calabashes, and perhaps a chair or two and a table, with a chest for clothing. The whole establishment is without cleanliness or comfort, and it indicates but an incipient state of civilization. Still, he is as well off as his neighbors; and he is, therefore, respectable in his own eyes and also in theirs. He feels no sense of degradation, because he compares himself only with his own people. He feels, too, that his present condition is much elevated above that of his fathers, or of himself as he was a few years ago. He has a seat of his own in the chapel, and comes to church with his family on the Sabbath, well dressed and clean. He has a horse to ride to and from the service, and he carries his Bible and hymn-book at his side.

"This is the bright side of the picture; but his old habits o aversion to labor, his want of forethought, his proneness to deceive and take undue advantage of his neighbor, and his facility to fall into temptation, cling to him still, and are often contending for the mastery.

"In truth, he is made up of two natures; one being that of a Christian, lately assumed; the other that of the old heathen, with all his prejudices and superstitions. It can not be expected that his walk and conversation will be as if he had been born and nurtured in the bosom of a Christian family.

"He may be better compared to some Washingtonian, once the wretched victim of vice and the inhabitant of the gutter, but now washed and cleaned, and admitted into decent society, still struggling, however, against his former appetites and habits, perhaps manfully, and anon overtaken in an unguarded moment and falling into the snare. He still struggles, and, on the whole, he is able to hold on his way. There is much to lament in his course; but he holds on to the end, dies in peace, and in the hope of immortality.

"Compare a Hawaiian Christian to this brand plucked from the burning, and you have his character. From the world he gains the name of a hypocrite, because of the frequent mastery of his former habits over him. His pastor and his more established brethren stand in fear of him, exhort him, and pray for him, because his light does not shine as it ought, and his faith is too feeble, and Satan's temptations are strong. But the Lord is gracious unto him, while he lingers like Lot on the plain; and he is finally carried through in safety, a ransomed heathen, a sinner saved by grace. Bless the Lord, and give him all the glory!

"The ground of hope that a remnant of this people will be left to perpetuate the race, rests on the facts that there are many virtuous men and women among them. God is hearing their prayers, and blessing their endeavors to promote the welfare of the nation. He has already interposed his kind providence, by delivering them in repeated instances, when their enemies were ready to swallow them up.

"The severe ordeal through which the government and people have just passed, during the embraces of French 'liberty, equality, and fraternity,' is an instance in point. During the late visit of the French admiral, prayer was offered up in every Christian family, and in social and public meetings, for the government and nation; and God turned the heart of the admiral from his first design to burn, plunder, and massacre, and sent him away in chagrin at what he had so wantonly and unavailingly done. Why should the Lord thus interpose, if it be not that he has purposes of good in store for the Hawaiians, even for the remnant, the chosen vessels of his mercy?"*

We say, finally, respecting the depopulation at the Sandwich Islands, that it will undoubtedly be arrested whenever the lands shall be properly subdivided, and a homestead exemption be secured to owners, and the time and employments of the people of both sexes shall be suitably methodized, and habits of industry fairly formed.

The late orders of the Privy Council at Oahu, in 1850, designating the rights of the common people to the lands they occupy, and the mode of establishing their claims, together with the stimulus given to native industry by the opening of the California market for native products, are already producing marked effects. A writer in one of the March numbers of The Polynesian for the present year, 1850, says that, in the region where he resides, the call for the products of the earth, created by the *California scarcity*, have aroused almost the whole population to action; and already are the fields beginning to be verdant and to give promise of a more abundant harvest than has been known there for many years. "I hazard nothing in saying that there has, throughout the whole of our district, been ten-fold more planting done this year, thus far, than for the same time during my acquaintance with the people. There seems to have been a general waking up on the subject, so much so as to destroy my incredulity as to their incapacity for industry, if they could be pressed with proper

* Rev. Artemas Bishop, Missionary Herald, May, 1850.

motives. Even the women are engaged in planting, and are flushed with the high hopes of reaping a golden reward for their labors. Of the common Hawaiian vegetables, such as Irish and sweet potatoes, onions, squashes, melons, cucumbers, tomatoes, bananas, &c., we shall, I hope, soon have an abundance for ourselves and to spare. It pleases me to see so great an improvement in the industry of the people with only the very partial stimulus by which it has been effected, and I can but look forward to the time when, encouraged by the experience that the fruits of every man's labor are his own, the Hawaiian will stand forth high in the ranks of enterprise and thrift, and thus repel the common but unjust imputation of *inborn* laziness."

The following papers are translated from THE ELELE HAWAII, a native newspaper, which were written upon the occasion of the government conferring upon the people, by proclamation, the FEE-SIMPLE of their lands.

Judge Lee's Remarks on the Lands of the Common Natives.

Salutations to you, the common natives of this kingdom.

It has pleased the Hawaiian government, the king, and chiefs, in privy council, to pass certain resolutions requiring the board of land commissioners to give you fee-simple titles to the lands which you personally occupy; and when surveyed, you can obtain your patents.

The king, chiefs, and commissioners also recommend you to exchange lands or parts of lands with each other, and with the Konohikis, so that each may have his land all in one place. Go to them peaceably, and agree well among yourselves before your lands are surveyed, that upon the arrival of the surveyor he be not delayed, but be enabled to proceed immediately with his work.

All that the commissioners will require you to pay for the settlement of your claims will be the costs of the land commission, *i. e.*, from $3 to $5 for each patent.

The king and chiefs have also resolved to set apart certain of the lands belonging to government, and intrust them to agents, to be sold to those natives who have no lands, or only very small ones. Nothing, therefore, remains to be done that you may obtain fee-simple titles to your lands. When you have secured your lands and taken your patents, your *poalima* (or landlord) tax will be at an end.

Two courses, then, are open for you: either to secure your lands, work on them, and be happy, or to sit still, sell them, and then die Which do you choose?

WILLIAM L. LEE.

Mr. Armstrong's Remarks on the Granting Lands to Common Natives, in Fee-simple.

Be joyful, ye common natives of this kingdom, for the king and government have conferred upon you a very great worldly blessing by granting to you the lands which you occupy in fee-simple; so that, when you have obtained your patents, the lands will belong to you and your children forever. The meaning of this term, "in fee-simple," is, that the patentee alone is the owner of the land, and no one else has any remaining right to it. The konohiki has no claim upon the tenant, and the poalima tax is at an end. Each man will be his own konohiki.

The government can, nevertheless, impose a tax upon lands held in fee-simple, should it hereafter be thought proper so to do. That is the custom in all enlightened countries. The *poalua* tax, however, which is not imposed upon land, and is set apart for the benefit of schools, is still to be enforced, unless commuted. The commutation system, paying half a dollar quarterly, is very generally introduced at present, so that there is no *poalua* work done at Oahu.

Formerly the land belonged to the chiefs only, and the common natives had no well-defined rights. The chiefs gave lands to whom they pleased, and took them away at pleasure. Thus it was till 1836 At that time the chiefs settled the rights of tenants, so that each man could continue upon his land, unless he were guilty of some wrong. Ever since it has been unlawful to expel any one from his lands unless he had been convicted of some offense; afterward, also, in 1846, six commissioners were appointed to ascertain the claims of every one to land. The lands were also divided between the king, the konohiki, and the common native, a third to each. The king and government also made a separation between the king's private lands and those belonging to the government. The board of commissioners have been, and still are, diligently engaged in their business of granting land titles.

The resolutions of the privy council, which are published in this paper, are the first which have clearly designated and settled the rights of the common natives to the land which they occupy. Read them attentively. One thing only remains, the proper surveying of the lands; but have a little patience, and that, too, will be attended to.

Now then, my dear fellow-subjects, let me advise you in respect to some things.

1. Be not obstinate in insisting upon every little crook and corner in your land, but consult together, and unite one piece with another,

so that several may be inclosed in the same patent, so as to accommodate yourselves. This uniting of your several pieces in one lessens the charges of the land commission. Do it quickly, and don't put it off.

2. When you have obtained your patents, what will you do? Just as you did before, eh? Ride around from place to place, work a little and idle about a great deal; sleep, talk, and loaf about? If so, your trouble and expense in obtaining patents will all be utterly useless.

You should act thus. Let the wife remain at home and put the house in order, and the husband go out and cultivate the land, day by day. Be industrious, and fit up your houses and house lots, furnish yourselves with seats, beds, plates, bowls, knives, spoons, and glasses; provide separate sleeping-rooms for parents and children; and increase the produce of your lands. Rest not until you are comfortably supplied with all good things. Plant all kinds of good trees on your lands, as the fig, coffee, guava, orange, bread-fruit, cocoa-nut, koa, kau, viapple, and all kinds of flowering shrubs and fruit trees, so that your lands may be embellished with beautiful plants and trees.

Take proper care, also, of your children, that you be not destitute of heirs. Let the daughters remain at home with their mothers, and learn to sew, wash, iron; to make mats and hats, and to seek after knowledge. The little girls should go to school. The older boys should go out to work with their fathers; for, as the land will become theirs, should they behave themselves properly, they should work upon and improve it.

You should, also, live in accordance with the word of God, for your lands will do you no good if you disregard His commands, by quarreling, drinking, licentiousness, devoting yourselves to pleasure, and breaking the Sabbath.

Furnish your children with books, pens, ink, maps, and other things to help them in acquiring knowledge.

Finally, the government will have done all in its power for you in giving you fee-simple titles for your lands, and the rest remains for you. If, now, you continue poor, needy, living in disorder, in miserable huts, your lands lying waste and passing into other hands, whose fault will it be? Whose but yours? Some say that this country is going to ruin through your laziness and ignorance. Is it so? Then be it so no longer. Rouse up and act as those wish you to do who have a real regard for your welfare. Let all natives witness your revivification. Thus wishes your sincere friend,

R. ARMSTRONG.

The preceding documentary statements and considerations, together with the facts developed along the pages of this book, will have given, as we believe, a correct picture of native Hawaiian society. The character of the foreign society at the Sandwich Islands, especially at Honolulu, is now rapidly rising in enterprise, intelligence, refinement, philanthropy, and piety; and the ports of the Hawaiian Group generally are fast becoming the most desirable places of residence to be found through the whole Island World of the Pacific.

While this improvement is to be ascribed mainly to the changes effected by the labors of American missionaries, much, also, is to be attributed to the beneficial influence of the seamen's chaplains there stationed, and to the permanent domestic circles that are gradually being established. The salutary, though silent, effect of this latter agency it would be impossible to over-estimate. In modern Protestant missions the influence of woman and of the family is an element of success in taming barbarians and Christianizing society, which Jesuit missionaries not having employed, have for that reason, among others, failed of realizing such beneficial and large results as have followed in the train of aggressive missionary Protestantism.

The present plan of the American Board of Missions, therefore, wisely, is to facilitate the independent settlement of the members of the Sandwich Island Mission, as pastors and teachers at the islands, and to place those who can not yet obtain a living on the same footing with home missionaries. They expect by this means to enable and induce the missionaries generally to remain at the islands *with their families,* and thus to insure a thorough Puritan basis for the future community, whatever that shall be, which is to occupy those islands.

The seamen's chaplain says of the foreign society at Honolulu, in 1850, that they are justly to be commended for liberality. In a little over one month of the present year, $750 had been collected there for benevolent purposes, and the community is declared to be ready to extend liberal aid to all worthy objects. Let this be true, and let a generous and wise spirit of public improvement, and a unanimous, patriotic devotion to the welfare of the island kingdom, prevail generally among the foreign residents of Honolulu, and they will soon make their "FAIR HAVEN" the favorite Watering-place of the Pacific.

We conclude this exhibit of the Sandwich Islands with a tabular synopsis of the schools and churches under the supervision of missionaries for the year 1849. The last yearly report from the mission says, in regard to the schools, that, under the rigorous administration of Mr. Armstrong, the Minister of public instruction, it is expected that the revenue appropriated by government for the support of schools will prove amply sufficient to carry them forward on an enlarged and liberal scale. School-houses are getting to be nearer what they ought to be. The buildings now erected are generally on an improved plan, and they are of more durable materials than they have been in years past. The ordinary apparatus of common country schools in New England is gradually finding a place in Hawaiian school-houses. The black-board has become a familiar object in many places, as are seats, tables, &c. Books, likewise, are more generally procured than formerly, and, as the natural consequence, they are more highly prized.

The experiment of devoting one half of each day to manual labor has been successfully made in many of the districts. The proceeds of the labor, performed by the pupils, have been laid out for their benefit, in procuring books, slates, and such other articles as they may desire for their convenience or comfort. This plan of uniting work with study, it is hoped, will have a happy influence upon the character of the rising generation; indeed, this effect is already apparent, wherever the experiment has been fairly tried; but the mass of teachers are but imperfectly qualified for the work which they have undertaken. The school-houses are often unsuitable; the books used are insufficient; the needful apparatus is wanting; and multitudes look supinely upon the whole subject of education, because they are grossly ignorant of its utility and end. But these obstacles are steadily diminishing, and they confidently expect the time when true knowledge shall be increased, and fill and bless the land. Their present school system continues to recommend itself by its admirable simplicity, and by its adaptation to the wants of the people. It works well, so far as is known, in all the islands.

STATISTICS OF SCHOOLS FOR 1849.

Stations.		Number of schools.	Scholars.	Readers.	Writers.	Arithmetic.	Geography.
HAWAII.	Hilo and Puna	48	2,091	1207	860	1037	802
	Waimea	21	841	400	285	366	166
	Kohala	21	1,116	605	260	759	276
	Kailua	21	972	381	100	374	233
	Kealakekua	26	925	404	202	265	141
	Kau	13	355	101	45	155	54
MAUI	Hana	27	1,149	579	317	430	411
	Wailuku	24	837	434	377	174	304
	Lahaina	15	899	424	282	341	377
	Kaanapali	10	333	117	69	133	101
	MOLOKAI	—	—	—	—	—	—
	LANAI	7	184	162	104	127	103
OAHU	Honolulu 1st	23	1,068	407	248	377	292
	Honolulu 2d	12	445	203	108	225	102
	Ewa and Waianae	27	820	496	312	436	535
	Waialua	26	735	361	247	371	263
	Kaneohe	11	529	386	287	356	380
KAUAI	Waioli	20	515	331	170	258	179
	Koloa	15	437	267	135	223	175
	Waimea	15	400	221	68	167	93
	NIIHAU	6	141	69	47	29	14
	Total	388	11,792	7655	4523	6603	5001

Seminaries, &c.	Now in school.	Received the past year.	Graduated and left the past year.	Expelled the past year.	Died the past.	Sent forth as teachers.
Royal school	11	—	2	—	—	—
Lahainaluna	64	—	14	2	1	14
Wailuku	35	—	3	—	5	—
Hilo	62	23	12	—	1	8
Waioli	48	4	14	—	—	7
Total	220	27	45	2	7	29

Statistics of Churches for 1849.

Stations.		On examination the past year.	Whole number on examination.	Dismissed past year.	Whole number dismissed.	Deceased past year.	Whole number deceased.	Excluded past year.	Remaining excluded.	In regular standing.	Children baptized past year.	Whole number baptized.	Marriages past year.	Average congregations.	Population in the field.	Deaths.	Births.
Hawaii	Hilo and Puna	265	9,647	28	453	703	3301	25	387	5,906	108	3,19	91	—	9,031	934	173
	Waimea	96	5,955	12	812	264	1464	51	800	2,292	39	1,226	62	200	4,114	550	100
	Kohala	26	1,791	19	188	130	500	23	80	1,264	27	793	80	900	4,712	415	189
	Kailua	—	2,339	67	466	139	575	33	95	1,465	12	1,692	22	450	3,544	273	51
	Kealakekua	—	2,694	16	841	59	574	14	—	1,265	23	—	46	—	3,522	283	32
	Kau	97	1,294	26	236	130	377	2	51	924	25	395	40	—	2,281	271	40
Maui	Hana	—	626	2	20	58	98	10	51	566	—	276	78	—	5,583	450	97
	Wailuku	55	1,573	9	319	58	212	18	—	1,262	17	979	73	—	4,226	361	67
	Lahaina	90	1,119	48	222	126	363	5	20	762	53	1,105	55	—	5,646	524	67
	Lahainaluna	—	—	—	—	—	—	—	—	—	—	—	—	—	—	—	—
	Kaanapali	—	—	—	—	—	—	—	—	—	—	—	—	—	—	—	—
	Molokai	276	1,401	8	45	85	235	40	16	1,129	—	—	52	—	3,429	412	52
Oahu	Honolulu 1st	306	2,280	16	184	164	486	14	—	1,595	34	636	134	1200	7,389	627	132
	Honolulu 2d	126	2,121	26	273	134	624	14	458	1,131	24	626	137	1000	6,375	793	122
	Ewa	10	1,914	18	290	111	356	8	167	1,430	35	559	44	900	3,308	323	37
	Waianae	5	256	8	21	49	79	6	13	334	4	—	—	—	—	—	—
	Waialua	151	924	5	70	52	155	8	—	610	36	654	35	—	3,241	298	54
	Kaneohe	36	326	3	22	21	90	1	22	203	2	151	37	450	2,832	368	51
Kauai	Waioli	40	292	1	29	20	78	4	17	259	12	102	40	—	2,340	216	57
	Koloa	8	269	1	79	11	56	—	—	201	3	160	—	—	2,732	259	68
	Waimea	7	403	2	82	32	134	2	29	233	8	179	58	350	1,869	211	29
	Total	1594	37,224	315	4652	2352	9754	278	2206	22,831	462	12,724	1084				

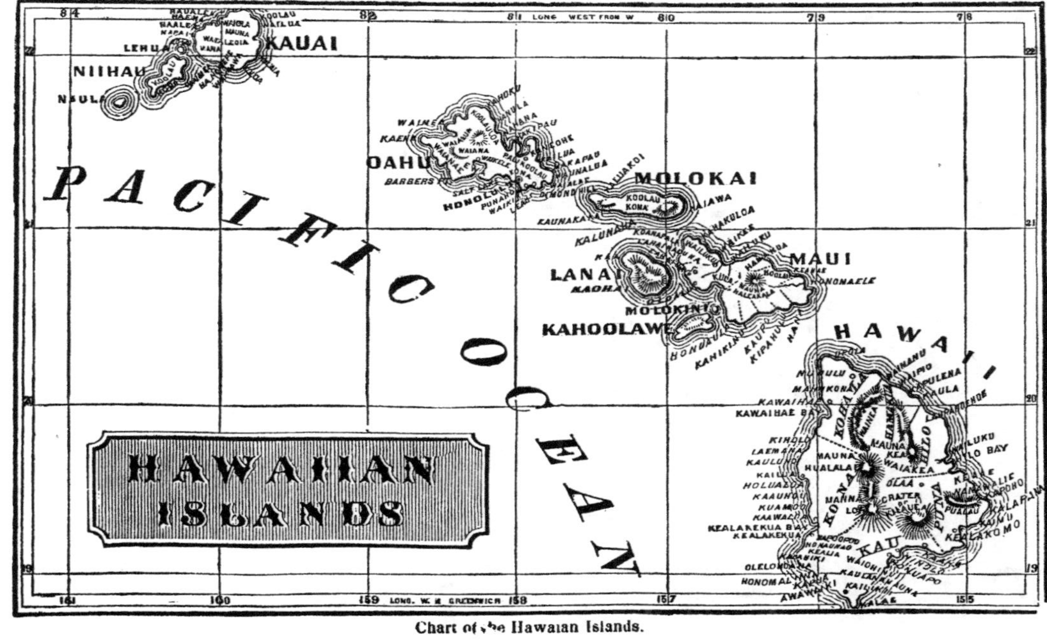

Chart of the Hawaiian Islands.

www.ingramcontent.com/pod-product-compliance
Lightning Source LLC
LaVergne TN
LVHW020058110826
845151LV00001B/16

* 9 7 8 1 4 2 5 5 4 5 1 3 0 *